WELL-BEING AND WORK

WELL-BEING AND WORK

Towards a Balanced Agenda

Philip Dewe

Professor of Organizational Behavior,
Birkbeck University London

and

Cary Cooper, CBE

Distinguished Professor of Organizational Psychology
and Health, Lancaster University

palgrave
macmillan

First published 2012 by
PALGRAVE MACMILLAN

Palgrave Macmillan in the UK is an imprint of Macmillan Publishers Limited, registered in England, company number 785998, of Houndmills, Basingstoke, Hampshire RG21 6XS.

Palgrave Macmillan in the US is a division of St Martin's Press LLC, 175 Fifth Avenue, New York, NY 10010.

Palgrave Macmillan is the global academic imprint of the above companies and has companies and representatives throughout the world.

Palgrave® and Macmillan® are registered trademarks in the United States, the United Kingdom, Europe and other countries.

ISBN 978–0–230–24352–1

This book is printed on paper suitable for recycling and made from fully managed and sustained forest sources. Logging, pulping and manufacturing processes are expected to conform to the environmental regulations of the country of origin.

A catalogue record for this book is available from the British Library.

A catalog record for this book is available from the Library of Congress.

10 9 8 7 6 5 4 3 2 1
21 20 19 18 17 16 15 14 13 12

Printed and bound in Great Britain by
CPI Antony Rowe, Chippenham and Eastbourne

CONTENTS

LIST OF FIGURES AND TABLES

FIGURES

TABLES

Note

The figures and tables should be read in conjunction with the text. Each has been constructed from the cited articles in the text and reading them together gives a much richer understanding of the points different authors are making. Each gives an overview and brings together many of the points made in the articles cited: these are all fully acknowledged and referenced in the text. Where references are cited in the table they offer the opportunity to read around the point being made.

INTRODUCTION

In a speech given by Robert Kennedy at the University of Kansas in 1968, whilst he was on the campaign trail, he reflected on the state of the nation:

> Too much and for too long, we seemed to have surrendered personal excellence and community values in the mere accumulation of material things. Our gross national product is now over $800 billion dollars a year, but that gross national product – if we judge the United States of America by that – that gross national product counts air pollution and cigarette advertising, and the ambulances to clear our highways of carnage. It counts special locks on our doors and the jails for the people who break them. It counts the destruction of the redwood and the loss of our natural wonder in chaotic sprawl. It counts the napalm and counts nuclear warheads and armored cars for the police to fight the riots in our cities...Yet the gross national product does not allow for the health of our children, the quality of their education or the joy of their play. It does not include the beauty of our poetry or the strength of our marriages, the intelligence of our public debate or the integrity of our public officials. It measures neither our wit nor our courage, neither our wisdom nor our learning, neither our compassion nor our devotion to our country, it measures everything in short, except that which makes life worthwhile.

This is a profound declaration of what a society should aspire to, and is reflected today in the speeches of British Prime Minister David Cameron and President Sarkozy of France, where they extol the virtues of well-being and emphasize the need to enhance our gross national well-being. Indeed, to reinforce this, the United Kingdom government has introduced a number of well-being categories to the national citizen's survey carried out by the Office of National Statistics, an effort to track the nation's well-being or lack thereof. This will help to identify areas in which social and economic policies could be directed in the future. In addition to this development, in 2011 the World Economic Forum created a Global Agenda Council on Health and Well-Being, which gathers senior people from around the world to examine the issue in a global context, and discuss what can be done to enhance it.

WORK STRESS

Over the last few decades, we have seen enormous societal change. The British workplace has altered beyond all recognition. First, we had the industrial relations strife of the 1970s, with the "them and us" mentality of management and unions; then the entrepreneurial 1980s with mergers and acquisitions, and the privatizing of the public sector. This was followed by the short-term contract culture of the 1990s, where jobs were no longer for life, working hours were longer, and the outsourcing of staff became more and more routine as the psychological contract between employer and employee was broken. Now, when the materialism and striving of the last decade has led to the virtual collapse of the world economic order, we are in the most severe recession experienced for over 80 years. Perhaps this is just a natural corrective for the excessive striving of the decades when we thought that material goods would make us happy. The evidence from the "happiness" researchers shows just the opposite: that we need a minimum amount of financial security, but beyond that level the increasing amounts we earn do not contribute significantly to happiness. The more "work-consumed" a person is, the less likely they are to invest in their significant relationships, which in the long term undermines their overall happiness (Burke and Cooper 2008).

Indeed, in the Mercer Engagement Scale, devised across a range of countries (e.g. China, France, Germany, India, Japan, the United Kingdom and the United States), it was found that "base pay" as a motivator comes low down a list of 12 factors that engage workers and make them job satisfied. The aspect of work that is most motivating, and most satisfying for workers in the United Kingdom, is "respect," which is about how much you feel your organization values you. This is followed by the "type of work you do," how stimulating and interesting the job is. Then we have your feelings about the service or product you provide to your customers, followed closely behind by the nature of the relationships you have with your work colleagues (the better the relationships are, the more engaged and satisfied you are). Work–life balance comes next, where workers are trusted enough to be able to work more flexibly, and are able to invest time in their personal relationships outside of work (the opposite of a long working-hours culture). Only after these, does what you get paid come into the engagement and satisfaction equation. And at the bottom of the list comes "bonuses or variable pay" as a motivator (Bowles and Cooper 2009).

With the recent dramatic changes in the workplace we have seen a significant increase in the costs of stress at work, not only for the country as a whole, but also in a range of public and private sector organizations. In 2007, the Centre for Mental Health reported that mental ill-health and stress costs the United Kingdom economy about £26 billion per annum due to sickness absence, presenteeism (defined as "lost productivity that occurs when employees come to work ill and perform below par because of that illness") and labor turnover, with presenteeism double the cost of absenteeism. In addition, if you look at the costs of incapacity benefit (people unable to work due to illness) for the United Kingdom economy the national bill is roughly £12 billion per annum, with the biggest single cost being mental ill-health and stress, 40 percent of the total. The Confederation of British Industry estimates that the direct cost of absence to industry in the United Kingdom is £537 per employee per year, with the indirect costs estimated at an additional £270 per employee. The Chartered Institute of Personnel and Development estimate the costs of labor turnover amongst staff at £7750 per employee replacement, for recruitment, retraining, and lost staff development investment. It has been estimated by the National Institute of Occupational Safety and Health that stress is likely to cost the United States economy between 5 and 10 percent of gross national product, due to absence and lost productive value. This doesn't even take into account the cost of medical treatment for those who are incapacitated, or leave early (Cooper and Dewe 2008).

The job insecurity resulting from the downsizing of employee numbers during this time of global downturn has also had an impact on employee well-being. Lundberg and Cooper (2010) report studies which highlight the negative impact of this. Sora *et al.* (2009) explored the impact of an "insecurity climate" on 1,000 employees in Spain and Belgium. They found that employees who felt job insecure had significantly lower levels of job satisfaction and organizational commitment; Kivimaki *et al.*

(2003) found that temporary workers in Scandinavia had significantly higher mortality rates than more secure and permanent workers.

TOWARDS WELL-BEING

As we move away from an era of coping with the stresses and strains of the constantly changing landscape in private and public sector organizations, and the fast pace of working life, there is a desire to assess the previously neglected positive aspects of work. Economists and occupational psychologists have made a significant contribution here, showing that happiness requires more than just a good salary or a high-status job, but is about having meaningful relationships at work, feeling valued at work, being trusted by employers, having some autonomy at work, and having the capacity to get better work–life balance and flexibility (Lundberg and Cooper 2010; Oswald and Wu 2010). Work economists like Layard (2006) and Dolan *et al.* (2008) have more broadly highlighted factors that contribute to overall well-being and happiness. They involve work factors, such as hours worked, type of work, commuting, unemployment, exercise, relationships at work, etc. However, there are numerous other societal factors that are related to one's subjective well-being, such as marriage, seeing family and friends, volunteering, religious activities, community involvement, etc. Powdthavee's (2010) book on the "happiness equation" highlights the various dimensions of our lives that lead to great contentment and happiness, with work or nonwork being one of the most important components. He uses an interesting quote from Rabbi Hyman Schachtel to capture the qualitative notion of well-being: "happiness is not having what you want, but wanting what you have."

WHAT CAN WE DO?

Can we do anything about enhancing our mental capital and well-being, or is it an inevitable part of living in an increasingly thrusting and global economy that stress, and its consequences, are here to stay? Are Europe, China, and India following the United States into becoming the workaholics of the world? Many countries have been Americanized to a large extent, but that doesn't necessarily mean that we have to suffer the nefarious consequences (e.g. inner city violence, drugs, extensive gun crime, and large-scale social exclusion). In an article entitled "America: A Toxic Lifestyle," the author (DeAngelis 2007, p. 50) summarized the evidence by saying "the way we value wealth and work over social connectedness may be compromising our long term health." The good news, for British industry at least, is that we now have better-trained and more authentic business leaders, who are increasingly aware of the dangers of driving towards the American agenda of being work-obsessed and ignoring other important aspects of our lives like the family, the community and our own health and well-being. The issues of work–life balance, well-being and positive organizational behavior are now on their radar, possibly due to these difficult economic times.

THE IDEA OF BALANCE

This book attempts to explore the tensions between workplace stress and the desire for greater positive psychology to help achieve a greater balance in the "happiness equation." When we think about balance we are drawn to the idea of equilibrium. But the idea of balance, or of achieving it, is more complicated. Balance requires us to think in terms of "something that brings about such a state [of equilibrium]; a harmony in the parts of a whole; the idea of weighing factors against each other" (*Collins Dictionary and Thesaurus* 1992, p. 71). Balance is also about matching, adjustment, evenness, comparison and consideration. When, as in the subtitle of this book, we talk about moving "towards a balanced agenda" we are using balance to express not necessarily equilibrium but more a need to weigh up, adjust, compare, and consider moving towards achieving a sense of evenness. In this way we hope to create a better understanding of why different theories emerge when they do, their emphasis and focus, and why they become more acceptable at one time than another. We look at the values they represent, the organizational structures they reflect, the contribution they make, the creative tensions they produce for change, the knowledge they give us, the use we make of that knowledge, and how they express and reflect our duty as researchers.

Running through this book are a number of themes that capture our idea of balance. None of these themes are mutually exclusive. Each adds to the other, providing a rich context within which ideas can be expressed, critically evaluated, and debated. In this way we can begin to gauge how we continue to move towards a sense of evenness in what we do; matching where we are against what we want to achieve, and considering how we get there whilst maintaining the integrity of what we have already achieved, the inclusiveness with which we have achieved it, and the comprehensiveness we need to develop a robust understanding of the experience of work. We outline below some of the themes that emerge.

From the negative to the positive

At the heart of the positive psychology movement is an argument that the body of knowledge that best expresses the discipline of organizational psychology, needs now, as is the case for other disciplines, to be reviewed and revisited, allowing the positive aspects of the work experience to emerge as a legitimate study in its own right. The debate accompanying this movement, has centered around the issue of how more attention can be given to this much-needed positive perspective, not at the expense of the negative, but in a more inclusive way that examines both the positive and the negative, offering a more comprehensive approach to understanding work experiences.

From description to meaning

Any attempt to capture the nature of the work experience cannot be separated from the issue of measurement. Researchers are continually confronted with the questions of "Where are current methodologies taking us?" and "What can alternative methodologies provide?" What is being called for is a period of quiet reflection, where consideration is given to exploring how the richness and complexity of the work experience can best be measured. Traditional measurement techniques should be considered in terms of "whose reality is being measured," and measures that describe relationships recognized as being substantively different from those that give meaning to such relationships. Description and meaning are both part of a researchers' toolkit, the issue is not that of replacing one methodology with another, nor is it one where by describing a relationship we are misled into believing that we are giving that relationship meaning, but one where we are concerned about what it is that we are measuring, and whether now more ecologically sensitive measures may give us the meaning of the work experience we are searching for.

From theory to practice

The issue here is two-fold. The first issue concerns not just what makes a good theory, but for how long it remains relevant. Whether the turbulent and dramatic changes to the nature of work raise the question: "When is it timely to reshape theory so that it best expresses, integrates and accounts for such changes?" With this question the issue is one of adjustment and matching, so that theory is aligned with, and reflects, the critical issues of context and change in order for it to uniquely express contemporary work experiences. The second issue is not dissimilar. It concerns the ideas and assumptions that lie behind different management practices. The issue here is that the language of the "economic imperative" has come to dominate the practice of management, portraying it in such a narrow, rational, and instrumental way that the practices themselves have become separated from the social context within which they take place (Ghoshal 2005). This raises the question of whether such a focus can express what makes good management practice. Now is the time to integrate the context back into the practice of management, so that the social, ethical, and leadership realities of organizational life are no longer separated from those practices that express what good management represents.

From developing knowledge to applying it

Exploring the relevance of theory and the ideas and assumptions that lie behind the practice of management cannot easily be separated from our responsibilities in terms of knowledge transfer. Here the idea of the "pragmatic contribution" of theory becomes important (Corley and Gioia 2011). When considering the utility of theories we need to give as much emphasis to how our theories connect with the issues facing organizations as has been given to the critical contribution they make. How do we progress this? The answer is that there must now be much more focus on "problem domains with significant input for future practice; balancing methodological rigor and practical relevance" (Corley and Gioia 2011, pp. 27–28). The dissemination of knowledge must now be regarded as equally important as its creation. We need to recognize that evidence-based practice relies as much on the methods used to create such evidence, as it does on working closely with practitioners to determine what constitutes evidence, and what problems need to be worked on.

From the status quo to change

It is clear that our role as researchers carries a moral responsibility to ensure that what we are researching is relevant to those whose working lives we study. Maintaining the status quo is not an option. The challenge must be to avoid the convenience that accompanies the use of established practices and methodologies, which discourage the need to consider more creative and alternative ways that can better capture the reality of what we are trying to understand. It is the exploration of new and innovative approaches that helps to develop the "creative tension" necessary to advance our understanding and move the field forward. Unless we accept the responsibility of change and the critical debate that goes with it, we are left with a methodological and conceptual narrowness that allows the gaps to widen between what we want to achieve, how we want to get there, and the expectations of those whose working lives we study.

From stress to well-being

While we use the phrase "from stress to well-being" we are not suggesting that the relationship is simply a linear one with each positioned at opposite ends of the same continuum. Stress research has always been about well-being, though the lens through which this has been explored has focused more on reducing its effects than explicitly focusing on how people flourish. The positive psychology movement now presents researchers with the case for exploring the psychology of positive human functioning. Stress and well-being are intimately linked to each other, so the challenge facing researchers is to achieve an evenness in our research that recognizes not just how one contributes to the understanding of the other, but how each separately continues to offer a unique contribution to our understanding of how individuals achieve their potential. The answer may lie in the emphasis we give to each, not just in the way we research them independently, but in the way we research them together.

THE STRUCTURE OF THE BOOK

The first two chapters set the context for the book. Chapter 1 ("Setting the Scene") sets the scene by first questioning whether we are now entering a new phase in how the work experience should be understood. This new understanding stems from the view that what is now needed is a broader, more comprehensive view of the work experience, which gives as much emphasis to its positive qualities as has previously been given to its negative qualities. This change in emphasis has been driven by what is now described as the positive psychology movement. The chapter then turns to critically reviewing this movement and its impact on the study of work. The review begins by looking at what the positive psychology movement stands for, why it emerged at the time it did, and the debate that has embroiled it. The review continues by exploring whether the movement represents a new discrete approach or whether its aim is to better integrate the positive with the negative when it comes to exploring the work experience. From here the chapter explores the two work-specific aspects of the movement (positive organizational scholarship and positive organizational behavior) and the debate that surrounds them. Finally the chapter explores the "good work agenda," before concluding that a balanced approach to understanding the work experience must accept that the positive and negative are intimately linked, and that one cannot be fully understood without reference to the other.

Chapter 2 ("The changing nature of work and its challenges") continues to set the scene by turning first to exploring the changing landscape of work through the lens of three forces: internationalization and global competition, advances in technology, and the changing nature of the workforce. It explores how these forces have driven organizations to focus on economic returns, and by doing so fundamentally marginalized the social, human, and ethical sides of organizational life. The chapter then considers whether some responsibility for this state of affairs should lie with the way management theory has developed, and whether positive psychology has a role to play in providing a sense of balance. The chapter concludes by suggesting that if our theories and practice are going to best express the work experience, then the rediscovering of the social context within which organizational behavior takes place is critical, as it is through this context that the complexities of individual values and beliefs are developed, nurtured, and expressed.

Chapter 3 ("Work and well-being: Progress and prospects") begins a more detailed discussion of work and well-being. Much of the research on work has focused on identifying those job characteristics that have the potential to motivate employees, and how jobs should be designed to capture those qualities. Chapter 3 follows this route. It begins by offering a historical account of job redesign. In doing so, the aim is not just to show how early motivation and job design theories were products of their time, but how these theories are now being redeveloped in a way that makes them more expressive of organizational life in the twenty-first century. This redevelopment has led to: a more elaborate model of job design; a more complex system of socially interdependent behaviors that make the job context more important; an acknowledgment of the importance of proactive and prosocial behaviors; and the addition of new job dimensions that capture the changing nature of the work environment. The chapter then turns to well-being. This section starts with a brief historical interlude that traces the interest in well-being, before exploring current approaches to defining it. Defining well-being raises questions about what it means to be happy, and the possible routes through which happiness can be achieved. Two relatively distinct but overlapping routes to happiness – hedonism and eudaimonism – are identified and discussed, as are the social conditions that support each route. The section on well-being concludes by exploring the different directions being taken to understand the complexity of an emotion like happiness.

The two chapters that follow explore the role of work and its impact, both negative (Chapter 4: "Resource depletion") and positive (Chapter 5: "Resource accumulation"), on well-being using a framework based around the idea of conservation of resources (Hobfoll 2001). Chapter 4 opens with a discussion of the term "stress," the way it has been defined and how these definitions reflect and shape the way stress research has evolved. The chapter then moves to consider the concept of eustress (positive stress) and its role as an indicator of positive functioning. We then argue that, since stress implies emotions, it is discrete emotions, rather than stress, that should become the language of researchers. Focusing on emotions not only overcomes the ambiguity that surrounds the troublesome word "stress," but is more likely to capture the reality of the stress experience. We follow this discussion by examining the debate that surrounds the conservation of resources theory (Hobfoll 2001), and from this initiate a more detailed discussion on the nature of work stressors, their measurement, and how they express the changing landscape of work.

The issue of resource accumulation (Chapter 5) considers resources from the point of view of a process that emphasizes investing in resource conservation strategies that are designed, in the face of work demands, to protect, foster, build, and maintain a reserve that contributes to personal development, individual functioning and capability, health, and well-being. We begin our exploration of resource accumulation by first returning to the concept of well-being, and, using the framework offered by Warr (1990; 1994; 2007), explore what it is about work that makes people happy or unhappy. We then move to positive emotions, their adaptive significance and how these emotions through their ability to "broaden and build" offer opportunities to develop lasting individual resources (Fredrickson 1998). Continuing with this theme of positive human functioning, we explore the concept of positive psychological capital and how this acts as a positive resource that enhances motivational capabilities, identifies individual strengths, and develops their psychological capacities (Luthans *et al.* 2007). We then explore the resource-building concept of resilience. We conclude this chapter on resource accumulation by touching on positive health and positive growth, thriving and flourishing.

Chapter 6 ("Coping and stress interventions") begins by pointing to the debate, and at times controversy, surrounding how coping is defined and what actually constitutes coping. It then explores the different approaches to classifying coping strategies in terms of three themes: focus, mode, and time. This thematic analysis of coping highlights both the need to consider reactive and proactive forms of coping and whether our classification frameworks capture the different ways in which coping strategies evolve. The chapter then turns to the equally thorny question of how coping should be measured. It looks first at the operational and interpretive difficulties associated with coping checklists, before considering whether the way forward, if we are to capture the richness of the coping process, is through the development of more person-focused, process-oriented approaches. The final section on coping explores coping effectiveness. More particularly, it raises the questions of what is meant by coping effectiveness, who is making such judgments, how we know when coping has an effect, and how coping effectiveness should be measured. The chapter then turns to stress interventions, beginning by pointing to not just the social, mental, and economic costs of work stress, but also the generally widely underestimated extent of mental ill-health problems at work. Against this context this section explores what the evidence shows in terms of the effectiveness of different work-stress interventions, the challenges facing evidence-based practice, and the growing need for academic/practitioner/health-professional partnerships in the future. This section concludes with an examination of the influence of positive psychology on work-stress intervention.

The final chapter draws together the areas reviewed under four headings – meaning, measurement, membership, and moral responsibility. Any discussion on work and well-being cannot get away from the ever-present concept of meaning. Meaning is present whether we are talking about what it means to be stressed, to be happy, about meaning-centered coping, or what we mean by evidence, and what evidence should we be collecting. It is clear that to understand the role and importance of meaning in work-stress research requires that we consider where current research methods are taking us, and what methods will provide us with the rich description we are trying to capture. Measurement is at the core of much of what we discuss. Good, innovative work is being done, but if our understanding of the stress process is to advance we need to broaden our measurement practices to consider who should be involved in the design of research, the questions we ask, the way we use that knowledge, and how that knowledge is disseminated. This captures what we mean by membership: when we consider who should be involved we are better placed to consider the utility of the knowledge we produce, the problems worth exploring, the way they need exploring, and the moral responsibilities we have to those whose working lives we study.

CHAPTER 1

SETTING THE SCENE

This book is about work and well-being. It is this relationship that has defined the very nature of organizational psychology and left in its wake a rich and enduring history of how work is experienced. Yet, it is these descriptions of the experience of work that have, within the last decade, attracted a considerable amount of discussion, frequently punctuated by the passionately expressed view that what is needed is a shift in focus to embrace a broader perspective of the work experience, emphasizing and capturing its "positive" qualities, where individuals can be encouraged to flourish. The idea that positive work experiences have been largely ignored by psychology of the past is, of course, robustly debated (Lazarus 2003a). Nevertheless, the new millennium ushered in what is now described as a positive psychology movement (Snyder and Lopez 2007), which gives momentum to a more focused, positive approach to organizational behavior (Wright and Quick 2009). This has led to the emergence of the "good work" agenda, where fulfilling employment is seen as an issue in its own right (Constable *et al.* 2009).

It is against this backdrop that the relationship between work and well-being is explored. We begin this chapter with a brief history of the different phases of organizational psychology, and the different perspectives through which work and well-being have been explored. We then outline the debate that surrounds positive psychology, the ideas emerging in respect of positive organizational scholarship, the need to capture a fuller understanding of organizational life, and finally, what is meant by the "good work" agenda.

A TOUCH OF HISTORY

"Work behavior" is in itself a contentious phrase. Researchers have pointed to the ambiguity surrounding what we mean by work

(Rose 1988). Additionally, prefixes like work, industrial, occupational, and organizational have all, at one time or another, been used to express the way psychology has been used when developing our understanding of workplace behavior. Whilst it is true that, as Arnold *et al.* (1998, p. 44) explain, "psychologists regularly cross these rather artificial boundaries," it is also true that each prefix represents a history that expresses that phase's understanding of the work experience, the level of analysis adopted, and the types of issues confronted. Each provides a context, an anchoring point, for understanding why different approaches were taken, how those approaches were molded and shaped by social and economic conditions, why different ideas emerged and became important, and how they were explained. Without acknowledging this history, the "present becomes less [well] understood" (Cooper and Dewe 2004, p. 114), and we are left to take, almost on faith, the importance of new developments and contemporary ideas, allowing them to assume a significance that ignores the rich history that has preceded them, and the context against which they need to be debated and evaluated.

It is clear that our knowledge and understanding does not exactly "mirror historical circumstances" (Rose 1988, p. 1), and that the development of ideas does not occur in an orderly straightforward fashion, with one idea logically and uncritically "neatly building on another" (Cooper and Dewe 2004, p. 114) free from patronage, misunderstandings, controversy, and intense debate. Nevertheless, running through this history there is a constant and enduring theme, which captures – no matter whether the analysis is at the structural, individual, social, or organizational level – the essence of the psychological perspective; the nature of the work experience as expressed through the work and well-being relationship. It is clear that this relationship has been explored at different times using different lenses, with names that are as familiar to us – classical, human relations, sociotechnical systems, contingency – as the researchers who represent them (Mullins 2002). It is also clear that throughout history this relationship, and by extension the "work experience," has been expressed through a range of ideas, including managerial behavior and effectiveness, organizational goals and strategy, leadership, motivation, job redesign and the quality of working life, work-stress and coping, and the psychological contract.

The question now is whether we are entering a new phase in how the work experience should be expressed; a phase that is now represented by positive psychology, positive organizational scholarship, and the "good work" agenda. Such an idea raises considerable debate, it questions whether our work to date has been unduly focused on the negative, and whether separating the positive from the negative is a somewhat artificial dichotomy. This raises instead the need for synthesis, where both are integrated in a way that reflects the reality of everyday work experiences (Lazarus 2003a). In addition, it raises the point as to whether accentuating the positive is less of a movement and more of a change in emphasis, and asks whether the time has now come to argue for a broader approach, where as much attention is deliberately given to how employees "flourish" as has previously been given to how employees cope with adversity and stress. In reviewing these issues, our aim in this chapter is to set the context for exploring how, through the work and well-being relationship, the nature of the work experience now needs to be expressed.

POSITIVE PSYCHOLOGY

Positive psychology: The movement

The new millennium saw the introduction of positive psychology (Seligman and Csikszentmihalyi 2000). In the decade following its introduction "quite a lot has happened in what has become known as the positive psychology movement" (Gable and Haidt 2005, p. 103). Positive psychology has at times courted controversy, been vigorously criticized, and passionately defended. It continues to raise issues about the realities of life experiences, and how they should best be expressed and understood. If, by provoking this level of debate, positive psychology achieves "nothing more," as Csikszentmihalyi suggests, it "would have served a useful end" (2003, p. 113). So, what is positive psychology, and what is the nature of the debate that surrounds it?

In their millennium article Seligman and Csikszentmihalyi (2000, p. 5), describe three themes running through positive psychology, defining them as "a science of positive subjective experience, positive individual differences, and positive institutions." Taken together they represent a psychology of positive human functioning. Later Seligman and his colleagues go on to describe positive psychology as an "umbrella term for the study of positive emotions, positive character traits, and enabling institutions" (Seligman et al. 2005, p. 410). Csikszentmihalyi goes on to suggest that the aim of positive psychology is "to legitimate the study of positive aspects of human experience in their own right" (2003, p. 114). The message at the heart of these definitions is, as Seligman reminds us, that "psychology is not just the study of disease, weakness, and damage; it also is the study of strength and virtue" (2005, p. 4).

Others have also contributed by defining positive psychology as "nothing more than the scientific study of ordinary human strengths and virtues; positive psychology re-visits the average person" (Sheldon and King 2001, p. 216), and renews "attention on the sources of psychological wellness" (Lyubomirsky and Abbe 2003, p. 132). Rand and Snyder (2003, p. 148) add that the aim of positive psychology is to act as a catalyst for change by refocusing psychology away from its "preoccupation only" with the "worst things in life" to "also building positive qualities." If positive psychology is defined in terms of "the conditions and process that contribute" (Gable and Haidt 2005, p. 104) to human flourishing, then why has it arisen now, and is positive psychology really something new, or only a more innovative way of looking at what has long been the goal of psychology generally?

It is absolutely clear, argue Linley and his colleagues (Linley *et al.* 2006), from even the most "cursory examination" of the literature that "positive psychology has always been with us," but has "passed unrecognized" (p. 4), and has not always received the attention or recognition it deserves. In posing the question "Is positive psychology new?" Csikszentmihalyi responds with "of course not," and in explaining the current ascendancy of positive psychology suggests that, like all other bodies of knowledge, it needs to be reviewed and revisited so that it can be better understood within the context of our ever-evolving body of knowledge (2003, p. 113).

Yet while some contend that positive psychology, as currently expressed, builds upon and learns from earlier work, particularly the work of those who called for a more *humanistic* approach to psychology (e.g. James 1902; Maslow 1954; 1968; Rogers 1961), others are not so sure. Taylor (2001), for example, suggests that positive psychology should be more informed about its history, recognizing that the scientific culture that now allows positive psychology to flourish, is exactly that fought for and established by those early humanists. Similarly, although Bohart and Greening (2001, p. 81) applauded the mainstreaming of positive psychology as articulated by Seligman and Csikszentmihalyi (2000), they too wished that these authors had "done a more scholarly job," when discussing both the contribution made by, and the value placed on, research by humanistic psychology.

Parallels between these early works and positive psychology are – "yet again" – remarkably similar argue Tennen and Affleck (2003). The inspiration found in the work of humanistic psychology as to the nature of human flourishing (Rathunde 2001), and the "complementary human depth" that humanistic psychology can bring to positive psychology, are worth continuing with and engaging in (Resnick *et al.* 2001, p. 94). Recognizing that positive psychology is not new led Seligman to ponder why, with such "distinguished ancestors," the ideas of the humanists failed somehow to amass a body of research on the positive, suggesting that perhaps the power of the negative has traditionally been more compelling, with more of a sense of immediacy, leaving many to take for granted the power and "survival value" of the positive (2005, p. 7). This is why, argue Tennen and Affleck (2003), we need to learn from what has gone before, acknowledging what the issues were and building on why different aspirations failed to be met. While, as Seligman and Csikszentmihalyi suggest, positive psychology "will not need to start afresh," requiring more of a refocusing of "scientific energy" (2000, p. 13), this debate is not yet over, it has stirred up, and leaves in its wake, a number of other issues that question the direction and focus of the positive psychology movement.

Positive psychology: The debate

It is true that the positive psychology movement has come a long way since its manifesto was first introduced by Seligman and Csikszentmihalyi (2000). Its progress has been well charted and its achievements identified (Gable and Haidt 2005; Linley *et al.* 2006; Seligman *et al.* 2005; Simonton and Baumeister 2005). So, despite all this activity, is there still the danger, as Lazarus (2003a, p. 93) suggested, that positive psychology "is just another one of the many fads that come and go in our field?" Not so is the answer. It is not "a panacea for many modern ills" (Linley *et al.* 2006, p. 5), nor is it "happiology" (Seligman and Pawelski 2003), a "pollyanna view of the world" (Gable and Haidt 2005, p. 107), or "a cult" (Simonton and Baumeister 2005, p. 101). It is, argues King (2003), in every sense a movement, and its value as a movement lies in its ability to stimulate scientific endeavor across a range of human experiences, motivate new collaborations, and heighten the focus on new sources of growth and well-being, which can be applied more broadly to people's lives.

As a movement it provides a common vocabulary, a means of uniting and bringing together a number of contrasting lines of enquiry, which now need to be made viable and expressed through a new innovative paradigm (Peterson and Park 2003; Rand and Snyder 2003; Seligman *et al.* 2005). Yet, despite the value in being "a movement," and the idea that, although not new, positive psychology "is having a scientific coming out party" (Rand and Snyder 2003, p. 150), intense, and at times acrimonious, debate continues to swirl around what it is that the positive psychology movement stands for (Lazarus 2003a).

Three concerns confront those trying to understand what the positive psychology movement is really all about, and what is new about it (Lazarus 2003a). These three concerns include whether it makes sense to describe past research in psychology as negative, which in some way "short changes" the positive (Lazarus 2003a, p. 105). Whether those who argue for a declaration of independence for the positive psychology movement (Snyder and Lopez 2005b) are really agitating for a separate movement, distinct from those approaches that have preceded it, and, lastly, whether the positive psychology movement can survive without acknowledging that it, like psychology generally, must be ready to tackle persistent methodological difficulties that confront all researchers attempting to understand well-being (Lazarus, 2003b).

The first two concerns can be discussed together as they both stem from the belief that for too long there has been an imbalance in psychological research, where the focus on, and preoccupation with, human suffering and frailty has dominated, and pushed the study of human growth and individual flourishing into the background. As a result, positive psychology grew out of the need to study the "other side of the coin" (Gable and Haidt 2005, p. 105), to provide an "exciting counterweight" to the more traditional focus (Simonton and Baumeister 2005, p. 99), a "more complete and balanced scientific understanding of the human experience" (Seligman *et al.* 2005, p. 410). The question of human thriving has not received the attention it deserves or the resources needed to research it, this has prevented many in the field from even "recognizing the value" of engaging in such research (Sheldon and King 2001, p. 216), and stopped the positive aspects of human experiences from achieving the legitimacy they deserve (Csikszentmihalyi 2003).

The idea that this imbalance has meant that psychology's traditional focus made for more of a negative psychology, or a psychology preoccupied with what McCullough and Snyder (2000, p. 9) describe as its "dark side" is a moot point, although Lazarus makes it clear that the idea is "specious because it is an inaccurate reading of the literature" (2003a, p. 105). But despite the positive psychology movement's claim that it is offering a different and somewhat new focus, Lazarus argues that this focus is what psychology has always been about (2003a). It may now be possible to sense a shift in the nature of the debate away from the idea of a psychology that is generally negative, towards gauging how much, over the years, has actually been learnt about how individuals flourish (Sheldon and King 2001). That research has simply not produced enough on the experience of human thriving (Gable and Haidt 2005) meaning that we still know very little about human strengths (Snyder and Lopez 2005b).

Whatever its focus, there is still an underlying concern that the positive psychology movement should have done "a more scholarly job of investigating humanistic psychology" (Bohart and Greening 2001, p. 81), rather than giving only casual attention to the considerable contribution made by humanistic psychology (Rathunde 2001), the research tradition that embodies the humanist approach (Taylor 2001), and the common ground that exists between positive and humanistic psychology (Resnick *et al.* 2001). What Ryff describes as the "profound neglect" by positive psychology of past contributions and the "broad scope" of contemporary research that explores positive individual adaptation (2003, p. 155). While this debate will no doubt continue, there is still the equally contentious issue of whether the positive psychology movement is calling for a separate and distinct science.

Positive psychology: Discrete approach or better integration?

When writers appear to describe positive psychology in separatist terms, as being a distinct science (see Held 2004), or say that it has made a "declaration of independence" from "the weakness model of psychology" (Snyder and Lopez 2005b, p. 751), are they really talking about a breakaway movement, a separate science with its own research base? While Seligman and Csikszentmihalyi (2001) are clear that they had no intention of forming an exclusive movement, or of wishing to champion positive psychology as the only right way of thinking about psychology, others have found it important to reinforce the idea that positive psychology's independence lies in the fact that psychology generally now realizes that such a perspective exists, that its focus is on "the positive side of what it means to be human," and that it should now be able to grow and develop alongside the "science and practice of the pathology model" (Snyder and Lopez 2005b, p. 752). Held (2004) points to what she describes as a more integrative message that may now be emerging from the debate, where any sort of exclusivity of the positive from the negative may in the end result in the loss of a much-needed perspective, and fail to capture the full richness of the human experience.

Two views now seem to be emerging in respect of positive psychology's place in psychology. The first is nicely expressed by Folkman and Moskowitz (2003) who, taking up Lazarus's (2003a) plea for a more balanced approach, observe that there is no problem with paying more attention to the positive, but say it should not be at the expense of the negative. Similarly, Seligman and Pawelski (2003, p. 159) add to this view by affirming that they prefer to talk in terms "of psychology as usual," where the positive supplements the negative, providing yet another perspective in our armory, rather than one replacing the other. Snyder and Lopez (2007) also argue for a more inclusive approach which examines both the positive and the negative, making a more comprehensive and valid approach to understanding life's experiences, sentiments shared by Bacon (2005), who argues that the positive and the negative should not be seen as two competing cultures, saying that an understanding of both advances our understanding of the totality of experience and the goals that we pursue as psychologists.

These views arguing for a more integrative rather than a separatist movement begin to blend into the second view, where the hope is that positive psychology becomes nothing more than good psychology (King 2003; Peterson and Seligman 2003). In years to come, suggest Linley *et al.* (2006), positive psychology will no longer be viewed as a movement nor will those concerned about the positive define themselves as such. "A psychology in balance would not need advocates for positive psychology" (Brewster-Smith 2003, p. 162), it simply becomes another part of the very essence of psychology (Diener 2003), and, as such, the movement will have achieved its goal (King 2003).

Positive psychology: Methodological challenges

One final issue remains in the debate that surrounds the advent of the positive psychology movement; that is whether those championing the movement are prepared to acknowledge and tackle the methodological challenges faced by researchers in this field. The answer is emphatically "yes" for Seligman and Csikszentmihalyi (2001, p. 90), who describe themselves as "unblushingly scientists" producing work that is replicable, objective, and evidence-based. Further confirmation, should it be needed, comes from Simonton and Baumeister (2005, p. 99), who argue that the movement has engaged in "rigorous scientific research" with the same enthusiasm and commitment as is expected from all psychologists. Diener (2003) makes it clear that because rigorous measurement is fundamental to, and at the core of, scientific endeavor, then so it must be for positive psychology. Rand and Snyder (2003) argue that without rigorous research positive psychology will lose its credibility, but by applying this rigor to the high standards demanded of any movement creativity can emerge that offers new opportunities to expand horizons. No doubt much more will be written about the positive psychology movement, its message, focus, and meaning.

While the debate is far from over, it is clear that the motivation of many in this debate is to urge for a more balanced approach and a more "appreciative perspective regarding human potential" (Sheldon and King 2001, p. 216), where all are invited to join in and explore the positive side of life-experiences (Simonton and Baumeister 2005). While the nature of any imbalance has been intensely argued, what, by infusion, has emerged from this debate is the need for a "catch-up phase" (Folkman and Moskowitz 2003, p. 121), a focus that has always been present but arguably underemphasized. So, the context for understanding work and well-being now needs to be explored as much in terms of how individuals flourish and improve their lives, as it has been in terms of what has been described as its "deficit-focus" (Linley *et al*. (2006, p. 7). It is in the spirit of capturing the richness of life experiences that we embrace both the positive and the negative when exploring the work and well-being relationship.

POSITIVE ORGANIZATIONAL SCHOLARSHIP

It was only a matter of time before researchers in the field of organizational psychology/organizational behavior began to pay attention to

TABLE 1.1   **Positive psychology – some characteristics of a movement[a]**

- ***Three themes***
  A science of the positive experience, positive individual differences, and positive institutions – collectively they embody a psychology of positive human functioning (Seligman and Csikszentmihalyi 2000, p. 5).
- ***The aim***
  The refocusing and exploration of positive facets of individual experiences (Seligman and Csikszentmihalyi 2000).
- ***A catalyst***
  A mechanism for change – to reunite the field emphasising the role of the positive (Csikszentmihalyi 2003).
- ***Is it new?***
  It builds on what has gone before, capturing and focusing on positive individual qualities that have not always received the attention they deserve (Gable and Haidt 2005; Seligman and Csikszentmihalyi 2000).
- ***Is it a fad?***
  It is not a panacea, nor is it simply a cheery ideology – its importance rests in the way it motivates empirical investigations across a range of positive experiences (Linley *et al.* 2006; Seligman and Pawelski 2003; Simonton and Baumeister 2005).
- ***Where does it come from?***
  It stems from the belief that for too long psychology has had an "imbalance," emphasizing individual vulnerability and failing to capture the richness of individual flourishing. It is now time for this side of individual experiences to emerge to give a more balanced understanding (Peterson and Park 2003; Rand and Snyder 2003; Seligman *et al.* 2005).
- ***Is it a discrete approach?***
  It is a movement that is inclusive – it sees the need for both the positive and the negative being present to give a more comprehensive understanding of individual experiences and capture the richness of that experience (Bacon 2005; Gable and Haidt 2005; Held 2004; Sheldon and King 2001; Snyder and Lopez 2005b).
- ***Does it embody scientific rigor?***
  As scientific rigor is at the core of all psychology then so it is at the heart of positive psychology – it embraces the high empirical standards required of any movement (Diener 2003; Rand and Snyder 2003; Seligman and Csikszentmihalyi 2001; Simonton and Baumeister 2005).

[a] This table and all the others that follow should be read in conjunction with the text. Each table has been constructed from the cited articles in the text and reading them together gives a much richer understanding of the points different authors are making. Each table gives an overview and brings together many of the articles cited: these are all fully acknowledged and referenced in the text. Where references are cited in the table they offer the opportunity to read around the point being made.

the positive psychology message, although to be fair these researchers, as we will see, were quick to acknowledge the long history of research that has embedded the positive in their work. Definitions of positive psychology, as we have noted, rest on three pillars or themes: "positive experiences," "positive individual traits," and "positive organizations." It is this third theme, with its focus on ways of thinking about organizational processes and dynamics that can lead to and stimulate positive experiences, individual development, and opportunities for individuals to flourish, which now needs to be better integrated into organizational research (Gable and Haidt 2005; Roberts 2006).

This need to sharpen the focus on positive organizational experiences found its voice in what has become known as Positive Organizational Scholarship (Bernstein 2003; Cameron and Caza 2004; Roberts 2006). The aim of this perspective is to challenge researchers to reconsider the way they think about organizational experiences, the assumptions they make about individual needs and human nature, and the ideas that they have about the role of organizational processes and structures (George 2004). Its purpose is to lay the foundations from which can emerge a fresh focus on positive organizational experiences, which can then be thoroughly investigated by organizational researchers (Cameron *et al.* 2003).

Positive organizational scholarship: Towards individual flourishing

Describing positive organizational scholarship as an "umbrella term" (Roberts 2006), a "label" that brings together many different approaches (Bernstein 2003), and a "broad framework" (Dutton and Glynn 2008), makes it difficult, according to those who champion it, to capture its nature in "just a few sentences" (see Bernstein 2003, p. 267). Nevertheless positive organizational scholarship is described, if not defined, as a particular way of thinking that "focuses on the dynamics in organizations that lead to the development of human strength, foster vitality and flourishing in employees" (see Bernstein 2003, p. 267). Put simply, positive organizational scholarship is all about identifying and focusing on those organizational processes that promote positive states. It is not so much a new perspective, as a change in focus that "expands and enriches" the scope of organizational research making the field of study more "inclusive and expansive" (Cameron and Caza 2004, p. 732). It is not, as Cameron and Caza go on to add, "fashionable advocacy for the power of positive thinking" (2004, p. 731), but a perspective that has as its core assumptions: "individual flourishing;" the synergistic and complementary nature of the positive and the negative; the belief that new understandings will emerge about organizational behavior when the positive is unlocked and human resourcefulness is released; and that focusing on the positive is both legitimate and worthy of systematic investigation (Dutton and Glynn 2008).

To capture the way in which individuals may flourish, maximize their potential, and fulfill their capabilities, positive organizational scholarship researchers argue for a better understanding of what they describe as "positive deviance" (Bernstein 2003; Cameron and Caza 2004; Spreitzer and Sonenshein 2004). In every respect, the focus of positive organizational scholarship is synonymous with understanding positive deviance, simply because the latter provides the mechanism through which positive acts are investigated, and those organizational processes that produce them are identified (Cameron and Caza 2004). In the view of positive organizational scholarship researchers, organizations, and particularly managers, have failed to understand the concept of "deviance" and, by focusing on conformity through order and control, have unintentionally lost sight of the positive side to deviance, and how it can be managed and developed (Spreitzer and Sonenshein 2003).

Managers have, in their quest for equilibrium and by narrowing their understanding of deviance to mainly negative behaviors, ignored how "organizations and their members partake in positive behaviors" (Spreitzer and Sonenshein 2004, p. 829). They have failed to ask "what is positive deviance, how do you find it, how do you cherish it, how do you nourish and develop it?" (see Bernstein 2003, p. 268). Positive deviance is defined as "intentional behaviors that significantly depart from the norms of a referent group in honorable ways" (Spreitzer and Sonenshein 2004, p. 841). Positive deviance provides the language for understanding positive behaviors that depart from organizational norms, that are located at the very heart of what positive organizational scholarship stands for, and which have profound effects on organizations and individuals alike (Spreitzer and Sonenshein 2004).

Positive organizational scholarship: The debate

Positive organizational scholarship, like the positive psychology movement before it, has been the subject of much debate and critical concern. While these concerns reflect those already raised in respect of the positive psychology movement generally, they are still sufficiently important to be rehearsed one more time. They include whether in searching for the positive in individual performance, a "normative moral agenda" is presented which becomes prescriptive, failing to allow investigation of what positive behaviors may emerge that are free of any "a priori assumptions" (Fineman 2006, p. 281). Similarly, George (2004) in her review of the book *Positive organizational scholarship: Foundations of a new discipline* (Cameron *et al*. 2003), points to what she describes as a "single-mindedness" that pervades some writing on positive organizational scholarship, which seems to suggest that organizations adopt a particular type of positive "ideology," raising questions as to who is it that defines and sets this ideology, and what happens when there are disagreements as to its nature. Nevertheless, she concludes that despite her concerns "this is a serious book for serious scholars" that should act as a repository of knowledge for those who are prepared to engage in genuine reflection on much that is "thought provoking" about positive organizational scholarship (George 2004, p. 326).

Another concern that certainly resonates with the positive psychology movement is a sense that positive organizational scholars, by arguing for a greater emphasis on the positive, discount the negative, when both are mutually linked and inform each other, and "there is more to lose than to gain" by separating them (Fineman 2006, p. 281). Indeed, an understanding of both is needed if we are to capture the richness of organizational life. While the significance of the positive cannot be captured by regarding the positive as merely the reverse of the negative (Roberts 2006), it is "crystal clear" to those championing positive organizational scholarship that to exclude the negative would be unrealistic (see Bernstein 2003; Dutton and Glynn 2008; Roberts 2006). It is, as most advocates of positive organizational scholarship argue, a question of addressing the balance so that as much emphasis is now given to the positive as has, in the past, been given to the negative. In this way the aim is simply to expand the scope of organizational research, capture the dynamics of individual growth and development, better understand the human condition of flourishing, and mainstream what has previously been a somewhat disparate area of organizational study (Cameron and Caza 2004; Dutton and Glynn 2008; Roberts 2006).

Those who champion positive organizational scholarship readily acknowledge that this emerging field is not newly created, but builds on a long tradition of work that has emphasized the positive (see

Bernstein 2003). They also acknowledge that the momentum that has swept through their field, whilst partly explained by the wave of enthusiasm accompanying the positive psychology movement, also has its roots in a more fundamental shift towards developing a better understanding of individual "strength-based approaches," and the need to return to those ethical and social values lost "in the wake of highly visible and significant organizational scandals" (Dutton and Glynn 2008, p. 697).

What positive organizational scholarship stands for will undoubtedly continue to be debated. Amidst all this debate the question, argues Roberts (2006), that must be asked is whether in spite of these concerns the field is better off by exploring positive states and the organizational dynamics that create them? The answer lies simply in the fact that to understand those organizational mechanisms that enable individuals to flourish, then yes "a positive perspective is necessary to achieve this end" (Roberts 2006, p. 301), but that considerably more scholarship is needed in terms of conceptual clarity, theory development, and measurement if these goals are to be achieved (Roberts 2006). In working towards considering how the aims of positive organizational scholarship can be incorporated more closely into organizational life, our attention is directed towards the emerging but complementary perspective of positive organizational behavior.

POSITIVE ORGANIZATIONAL BEHAVIOR

Positive organizational behavior: Its origins

The origins of positive organizational behavior can be found in the work of Luthans (2002a; 2002b). Reflecting on his distinguished career as an organizational behavior scholar, Luthans found, in the positive psychology movement, ideas and concepts that could be used to reenergize and refocus organizational behavior, bringing a more positive approach to established organizational behavior concepts, whilst at the same time introducing new ways in which the positive could effectively be implemented in the workplace. While recognizing the early and auspicious beginnings of organizational behavior, Luthans (2002a; 2002b) argued that there was a growing sense that organizational behavior has, over time and for understandable reasons, given more attention to the negative than the positive. The moment has now come, argues Luthans, for organizational behavior as a discipline to engage with the proactive positive psychology movement, and by "drawing on its own strengths" begin to develop a sustainable positive approach that "builds on employee strengths" and can be put "to effective practice" (2002b, p. 58). These aspirations are encapsulated in what Luthans (2002a; 2002b) describes as "positive organizational behavior."

Luthans (2002a; 2002b) defines positive organizational behavior as "the study and application of positively oriented human resource strengths and psychological capacities that can be measured, developed, and effectively managed for performance improvement in today's workplace" (2002a, p. 698). What distinguishes positive organizational behavior from other more popular "self-help" approaches, he argues (Luthans 2002a; 2002b), stems from the deliberate inclusion of three definitional criteria; (a) being measurable; (b) demonstrating a contribution to improving workplace performance; and (c) an emphasis on "state-like strengths and positive capacities that can be developed and managed" (2002a, p. 698). It is this third criterion of the capacity and readiness to learn and develop that most critically distinguishes positive organizational behavior from other positively focused approaches (Luthans 2002a, b).

When asked what the positive psychological qualities that express these definitional criteria are, Luthans points to concepts like "confidence," "hope," "optimism," "subjective well-being," and "emotional intelligence" (2002a, p. 699). It is these states that become the positive psychological resource, the force that builds strengths, enhances performance, and generates satisfaction and well-being in the workplace (Quick *et al.* 2010). While there is still much more to be done in terms of theory development and research, there is a sense, argues Luthans (2002a, b), that positive organizational behavior is a move in the right direction, and a path that resonates with the way our discipline should be moving in what are challenging and changing times.

Positive organizational behavior: Its contribution

Wright (2003) agrees that the time for positive organizational behavior has now arrived, but goes on to explain that it is also time to balance the somewhat utilitarian approach underlying Luthans' approach with a broader agenda, one that is "proactive" in its support for individuals in their quest for greater well-being and more meaningful lives. To "make a truly valuable contribution," Wright suggests, positive organizational behavior needs to "include the pursuit of employee happiness, health and betterment issues as viable goals in their own right" (2003, p. 441). What emerges, argue Bakker and Schaufeli, when the "organization-centered" view of Luthans (2002a, b) and the "employee-centered" view of Wright (2003) are integrated is "a positive business value model of employee health and well-being" (2008, p. 148).

This more inclusive view is reinforced by Nelson and Cooper (2007), who suggest that the greater variety of approaches that fall within the rubric of positive organizational behavior, the more enriched the field becomes, giving it a legitimacy that will eventually see it accepted as just another facet of organizational behavior. To capture this inclusive characteristic, Nelson and Cooper define positive organizational behavior as "a focus on positive states, traits, and processes within organizations" (2007, p. 4). The inclusion of positive traits in their definition provides the opportunity to explore how traits like, for example "character," "reliance," "hardiness," and "resilience" enhance well-being and constructively contribute to organizations, and how positive interpersonal organizational processes like communications, forgiveness, and thriving contribute to individual exchanges, positive cultures, and individual growth (Nelson and Cooper 2007, pp. 3–4).

Positive organizational behavior is not without its critics (Fineman 2006) and those who adopt the role of the skeptic, highlighting a number of essentially troubling concerns (Hackman 2009a). While the debate – point and counter-point – flows back and forth (Hackman 2009b; Luthans and Avolio 2009b; Wright and Quick 2009), Hackman (2009b) offers two cautions. The first is to be mindful of pace when moving forward, recognizing that it is the quality of work, not the quantity, that will ultimately decide the contribution that positive organizational behavior makes. The second is to be aware that positive organizational behavior needs to do something more than just help people make do with a bad situation, but should help people prosper in work situations that in themselves promote well-being, growth, and development. While, as Luthans and Avolio point out (2009a), researchers are conscious of these concerns and recognize that positive organizational behavior can only progress through innovative theoretical development, strong measurement practices, and critical research findings, attributes already at the heart of the movement (Luthans and Avolio 2009a), there is still every reason to believe that positive organizational behavior adds value in a number of different ways.

This includes offering a more inclusive approach to organizational behavior at a time when the challenges facing organizations warrant such inclusiveness (Luthans and Avolio 2009b). Positive organizational behavior also continues to question what we mean by positive, allowing for a more comprehensive concept to emerge that embraces and is intimately linked to the negative (Bakker and Schaufeli 2008). It allows our understanding of positive states, traits, and processes to develop in a way that encourages new insights into how these mechanisms contribute to individual growth and development (Quick *et al.* 2010). Finally, positive organizational behavior helps to transfer this knowledge into practice so that we meet our moral obligation to those whose working lives we study.

THE GOOD WORK AGENDA

The growth of the positive psychology movement, and its translation into the workplace through concepts like positive organizational behavior, has led to two developments which are not mutually exclusive. As researchers began to explore the positive message, with its emphasis on individual flourishing and growth, attention turned to the associated issues of "what makes good work" focusing on what healthy work is, and what is meant by "a good work agenda" (Coats and Lekhi 2008; Quick *et al.* 2010). The quality that best captures the notion of healthy work is balance (Quick *et al.* 2010). The role of balance is to broaden our understanding of health so as to provide a more comprehensive context for identifying those features that articulate healthy individuals and healthy organizations (Quick and Macik-Frey 2007).

The idea of health, argue Quick and Macik-Frey, has increasingly moved away from the body–mind split, to one that now not only enthusiastically embraces both, but sets them within a much broader canvass that encompasses "emotional, spiritual and even ethical dimensions." This allows for a much more inclusive understanding of health that goes beyond the traditional concept to include prospering, flourishing, and thriving (2007, p. 27). When promoting in workplaces this broader, more positive, view of health three core features need to be present. They include, say Quick and Macik-Frey, "leading a life of purpose, quality connections to others and positive self-regard

TABLE 1.2 **Positive organizational behavior: An overview**

Its origins
- Positive organizational behavior grew out of the work of Luthans, who found in the positive psychology movement ideas that, he argued, could reenergize organizational behavior (Luthans 2002a, b).
- Positive organizational behavior is all about investigating positive individual strengths, resources, and psychological capacities that can be measured, developed, and managed for improving performance (Luthans 2002a, p. 698).
- Positive organizational behavior embraces three themes – qualities that can be measured, that contribute to workplace performance, and can be developed and managed (Luthans 2002a, p. 698).
- Positive organizational behavior provides an explanatory pathway that reflects the emphasis on the positive, the need for change and a direction that resonates with contemporary workplace challenges.

Its contributions
- Positive organizational behavior researchers take Luthans's (2002a) agenda and broaden it to integrate the organizational development performance focus with an individual view into a concept that provides a positive model that also captures employee health and well-being (Nelson and Cooper 2007; Wright 2003).
- Recognizing that in order to progress positive organizational behavior researchers need to ensure there is continuous theoretical development, rigorous measurement practices and critical empirical findings (Luthans and Avolio 2009a).
- In this way positive organizational behavior can add value by constantly exploring what is meant by being positive, how such meanings contribute to individual flourishing, and how this knowledge can be transferred into practice (Bakker and Schaufeli 2008; Luthans and Avolio 2009b; Quick *et al.* 2010).

The good work agenda
- This emphasis on the positive has meant that there is now a greater emphasis being placed on "what makes good work" and what needs to be done to begin to develop a good work agenda (Coats and Lekhi 2008; Quick *et al.* 2010).
- The emphasis on the positive has also resulted in a much broader understanding of health, and what this means for healthy individuals and healthy organizations, with policy that reflects meaningful work set within a life of purpose, quality interpersonal connections, and opportunities for positive self development (Quick and Macik-Frey 2007, p. 28).
- Job quality becomes important meaning that organizational policy and procedures need to develop and sustain a quality of working life that becomes an issue in its own right constantly emphasizing meaning and purpose (Bevan 2010; Coats 2009).

and mastery" (2007, p. 28). It is this framework that provides a more balanced, inclusive basis for understanding health, and, by extension, the basis for healthy individuals and organizations (Quick *et al.* 2010; Quick and Macik-Frey 2007).

The idea of "leading a life of purpose," one of the cornerstones of a broader view of health, is at the heart of the good work agenda with its focus on meaningful and "fulfilling employment" (Brown *et al.* 2006, p. 1). The good work agenda has at its center, the belief that "if we care about the capabilities of individuals to choose a life that they value then we should care about job quality" (Coats and Lekhi 2008, p. 6). The objective when it comes to good work, is to consider the design of jobs and the role of management in a way that leads to work becoming a source of "well-being, personal growth, fulfillment, autonomy and meaning" (Constable *et al.* 2009, p. 6). Embedded in this objective is the belief that good work "is a social act and a fully human activity" (Coats and Lekhi 2008, p. 23), and that in achieving this belief the goal should be to develop and sustain a quality of working life as an important issue in its own right (Brown *et al.* 2006). Working life should offer (a) a sense of self-worth (Black 2008); (b) a greater emphasis on meaning and purpose (Overell 2008), a focus on work that stimulates and challenges (Barber 2009); and (c) an acceptance that good work is good health (Bevan 2010).

Whether the good work agenda has been influenced by the positive psychology movement, is a moot point. The ideals characterizing the good work agenda are more likely to have their beginnings in the "growing and compelling" evidence that quality of work is clearly related to health and well-being (Bevan 2010, p. 3). Hence the argument that to understand the good work agenda you have first to begin by understanding the science (Coats and Lekhi 2008; Lundberg and Cooper 2010). Nevertheless, it is interesting to speculate on how one could be seduced into thinking that the good work agenda builds on elements of positive psychology. For example, in discussing meaningful work Overell (2008, p. 36) talks about "the ghost" of Maslow, and how "the contours" of meaningful work become much clearer when a more expansive, less traditional, approach is adopted, which embraces "more psychological types of issues like self-realization, self-esteem, expression, personal formation and psychological growth" (2008, p. 36). Similarly, at the heart of good work, argue Coats and Lekhi, lies the concept of "social capital"; the "bonding" and "bridging" between employees and employers that creates a positive culture of trust, where work "engages all our skills, talents, capabilities, and emotions" (2008, p. 20; 13). However, the reality is that good work, good health, and organizational performance are all linked, and we must remember that "work is good for us, but that work is only good for us if it is 'good work'" (Coats 2009, p. 10).

OVERVIEW

This chapter began by saying that this book is all about work and well-being. That remains true. We have presented an argument that to understand the relationship between work and well-being we now need to consider not just the negative aspects of work but also those aspects that capture the positive qualities of work, where individuals flourish and thrive, and are encouraged to do so. This required setting a context that explored the influence of the positive psychology movement, and the associated ideas of positive organizational scholarship and positive organizational behavior. We also drew attention to concepts like healthy work and the "good work agenda." While this chapter has emphasized these positive ideals, our aim in this chapter and those that follow is to present a balanced approach, which accepts that the positive and the negative are intimately linked, and that one cannot be fully understood without reference to the other. Nevertheless, it has been necessary to present the positive movement in some detail so as to capture the intensity of the debate, the passion that has been expressed, and the issues that have been involved. Our aim now is to go forward and discuss the work and well-being relationship in more detail, exploring both positive and negative aspects of work, and the range of emotions and behaviors, both positive and negative, that best capture a more contemporary understanding of well-being.

CHAPTER 2

THE CHANGING NATURE OF WORK AND ITS CHALLENGES

We begin this chapter by reviewing the changing nature of work, and use this as the context for the chapter that follows, to better understand how well traditional notions of work and well-being capture and express this changing landscape. We look first at how global competition and internationalization, advances in technology, and a more diverse work-force have led to an emphasis on higher value-added services and a "weightless economy" (Coyle and Quah 2002). We follow this discussion on the changing landscape of work by exploring: new challenges facing management practices, and the values and ideology that surrounds them (Ghoshal 2005), whether organizational research needs to become more relevant (Dutton and Glynn 2008), the changing nature of leadership (Podolny *et al*. 2005), the links between positive psychology, business ethics, and corporate responsibility (Giacalone *et al*. 2005), and the role and significance of Human Resource Management as the agent for organizational integrity, trust and authenticity (Sears 2010).

THE LANDSCAPE OF WORK

Over the last forty years we have seen dramatic changes across the whole of society. It is now generally accepted that three forces have been at the heart of these changes. These three forces are: (a) *internationalization and global competition*, which continues to bring dramatic and complex changes to the nature and structure of work, the distribution of capital, knowledge and skills, labor and consumer markets, where work is organized, where it is located, how it is managed, the leadership styles required, the opportunities to work, and the way in which we want to work and live. Economies, too, have changed from being based on manufacturing and production to being based on information and services. (b) *Advances in technology* also continue to influence how capital, products, and employment are managed, organized, and led, the types of management practices needed, the skills required, and how they are combined and located to produce goods and services that reflect a significant increase in their knowledge base, and the growing importance of value-added design, product differentiation, and fashion. Technology will continue to influence the nature of the social context within which work takes place, influencing the way in which we communicate, relate to one another, cooperate and work together, the blurring of boundaries between work, home, and other aspects of our lives, and changes in preferences as to where, when, and how we work. The intensity of competition and the continued rise in consumer expectations "place a premium on more rapid innovation, customized products and greater organizational responsiveness" (Jones *et al.* 2007, p. 9). (c) *Workforces are also changing*. Demographic changes point to an aging workforce, with generational differences in aspirations and values, the increasing number and importance of women in employment, and changing immigration patterns, all of which continue the trend towards a more culturally diverse workforce. These demographic changes mean that the work environment becomes more complex in terms of human resource legislation, more demanding in terms of flexibility, equity, fairness, and equal opportunities, and more responsible in terms of care, support, and development. Intergenerational differences and workforce diversity will present an array of values and expectations that will impact on the role of work in people's lives, the changing nature of careers and the meaning of career success, the intensity with which we work, the demands for flexible working, the maintenance of work–life balance, the ability to make choices and express individual preferences, and the growing tension between what we want from work and what work can provide. All will influence how organizations are structured, managed, and led.

Technology, the growth in service sector employment, and the emphasis on knowledge-based and innovative products, will inevitably require continuous reskilling and a more highly skilled workforce, one that is more flexible in terms of how work is arranged and organized, and how organizations are structured and managed. Work will assume more of an "emotional quality," with greater interaction between employees and customers. At the same time, employees will become a unique source of competitive advantage, and resource-based strategies (competing through people) will emphasize the central role of people in organizational success. While all advanced economies have witnessed and been shaped by these forces, there has been some debate as to how to describe the shift in employment from manufacturing towards services. Any attempt to describe these changes must encompass this move towards "higher value added services," a greater "investment in intangible assets such as software and human capital," and "an increase in the number of employees with higher levels of qualifications" (Brinkley *et al.* 2010, p. 5). While terms like "postindustrial society," and "network and knowledge-based economy" have been used, what is clear is that such a shift means that economies are "becoming increasingly weightless" (Coyle and Quah 2002, p. 8). The notion of "weightless" refers to the idea that "creating value depends less and less on physical mass, and more and more on intangibles, such as human intelligence, creativity, and even personal warmth" (Coyle and Quah 2002, p. 8).

Looking to the future, as globalization and technological change intensify, the nature of weightlessness, "people and tacit knowledge are likely to become increasingly important [along with] human resource factors – particularly management skills and development [becoming] even more crucial" (Confederation of British Industry 2007, p. 10). The future requires the "speeding up of human capital management" in "two very important areas": advancing the development of human resource accounting, coupled with more focused attention being given to the "human" in human resources, articulated through forms of employee engagement and organizational cultures (Chartered Institute of Personnel and Development 2007, p. 26). In respect of the latter, the important element here is partnership, where all in the organization work together as partners, developing new approaches to working relationships and accepting that partnership at work "should no longer be regarded simply as a well-meaning slogan" (Taylor 2005, p. 22).

FORCES OF CHANGE AND HUMAN RESOURCE MANAGEMENT

All of these changes will continue to influence human resource management, and we can expect to witness a new generation of practice that lays the foundations "for future [sustainable] success with a level of focus and priority that is new" (Sears 2010, p. 4). In order to stimulate debate about what the new generational practices may be, Sears puts forward three themes built around emerging practices and views from human resource and management professionals. Sears describes the first of these themes as the "future-proofing" of organizational cultures. By recognizing the importance of employee engagement, and its key component trust, and by developing this further by taking it to its next level through a process that emphasizes "organizational authenticity," employee trust develops not just through what an organization stands for, but also through "day-to-day experience that reinforces this in numerous ways" (2010, p. 8). Future proofing organizational cultures includes not just recognizing the importance of healthy cultures, but also the need for such cultures to become more "agile" and "adaptable" (p. 10), more understanding of what talents, abilities, and values are needed, more aware of what behaviors are acceptable, how such behaviors are encouraged, how they reflect what the organization stands for, and how they all contribute to the building and valuing of equity (p. 12).

The second of these change themes points to what Sears describes as "an insight-driven approach to Human Resources," built around what supports or prevents organizational success. From both a strategic and operational perspective, this approach emphasizes how Human Resources can "shape solutions, challenge conventions, [and] find new solutions to old problems" by identifying just what it is that will make a difference (Sears 2010, p. 13). This insight, he argues, requires Human Resources to expand its horizons to ensure it understands the core values that drive the business, the nature of the market, social and economic trends influencing the business, and the "change dynamics" that need developing to bring about sustainable success (pp. 15–16).

The third and final theme identified by Sears in his research, describes a "new breed" of Human Resource leaders who are able to operate as "partners and provocateurs," because their knowledge and skills provides them with a "real share of voice and influence" (2010, p. 17) that goes beyond their traditional organizational position. This offers the organization a perspective and a sense of purpose that challenges, builds on core values, and clearly understands the wider role that human resources must adopt if it is to contribute to sustained organizational performance. However, as Wong and his colleagues make clear (Wong *et al.* 2009), any future changes in human resource practice rely on the profession itself drawing on available research knowledge, otherwise despite pockets of innovation and the recognition that cultures, values, and engagement can all help to transform practice, "the profession will continue to react to external pressures with only limited scope to be strategic about its own development as a profession" (2009, p. 30).

TABLE 2.1 **The changing nature of work**

The forces of change
- Internationalization and global competition.
- Technological advances.
- Workforce diversity.

Structural and organizational change
- From mechanistic to organic structures.
- From control-driven to value-driven organizations.
- From bureaucracy to network structures.
- From transactional, transformational, leadership to authentic leadership.
- From personnel management to sustainable human resource management.
- From an economic imperative management style to a more inclusive, socially responsible management style.

Management challenges
- Managing the intensification of work in terms of how it is organized, planned, rewarded, controlled, and evaluated.
- Managing the nature of work as it takes on more of an emotional quality.
- Managing the demand for flexible working and work–life balance.
- Managing a more diverse workforce in terms of ethnicity, age, generational differences, and gender.
- Recognizing that the nature of management is itself changing, with managers needing to act more as facilitators.
- Recognizing the importance of resource based strategies (competing through people) and the responsibilities this brings with it in terms of individual competencies, learning and development, and proving meaningful work.
- Recognizing the changing nature of careers, and how for both individuals and organizations advice and guidance will be needed in terms of how careers are structured, how career expectations are met, how such expectations are managed, and how careers are evaluated in contemporary organizations.
- Recognizing the importance of the "green agenda" and its management needs in terms of environmentally friendly strategies, sustainability, work patterns, and carbon initiatives.

Global competition, technology, and the "weightless" economy have undoubtedly led to radically changed organizational structures and management styles. The extent to which the structural and managerial changes brought about by these forces can now be held responsible for the excesses that fuelled the financial crisis, the corporate scandals, and the large-scale organizational failures that have "cast a chilling pall over the way business is conducted" (Fry 2005, p. 48), remains somewhat of a moot point. Nevertheless, there is little doubt that the emphasis on, and drive for, economic and financial gain at all cost has increasingly and fundamentally marginalized the social, human, and ethical side of organizations, and created "seemingly intractable issues that must [now] be addressed" (Fry 2005, p. 48).

What is clear is that in dealing with these "intractable issues," organizational research needs to become more relevant (Dutton and Glynn 2008), we need to revisit what we mean by leadership (Podolny *et al.* 2005), the critical links between positive psychology business ethics and corporate responsibility need exploring (Giacalone, *et al.* 2005), and human resources need, more than ever, to become the innovators and distillers of organizational integrity, trust, and authenticity (Sears 2010). In pursuing the changing nature of work and organizations, it is to these issues that we now turn.

MANAGEMENT THEORY AND ITS IMPACT ON PRACTICE

In his seminal paper on whether bad management theories are destroying good management practices, Ghoshal raises the concern that management research, and the values and ideologies that surround it, "have had some very significant and negative influences on the practice of management," not least because they have freed those practicing such ideas from "any sense of moral responsibility" (2005 p. 76). From his detailed analysis, Ghoshal argues that the ideas and assumptions dominating theories surrounding management practice present a gloomy pessimistic vision of individuals and organizations. They focus on limiting the cost of negative problems, allowing managers to legitimize such practices as the norm, because as they "gain currency," often through "theorists persuade[ing] managers to use them" (Kanter 2005, p. 93), managers believe not just that it is the way to manage, but that they are managing in accordance with some reliable and testable theory. This sets in motion "processes that tend to ensure they become self-fulfilling" and make assumptions about people and organizations that "can be harmful" (Pfeffer 2005, p. 96).

The rethinking of management theories

While the depth, rigor, and cogency of Ghoshal's argument, and the passion with which it is expressed, may not be apparent from this summary, it can be captured in Ghoshal's description and argument about the dominant reductionist and methodological narrowness that prevails when conventional managerial theories describe human nature, behaviors, and values. In many respects, as Ghoshal portrays, behaviors are driven by, reduced to, and evaluated against the language of economic imperatives that describe behaviors in terms of their instrumental, rational, impersonal, self-interested, and emotionally detached qualities, isolated and separated from the social context of the organization itself. Is it not time, argues Ghoshal, to revisit and "fundamentally rethink" some of these issues? (2005, p. 81).

What if, Ghoshal asks, we were not only to broaden our thinking about the nature of managerial scholarship, reinvent "our taste" (p. 82) for pluralism, pay more attention to synthesis, and be more inclusive in our outlook, but also recognize in our scholarship the complexity of human behavior, focus not just on the negative but allow the positive to emerge as a legitimate area of study, pay attention to issues of context, choice, meaning, and process? Then, argues Ghoshal, we could build management theories "that are broader and richer than the reductionist and partial theories we have been developing over the last 30 years" (2005, p. 87).

Ghoshal makes it clear that, although it will not be an easy task, business and management schools need to own up to their role and explain why they have contributed to, or at best allowed, such research, and its accompanying ideology to emerge as victorious in corporate boardrooms. To prevent "bad management theories" from "destroying good management practices" (2005, p. 86), Ghoshal suggests that we need to "think more broadly, more inclusively about what constitutes valuable scholarship" (Hambrick 2005, p. 104). He points to the emergence of new initiatives such as positive psychology, positive organizational scholarship, and the move by some economists to explore the interaction between economics, institutional values, individual well-being, and ethics. These new initiatives are still some way from being described as mainstream, and are yet to achieve a significant and much needed shift in thinking. However, of the eminent scholars who were offered the opportunity to comment on Ghoshal's paper (Donaldson 2005; Gapper 2005; Hambrick 2005; Kanter 2005; Mintzberg 2005; Nord 2005; Pfeffer 2005), whilst some suggested that Ghoshal may have overstated the influence of management scholarship, all, as Nord so neatly summarizes, "agreed so strongly with the basic claims of a work that challenged so deeply the major tenets of the status quo in our field" (2005, p. 92).

WHAT HAS BECOME OF LEADERSHIP?

The need to think about where current methodologies are taking us, and what alternative methodologies could provide, is not just a call to management researchers, but to all researchers. Such arguments can be found in other branches of organizational research, where commentators ponder how to "breath life [back] into organizational studies" (Dutton 2003, p. 5), inviting researchers to pursue new ways of explaining patterns of life in organizations that arise from a need to improve the quality of the work experience. Or ask what is needed "to reconstruct" research so that balance is restored and both the social and the economic are served when trying to answer what is the nature of organizational life (Walsh *et al*. 2003). If bad management practice has become self-fulfilling then what has become of leadership? Leadership theory and practice has, it seems, lost its way (Podolny *et al*. 2005). Arguments with which we are already familiar point to leaders being so obsessed by short-term results that they fail to recognize and create sustainable organizational performance (May *et al*. 2003).

Similarly, business schools have to shoulder some of the blame since "the desire to elucidate the causes of performance is very strong in the marketplace of ideas" (Podolny *et al*. 2005, p. 10). Arguments can also be made for leaders to step up and take the blame for organizational wrongdoing, by accepting responsibility for building organizational cultures based on "self-serving ideologies" that "institutionalize and socialize" employees to routinely engage in wrong behaviors (Ashford and Anand 2003, p. 1). In this context, it should not come as a surprise that when questions like "Why do leaders want to lead?" are raised, answers invariably emphasize egotistical motives like self-interest, personal achievement, power, and control, leaving altruistic motives like concern for others, empowerment, and the "desire to serve" out in the cold (Whittington 2004).

Theories surrounding leadership have, argue Podolny and his colleagues, gone awry, because they have been contaminated by the belief that if leadership cannot be seen to contribute directly to organizational performance then "leadership does not matter to organizational life" (2005, p. 4). Podolny and his colleagues go on to suggest that "when decoupled," the different behaviors and attributes that combine to define leadership make it easy to relate to performance, satisfying the concern for economic outcomes. However, what lies at the core of their argument is that you cannot judge the importance of leadership to organizational life by simply focusing on economic performance alone. Leadership is something more than that. What is missing, argue Podolny and his colleagues, is the "importance of leadership in terms of its ability to infuse purpose and meaning into the organizational experience" (Podolny *et al.* 2005, p. 5). To regain our understanding of the importance of leadership in organizational life, the focus must shift back to exploring what meaningful actions are, how they become instilled in organizations, how they affirm organizational purpose, and how they are expressed through the meanings individuals derive from work (Podolny *et al.* 2005).

What constitutes genuine leadership?

Challenging times, and the turbulence they create for organizations, call for a "refocus on what constitutes genuine leadership" (Avolio and Gardner 2005, p. 316). Leadership scholars and practitioners alike are familiar with the development of leadership theories. They are also familiar with the different styles of leadership, and how these are described in transactional, charismatic, transformational, and global terms. Yet despite the currency of these styles, and their examination in terms of the values they express (Kanungo 2001; Price 2003; Whittington 2004), new ways of thinking and adaptation of styles are called for, styles that begin the process of rekindling trust in organizational governance, recapturing the full meaning of leadership, developing a more positive approach to leadership, and restoring the balance that has been lost to economic and performance indicators. By building on those leadership styles that have gone before, and searching for such characteristics as "transparency, trust, integrity, and high moral standards" (Gardner *et al.* 2005, p. 344), what emerges is a call for a more authentic style of leadership (Avolio and Gardner 2005).

"Authentic leadership" has its roots in the positive psychology movement and represents what Luthans and Avolio describe as "the confluence" of positive organizational behavior, transformational and moral/ethical leadership (2003a, p. 243). The synergy of these three approaches channeled into the concept of authentic leadership offers a new beginning, and a shift in emphasis in the way organizations need to be led if they are to meet the challenges they face from the recent unparalleled changes (Luthans and Avolio 2003a). Authentic leadership is defined as "a process that draws from both positive psychological capacities and a highly developed organizational context which results in both greater self-awareness and self-regulated positive behaviors on the part of leaders and associates, fostering positive self-development" (Luthans and Avolio 2003a, p. 243).

The necessary qualities of authentic leadership include self-awareness, being true to your personally held values and beliefs, and basing actions on those beliefs (Avolio and Gardner 2005; Gardner *et al.* 2005; May *et al.* 2003), drawing on such positive psychological resources as "confidence, optimism, hope and resilience" (Avolio and Gardner 2005; Gardner and Schermerhorn 2004; Luthans and Avolio 2003a). Gardner *et al.* (2005) suggest that this style of leadership should not be thought of as just about the authenticity of the leader. It also involves developing and sustaining authentic relations with followers, or "authentic followership," built around "transparency, openness, and trust," working towards laudable goals and recognizing the significance of, and engaging in, follower development (Gardner *et al.* 2005, p. 345).

THE SHAPING OF POSITIVE LEADERSHIP

As Luthans and Avolio (2003a) make clear, there is still much to learn about what shapes positive leadership development. What is also clear, however, is the need to recognize the potential of positive leadership as expressed through an authentic style in building sustainable futures and sustainable performance (Avolio and Gardner 2005). The urgency of the challenges facing organizations has led others to explore the notion of positive leadership. Researchers have over the last decade, for example, been attracted to, and given attention to, "spiritual leadership" in organizations, and its power in giving meaning and purpose. Spiritual leadership promotes "transcendence through work" (Dent *et al.* 2005, p. 627), and the role it can play in providing ethical and spiritual well-being, and corporate social responsibility (Fry 2005).

There are many more perspectives in the field focusing on: the challenge of ethical leadership (Fulmer 2004), managing for the common good and prosocial leadership (Lorenzi 2004), developing a construct of ethical leadership (Trevino and Brown 2007), exploring the ethics of authentic transformational leadership (Price 2003), ethical values of transactional and transformational leaders (Kanungo 2001), integrating leadership styles and ethical perspectives (Aronson 2001), and personalism and moral leadership through the "servant leader" with a transforming vision (Whetstone 2002).

TABLE 2.2 **What's happening to leadership?**

The climate for change

- It is clear that researchers are being invited to explore new ways of explaining organizational life; to restore a sense of balance where as much attention is now given to the social aspects of organizational life as has been given to the economic (Ghoshal 2005).
- What is now needed is a broader view of organizational life that captures the richness of the work experience where organizational behavior is seen and understood in terms of the social context within which it is embedded, recognizing that such behavior is complex and has attached to it a range of social and ethical responsibilities (Ghoshal 2005).
- There is every sense that leadership has lost its way seeking short term results in a way that has given little attention to how those results are achieved, little emphasis on the wider more inclusive responsibilities necessary to lead, and had little responsibility for the cultures and values that emerge (Ashford and Anand 2003; May *et al.* 2003; Podolny *et al.* 2005).

What needs to happen?

- What is missing is the need for leadership to once again "infuse a sense of meaning and purpose" (Podolny *et al.* 2005, p. 4) that affirms organizational values, that reflect a broader spectrum of behaviors that give a greater meaning to the organizational experience.
- While leadership theories cover transactional, charismatic, and transformational styles, the call by researchers is for new ways of thinking about leadership, or redevelopment of established styles – to rebuild a sense of trust in the way organizations are managed, and restore a balance that has been lost to the economic imperative (Avolio and Gardner 2005; Gardner *et al.* 2005; Kanungo 2001).
- What emerges is a more authentic style of leadership, where leaders exhibit a more highly developed sense of self-awareness, where actions are based on transparency, openness, and trust, and emphasis is placed on sustainable individual and organizational development (Avolio and Gardner 2005).
- Researchers have also been attracted to spiritual leadership (Dent *et al.* 2005) and the way it offers meaning and purpose, ethical leadership, (Fulmer 2004) and management for the common good through prosocial leadership (Youssef and Luthans 2005).
- What is needed is for the balance to be brought back into leadership – research now has to determine what is needed to bring about this balance, establishing the organizational dynamics that facilitate achieving a greater balance in leadership style, and develop in leadership practice a sense of valued meaning, purpose and responsibility (Waddock 2005).

While Luthans and Avolio (2003a) make the point that the time is now right, and that never has the need for authentic leadership been greater. They are also quick to remind the reader that creating awareness of what constitutes authentic leadership is only the first step. What is now needed, they add, is research that proactively identifies ways to develop the practice of such a leadership style. There is, in the writings of Luthans and Avolio (2003a), a strong self-development theme, which points to those qualities that need developing if authentic leadership is to take a hold on practice, just as there is in positive psychology more generally the belief that creating such positive knowledge and practice has self-reinforcing qualities (Lee *et al.* (2003).

Whether these qualities are sufficient to capture and take forward the balance that is missing in leadership development depends as much on how well such research and beliefs are disseminated as it does on corporate leaders recognizing, taking forward, and instilling such qualities and styles in their organizations (Peterson and Seligman 2003). Much is still to be done, not least of which is determining what is needed to drive this call for "balance" forward, identifying the organizational dynamics that facilitate such a shift in leadership style, infusing into leadership practice a sense of meaning and purpose, and determining how, through these leadership qualities, organizational performance and survival can best be sustained.

LEADERSHIP AND THE ROLE OF POSITIVE PSYCHOLOGY

The positive psychology movement grew out of a need to emphasize the value of exploring today's challenges in terms of people's strengths, and instilling, through a greater sense of positivity, new perspectives in theory research and practice. This craving for positivity, as Youssef and Luthans (2005) describe it, draws attention to the role that the positive psychology movement and, more particularly, positive organizational behavior can play in helping meet the challenges facing organizations. Meeting these challenges is as much about developing alternative approaches, and the application of those approaches, as it is about overcoming "the prevailing preoccupation with negativity" (Youssef and Luthans 2005, p. 2). The call for more attention to be given to authentic leadership (Avolio and Gardner 2005) represents just one way in which positive psychology has offered an alternative approach to meeting the challenges facing today's organizations. Another, stemming from the work on authentic leadership, is the role positive organizational approaches can play in providing "proactive and creative" approaches to the ethical performance of organizations (Youssef and Luthans 2005, p. 2).

The fraudulent behaviors and socially and ethically irresponsible scandals that have swept through organizations over the last decade demand, argue Youssef and Luthans (2005), new approaches that go beyond the remedial solutions that have dominated the past. At the heart of these new approaches lies the belief that individuals need to develop within themselves and their organization a greater capacity to act ethically; a capacity that is built around individual strengths and from which "deeper meanings" are derived (Youssef and Luthans 2005). As their contribution to building ethical capacity, Youssef and Luthans (2005) introduce the idea of "positive psychological capital." Positive psychological capital is the combination of a number of positive organizational behaviors – capacities that are unique, measurable, developable, and performance-related (Luthans *et al.* 2004; Luthans and Youssef 2004).

Positive psychological capital is defined as "an individual's positive psychological state of development" (Avey *et al.* 2009, p. 678) "to which each of the individual resources of efficacy, hope, optimism, and resiliency synergistically contributes" (Avey *et al.* 2009, p. 434). Youssef and Luthans (2005) go on to illustrate how each of these different positive psychological resources can be developed, not just to build a capacity to act ethically, but to establish an ethically driven culture that reinforces the significance of such resources as powerful strengths in sustaining ethical behaviors. To validate this approach more research is needed, but, as Youssef and Luthans go on to conclude, work to date suggests that such an approach "can make meaningful inroads in the complex mosaic of ethical performance" (2005, p. 18).

POSITIVE PSYCHOLOGY AND THE RESPONSIBLE ORGANIZATION

Positive psychology offers a number of other approaches that deal with the issue of ethical behaviors in organizations. Waddock (2005), for example, builds her work around the idea that organizations need now to relearn what it means to be a responsible organizational citizen, developing the concept of "positive corporate citizenship." While Waddock acknowledges that knowing what to do to be a good corporate citizen is one thing, she states that making it happen is perhaps more difficult when set against present organizational realities. Nevertheless, Waddock (2005, pp. 25; 28) identifies a number of "foundation values" (integrity, mindfulness, and respect) upon which positive corporate citizenship is built, and from which vision and values emerge that add positive value by developing, for example, trust, shareholder engagement, responsibility, transparency, and accountability. While Waddock (2005) emphasizes the normative, "what might be," nature of her concept and the long-term "journey" that is involved, there is no doubting the value added by being positive, and the need for developing such positive insights in organizational research.

Logsdon and Young also argue for the need to improve organizational ethics. For them, positive psychology offers, through the concept of transcendence, an opportunity to develop in individuals much more of a "worldview or perspectives larger than themselves" (2005 p. 112), motivating and developing the "capacity for empathy and interest in creating a positive ethical culture" (p. 118). In the same vein, Pawelski and Prilleltensky (2005) suggest that exploring the theoretical nature of the concept of "good" in positive psychology also aids our understanding of organizational ethics, while Shorey et al. (2005) argue that through the ethics of "hope," individuals and organizations can build a socially responsible way of doing business.

The role that positive psychology can play in developing the "critical linkages" that foster business ethics and corporate responsibility is thoroughly explored by Giacalone et al. (2005) in their edited book from which much of this discussion is drawn. Yet, as we will continue to see, the influence of positive psychology, positive organizational scholarship, and positive organizational behavior extends into all facets of organizational life. It is through expressing the need for a more balanced agenda that the positive psychology movement contributes to the debate surrounding the goodness of fit between organizational theories and research, and the changing nature of work and organizations.

OVERVIEW

The meaning of work and the management of organizations constantly challenged by globalization, technological advances, and workforce diversity has led researchers, practitioners, and commentators to question current methodologies and to raise the issue of what can be learnt from alternative methods. This is at a time when many of these "macro forces," which were generally applauded, overwhelmingly accepted and robustly endorsed as vital for growth and prosperity, have now wreaked havoc across societies, economies, industries, and the workforce. Rather than growth and prosperity, the general economic outlook is now best described by terms like "economic downturn," "credit crunch," "double-dip recession," "deficit cutting," "reduced public spending," and "private sector uncertainty." Managing through all this turbulence and change is further challenged as traditional organizational practices and techniques are questioned, old managerial structures disaggregated, working relationships redefined, markets become more complex, traditional boundaries more blurred, and transacting business more demanding.

Managing any change has, of course, to be juggled against a backdrop of social and environmental issues, calling for more social and ethical responsibility, eco-friendly management, fair trade innovations, greater equality and fairness, high-efficiency–low-carbon initiatives, meaningful work, good work agendas, and enabling work environments. What has become clear, as researchers, practitioners, and commentators consider the way forward, is that theories and practice must now be relocated into a broader framework and engage with a wider, more inclusive perspective. The perils of a single dominating focus have been identified and their results exposed. If our theories and practices are going to best express the changing nature of work and organizations they need to achieve much more of a sense of "balance."

Balance means rediscovering the importance of the social context within which behavior takes place, being more accommodating of concepts like pluralism and synthesis, recognizing the complexities of individual values and beliefs, embracing both the positive and the negative, allowing individual realities to emerge that express the richness and variety of organizational life, encouraging the benefits of the free flow of knowledge between scholar and practitioner, and accepting that individual contributions flow from a range of activities. How far such ideas have filtered through and influenced our understanding of work and well-being is explored in more detail next.

CHAPTER 3

WORK AND WELL-BEING: PROGRESS AND PROSPECTS

In this chapter, we explore in detail the constructs of work and well-being. By exploring the motivational properties of work through the lens of job design we investigate how traditional views of jobs have been challenged (Grant and Parker 2009), how the behaviors valued by organizations are being reshaped (Griffin *et al.* 2007), and how jobs can be designed to do good (Grant 2008b). In terms of well-being, we explore the pursuit of happiness and the changing nature of positive individual functioning in organizations (Kesebir and Diener 2008), the structural components of well-being (Diener 1984), the shifting orientations of happiness through pleasure, fulfillment, and engagement (Peterson *et al.* 2005), and the change in emphasis of those processes underlying well-being (Diener 2000).

WORK

The nature of the work experience, and those aspects of the job which contribute to that experience, has had "many organizational scholars spend[ing] the majority of their waking hours trying to understand the trials and tribulations of work" (Grant and Parker 2009, p. 318). Much of this work has focused on identifying which job characteristics have the potential to motivate employees, and how jobs should best be designed to capture those qualities. The field of job design has "generated substantial theoretical and empirical interest in the twentieth century" (Fried *et al.* 2008, p. 586), and has played a key role in contributing to our understanding of work motivation and performance. For almost half a century, job design theories and practices have offered researchers and practitioners a context for explaining work experiences. We begin our discussion by reviewing this "golden age" (Grant and Ashford 2008) of job design and the contributions it has made.

This historical interlude leads us to consider whether, as Ambrose and Kulik suggest, "after twenty years of research a clear picture of the psychological and behavioral effects of job design has [now] emerged" (1999, p. 262), and whether, therefore, work is finished in this area. Not so, argue reviewers, quite the reverse in fact (Parker *et al.* 2001; Grant and Parker 2009). The turbulence and dramatic nature of the changes to work that ushered in the new millennium raise "timely question[s]" about job design (Fried *et al.* 2008, p. 587), clearly requiring it to remain as a significant item on the research agenda (Parker *et al.* 2001). We review how these changes to the nature of work affect the "role and characteristics of job design" (Fried *et al.* 2008, p. 587), and the way researchers have begun, as Grant and Parker suggest, "to redesign theories of work design" (2009, p. 319) in the light of these changes. It is clear that in this rapidly changing work environment if individuals are to achieve meaningful work and experience intrinsic motivation (Deci and Ryan 2000; Humphrey *et al.* 2007) advances must continue to be made in how work is "crafted" and designed to "capture the work context of the twenty-first century" (Grant and Parker 2009, p. 319).

Job design – A historical interlude

Job design has a long and rich history, with roots that can be traced as far back as the Industrial Revolution. But it took until the beginning of the twentieth century to establish the significance of job design, helped by the work of Frederick Taylor and the growth of the Scientific Management movement, with its emphasis on efficiency of effort and the practice of job specialization. The seeds, once sown, quickly flourished and it wasn't long before "the intuitively evident view" that poorly designed jobs had harmful consequences for health and well-being was confirmed by research (Parker *et al.* 2001, p. 414). While by the 1950s, techniques like job enlargement and job rotation had achieved a level of popularity, it was in the 1960s that there was a shift in focus, with developments in motivation theory and practice, and the emergence of the quality of working life movement to usher in the drive for a more theory driven approach to job design. During a time that offered economic growth, prosperity, and stability, values which embraced beliefs about work as a central life interest and the primary source of self-actualization, and led to calls for the quality of the work experience to be improved, job design emerged as a dominant focus.

Maslow revisited

The job design literature has been comprehensively reviewed (Fried *et al.* 2008; Grant *et al.* 2008; Grant and Parker 2009; Grant *et al.* 2010; Humphrey *et al.* 2007; Oldham 1996; Oldham and Hackman 2010; Parker and Ohly 2008; Parker *et al.* 2001). We draw on these reviews to provide the backdrop for exploring how the proposed extensions being recommended to job design theories reflect the changing nature of work and organizations. We begin our historical backdrop and scene-setting by revisiting the work of Maslow (1954). The aim here is simply to acknowledge his influence on motivational and job design theories, recognize that, through his humane approach to science, his work represents a strong statement about individual growth, development, and self-fulfillment, and more importantly "rediscovery" through his work on the concept of "self-transcendence" (Koltko-Rivera 2006). It is Koltko-Rivera who draws attention to how, in his later writings, Maslow comments that self-actualization was not sufficient to fully develop individual growth because "it works to actualize the individual's own potential" (2006, p. 306).

Some individuals, according to Maslow, "seek a benefit beyond the purely personal [where their] own needs are put aside, to a great extent in favor of service to others" (Koltko-Rivera 2006, p. 306). Putting oneself aside for the greater good captures the notion of "self-transcendence," represents the highest level of human need, and provides a more broad and inclusive appreciation of human behavior (Koltko-Rivera 2006). Koltko-Rivera's analysis of Maslow's writings, particularly Maslow's need to distinguish between self-actualization and self-transcendence when considering the further reaches of individual development, captures those humanistic qualities that contribute, and add value, to positive psychology. It allows his work to continue to find expression in one form or another in contemporary concepts like meaningful work (Pratt and Ashforth 2003) and the redesigning of jobs to do good (Grant 2008b).

Herzberg and two-factor theory

Notwithstanding Maslow's enduring influence, or maybe because of it, the 1960s, as Oldham and Hackman (2010) point out, belonged to Frederick Herzberg (1966) and his two-factor theory of motivation. The power of Herzberg's theory lies in the argument that it is a set of intrinsic job characteristics called *motivator* variables (e.g. recognition, achievement, responsibility, advancement, growth, the work itself) that have the greater potential to produce job satisfaction over a second set of extrinsic job characteristics called *hygiene* variables (e.g. colleague relationships, working conditions, salary, status, security). Herzberg takes his theory a step further by arguing that motivator variables, if perceived as being present in a job, lead to job satisfaction, but their perceived absence does not lead to job dissatisfaction. It is, argues Herzberg, the perceived absence of hygiene variables that leads to job dissatisfaction, yet their perceived presence does not lead to job satisfaction but places the worker in a neutral state.

For Herzberg, motivated behavior comes from enriching the job with motivator characteristics rather than enlarging the job or engaging in job rotation (Oldham and Hackman 2010). Herzberg's work generated an enormous amount of interest and almost a decade of discussion and debate. However, the power of his two-factor idea, "its simplicity and intuitive appeal," was not enough to withstand the empirical weaknesses that surrounded his work, and his theory "lost credibility" (Parker and Wall 1998, p. 11). Nevertheless, the issue of how jobs can be enriched through characteristics that include opportunities for personal growth, achievement, and development still "remains current" (Parker *et al.* 2001, p. 415) and represents what must be Herzberg's more enduring legacy.

Enriching jobs through the presence of motivator variables still left researchers pondering what the key characteristics of a job were, how significant changes to the job had to be to ensure changes in behavior, what were the short- and long-term benefits of job design, and what role did individual difference play in job design (Fried *et al.* 2008). Researchers had already begun to identify the impact of core task attributes on performance (Turner and Lawrence 1965), and the need to develop in parallel, when considering job design, the social and technical aspects of the job (Emery and Trist 1960). It was through their "synthesis and expansion" (Grant and Parker 2009, p. 320) of these ideas that Hackman and his colleagues developed the

Job Characteristics Model of job design (Hackman and Lawler 1971; Hackman and Oldham 1976; 1980) leading to the next, and probably most fruitful, phase in job design research.

Hackman and Oldham's job characteristic model

Hackman and Oldham's job characteristics model (see Fried *et al.* 2008; Grant and Parker 2009; Oldham and Hackman 2010; Parker and Ohly 2008; Parker and Wall 1998; Parker *et al.* 2001) identified five key job characteristics, or core job dimensions. These were: skill variety, task identity, task significance, task autonomy, and task feedback. The perceived presence of these core dimensions in a job was predicted to lead to three critical psychological states: variety, identity, and significance leading to the experience of meaningfulness in the job, autonomy leading to the experience of responsibility for outcomes, and feedback leading to knowledge of results. Experiencing these critical psychological states led to increases in intrinsic motivation and job satisfaction, enhanced job performance, and reduced turnover and absenteeism.

Those individuals with "higher order need strength" (e.g. greater need for challenge, responsibility, growth, and development), job-relevant knowledge and skills, and satisfaction with the work context (Oldham and Hackman 2010) were predicted to respond more positively to the relationships expressed in the job characteristics model than others. Oldham and Hackman argued that in the absence of higher order need strength the individual would not "seek or respond" to the energized motivational feelings that come, for example, through meeting challenges, without job-relevant knowledge and skills individuals "would experience more failure than success; never a motivating state," and when dissatisfaction with the work context is expressed "motivation would be muted" because of a preoccupation with such circumstances (2010, p. 464). Hackman and Oldham (1976) also provided, through their job diagnostic survey, a measure for estimating the motivating potential score of a job.

The 1980s and job design

The 1980s belonged to job design. Oldham (1996) illustrates the significance of job design research by pointing out that few topics have attracted as much attention in the field of organizational psychology as job design. It is not surprising, then, for reviewers to comment on the fact that "several hundred studies" have investigated the job characteristics model and its major propositions (Grant *et al.* 2008, p. 422). Reviewing many of these studies (Fried *et al.* 2008; Grant *et al.* 2008; Oldham 1996; Parker and Wall 1998; Parker *et al.* 2001) has allowed researchers to conclude that the expected relationships between the five core job characteristics and outcomes have generally been supported, although the stronger relationship is with affective reactions rather than behavioral-performance outcomes. Caveats surround the moderating role of the critical psychological states, with results being described as mixed and offering only partial support, leaving questions about the precise nature of the relationship between job characteristics and psychological states. However, reviewers (Fried *et al.* 2008; Grant *et al.* 2008) do suggest, albeit cautiously, partial support for the moderating role of growth need strength on the relationship between job characteristics, job satisfaction, and performance relationship. If, as Humphrey and his colleagues suggest from their analysis, some support exists for "experienced meaningfulness" providing "the greatest level of mediation" between job characteristics and work outcomes then this finding, however tentative, is encouraging as it goes to the heart of job design where "promoting intrinsic motivation is" essential if people are to experience meaning in their jobs (2007, p. 1346).

New directions in job design research

Because of the central role job design has played in organizational psychology research (Grant *et al.* 2008), the level of research activity that surrounds it, and the fact that for almost three decades it has been a key, and almost universally accepted, approach to motivation, many regard job design research as "case closed" (Humphrey *et al.* 2007, p. 1332). Once again this is not so. Global, economic, and social forces of change led researchers to question whether studies of job design reflected, accounted for, and integrated the "impact of the dramatic changes in work contexts that [had] occurred over the past few decades" into their work (Grant *et al.* 2010, p. 145). It was the changing nature of work that led to the next phase in the development of job design research. It was these local and global forces that "created new types of [service, knowledge/creative] jobs" (Grant *et al.* 2008), jobs that were emotionally more complex, used more flexible technologies (Humphrey *et al.* 2007), were set within a more contextually diverse work environment (Fried *et al.* 2008), generated new social and cultural norms (Parker and Ohly 2008), and required more demanding interpersonal skills, relationships, and strategic alliances (Parker *et al.* 2001). This led researchers to point to "two major changes" (Griffin *et al.* 2007, p. 327) in terms of "critical conditions of context" that must not only be managed, but accounted for within job design research. The two major contextual changes are uncertainty and interdependence (Grant and Parker 2009, p. 321).

As Grant and Parker discuss, when managing uncertainty, organizations now require individuals to be much more proactive in initiating how jobs can be restructured. The focus on interdependence reflects how jobs are now set in a more relationally complex system of socially interdependent behaviors, making the job context more important (Rousseau and Fried 2001) and an integral part of job design (Griffin *et al.* 2007). As a consequence, researchers' attention turned first to exploring elaborated models of job design, then to proactive behaviors, and finally, through the influence of positive psychology, to the role of prosocial behaviors in job design. Job design was to enter a new phase as it became "especially important to pursue and develop relational and proactive perspectives on work design" (Grant and Parker 2009, p. 322).

While the five core dimensions outlined by Hackman and Oldham (1976) remain relevant, researchers began, over a period of time, to see them as a relatively narrow subset of the job characteristics that influence individual experiences and behaviors and "expanded the basic model to better capture technological and social developments in the workplace" (Grant and Parker 2009, p. 321). So, prompted by the need to give more attention to the social context of work (Humphrey *et al.* 2007), to view jobs within the broader work environment (Morgeson and Humphrey 2006), to reconsider the changing meanings and roles of job characteristics (Fried *et al.* 2008), and by reinforcing that it is the changing work context that shapes organizationally valued behaviors (Griffin *et al.* 2007), researchers began to broaden the focus and comprehensively redevelop their job design models by expanding the range of job/work characteristics, considering new mediators/moderators to the relationship between job characteristic and outcomes and broadening the set of performance outcomes (see Fried *et al.* 2008; Grant and Parker 2009; Grant *et al.* 2008; Humphrey *et al.* 2007; Morgeson and Humphrey 2006; Parker and Wall 1998; Parker and Ohly 2008; Parker *et al.* 2001).

The issue of job characteristics

To address the job characteristics issue, Morgeson and Humphrey offered, through their Work Design Questionnaire, an expanded focus on work design "as opposed to the narrower term" job design, and identified, in addition to the traditional five core job characteristics, knowledge, social, and contextual characteristics (2006, p. 1324). In their effort to continue to adapt job design to the changing work context, Parker and her colleagues offered, for example, opportunity for skill acquisition, cognitive characteristics of work, emotional demands of work, and group level work characteristics (2001, pp. 422–423), categorized these within individual, group, and organizational dimensions, and considered them in terms of how they are influenced by factors external to the organization, internal organizational factors, and individual factors (Parker *et al.* 2001).

Further additions and expansions were to follow, including physical characteristics and task characteristics, such as work cycles, time pressures, virtual work (Grant *et al.* 2008), and self-directed teamwork (Fried *et al.* 2008). As new characteristics are added to an already expanded list of work characteristics, what needs to be continually borne in mind is that the relative significance and role of any work characteristic will ultimately depend on the broader social context within which it is embedded (Fried *et al.* 2008). In this respect, it is also important to continue to explore the meaning, nature, and structure of the original core job characteristics, as they too will need adapting to meet the changing work environment (Fried *et al.* 2008; Parker *et al.* 2001).

When it comes to those pathways that influence the relationship between job/work characteristics and outcomes, researchers have also identified the role of mediators/moderators that may now best express the changing work context. Fried and his colleagues (2008) considered, for example, culture, diversity, and the physical environment. Grant and his colleagues (2008) added uncertainty, proactivity, dynamism, and creativity, while Parker and her colleagues (2001) added intrinsic motivation, tacit and local knowledge, employee learning and development, and interpersonal interactions and interdependencies; remarking that while it is clear that such factors can influence outcomes "we have much less systematic evidence about *why*" (Parker *et al.* 2001, p. 428). The expansion of valued outcomes included, for example, well-being and role perceptions (Humphrey *et al.* 2007), innovation, knowledge transfer, collaboration, creativity, and proactivity (Parker and Ohly 2008; Parker *et al.* 2001), in an effort to determine how job design "might affect types of performance beyond the traditional emphasis on core task performance and productivity" (Parker and Ohly 2008, p. 245).

What emerges from these attempts to express through the different facets of the job design model the dramatic changes that have occurred, and are occurring, to the nature of work, is the importance of the social context, and that jobs and the tasks that characterize them are "embedded in interpersonal relationships, connections and interactions" (Grant and Parker 2009, p. 323). While earlier work on job design (Hackman and Oldham 1976) focused on the task structure of jobs in order to generate intrinsic motivation, for many researchers the aim now is to focus attention on the relational structure of jobs in order to "cultivate" proactive and prosocial behaviors (Grant and Parker 2009, p. 328; see also Grant *et al.* 2008; Griffin *et al.* 2007).

Proactive behavior

The challenges facing organizations, and the changing nature of work, led researchers to accept that such challenges and changes needed to be integrated into job design models (Grant *et al.* 2010). In doing so, it became clear that in such an environment employees "are increasingly likely to be – and increasingly need to be – active participants in work design" (Grant and Parker 2009, p. 342), challenging the assumption that managers design jobs and employees passively carry them out (Grant and Ashford 2008; Grant *et al.* 2008; Grant and Parker 2009), and heralding the beginnings of proactive behavior as a separate field of study (Grant and Ashford 2008). Building on the work around the proactive personality, and developing from the focus on proactive behaviors themselves that grew out of the work on personal initiative (Frese and Fay 2001), *proactive behavior* is defined as "anticipatory action that employees take to impact themselves and/or their environment" (Grant and Ashford 2008, p. 8). The essence of proactive behavior lies in taking the initiative to improve or create new conditions. It "involves challenging the status quo rather than passively adapting to present conditions" (Grant 2000, p. 436).

What distinguishes proactive behavior from more general ideas about motivated behavior is that it is about acting ahead; taking advance action and engaging in change-orientated behaviors, which

TABLE 3.1 **The road to job design**

Beginnings

- The rich history of job design has seen many researchers searching for those characteristics of the job that have the potential to motivate, and then review how jobs should be designed to capture this motivational potential (Fried *et al.* 2008; Hackman and Oldham 1976; 1980; Parker *et al.* 2001).
- The field of job design continues to capture the imagination of researchers and continues to be at the centre of our understanding of work, motivation, and performance (Grant *et al.* 2008, 2010).
- The story of job design is a continuous once, since changes in the nature and meaning of work require that job design theories are constantly redesigned to capture the contemporary way work is experienced (Grant *et al.* 2010; Humphrey *et al.* 2007; Parker *et al.* 2001; Parker and Ohly 2008).

The early years

- The growth of the Scientific Management movement with its emphasis on efficiency of effort led Frederick Taylor to pursue the ideas of job specialization, sowing the seeds that established the significance of job design.
- Job design theories were quick to flourish, encouraged by the view that poorly designed jobs had a detrimental impact on well-being, providing researchers in the 1950s with a context for emphasizing the importance of job rotation and job enlargement.
- It was the 1960s, with the arrival of the quality of working life movement and developments in motivation theories, that ushered in a drive for more theory driven approaches to job design (Herzberg 1966; Turner and Lawrence 1965).

The motivational years

- Need theories of motivation, with their emphasis on the forces within individuals that drive them to behave in certain ways, flowed from the work of Maslow and significantly influenced the development of motivation and job design ideas. Maslow's work, by emphasizing individual growth and development and the qualities of self actualization, resonated in one form or another with theories of job design (Maslow 1954).
- Maslow's idea of self transcendence – service to others – allows his work to continue to find expression, capturing the more contemporary need for meaningful work and the redesign of work to achieve this (Koltko-Rivera 2006).
- Herzberg's two-factor theory of motivation, with its idea that motivated behavior comes from enriching jobs with "motivator" characteristics, represented another step in the development of job design theories and reflects, perhaps, his lasting legacy (Herzberg 1966; Parker *et al.* 2001; Parker and Wall 1998).
- The shift in focus of motivation theories towards more process driven ideas, which emphasized what it is about jobs that energizes and sustains motivated behavior, simply helped to further enrich a context that was, in the 1970s, to lead to what could be described as the golden age of job design.

(Continued)

TABLE 3.1 **(Continued)**

The golden age of job design

- Out of this context rich in ideas expressing the motivational and meaningful aspects of work came the Job Characteristic Model of job design. The power of this model stems from the identification of five core job dimensions that when perceived as being present in the job lead to the experience of three critical psychological states – meaningfulness, responsibility for outcomes, and knowledge of results – which increase intrinsic motivation, satisfaction, and performance (Hackman and Lawler 1971; Hackman and Oldham 1976; 1980; Oldham 1996; Oldham and Hackman 2010).
- It should come as no surprise that the following decades have seen scores of studies that have investigated and reviewed the model's major propositions and over this time it has been almost universally accepted as the key approach to work motivation (Fried *et al.* 2008; Grant *et al.* 2008; Parker and Wall 1998; Parker *et al.* 2001).
- Despite all this work, it is not a case of job done as fundamental changes to the nature of work led researchers to conclude that it is now time to realign and redesign the job characteristics model (Grant *et al.* 2010; Griffin *et al.* 2007; Humphrey *et al.* 2007).
- So began a new phase in the development of job design research, with researchers accepting the view that it is now time to broaden our understanding of what the core job dimensions are, continue to develop our knowledge of those pathways that influence job behaviors, better integrate the social context of the job into job design, and give greater emphasis to understanding how job characteristics cultivate more contemporary job behaviors such as proactive and prosocial behaviors (Fried *et al.* 2008; Grant *et al.* 2008; Grant and Parker 2009; Morgeson and Humphrey 2006; Parker and Ohly 2008).

The road ahead

- Researchers will continue to innovate and develop the job design model so as to capture the nature of contemporary work experiences. Moving from those issues that focus on developing features of the job design model and their relationships researchers have begun to explore how organizations should prepare and plan for job design initiatives, how such initiatives are evaluated and outcomes assessed, what is meant by motivated behavior, and what distinguishes one form of motivated behavior from another (Grant *et al.* 2008; Morgeson and Humphrey 2006; Parker *et al.* 2001).
- There are also policy implications that need reinforcing. These include recognizing in policy initiatives that considerable benefits can be gained from making more jobs good jobs, looking at how a "good work agenda" translates into job design initiatives, and accepting that policy considerations depend as much on good management as they do on job design (Coats and Lekhi 2008; Constable *et al.* 2009).

are intended to have an impact (Grant and Ashford 2008). Proactive behaviors, while "self starting" and energetically engaging, also share personal initiative qualities like, for example, perseverance (facing up to and overcoming obstacles; see Rank *et al.* 2004, p. 523). Realizing the significance of these behaviors to job/work design has led researchers to explore the motivational processes and the drivers that initiate proactive behaviors (Parker *et al.* 2006). As Grant and Parker point out, there is a need to engage in three other types of investigation: exploring how proactivity can be encouraged through work design, how proactive individuals can take steps to redesign their work through concepts like job crafting and role adjustments, and how individuals initiate and propose design changes to their work through idiosyncratic deals and role negotiations (2009, p. 342).

Yet, could it be that despite the positive nature of proactivity, there is a "dark side" to such behavior (Belschak *et al.* 2010)? For example, Belschak and his colleagues suggest that the positive benefits of persistence need to be weighed against knowing "when to let go." Proactivity may not always lead to resolving interpersonal conflicts, being proactive may produce unanticipated consequences, particularly when it comes to performance, and such behaviors may be unwelcome by colleagues, particularly if they overstep the line in respect of socially and ethically acceptable behaviors (2010, pp. 268–269). Carrying on this theme of the "dark side" of proactivity, Bolino and his colleagues point to how expecting individuals to engage in proactive behaviors may cause stress, initiate conflict between colleagues, create difficulties in terms of undermining socialization activities, inhibit learning opportunities, and stifle leadership development (Bolino *et al.* 2010, pp. 326–327).

There is still more work to be done on understanding the architecture of proactive behaviors, the roles that different proactive behaviors play, how it is understood and interpreted by different levels in the organization, the trade-offs that individuals may make (Bolino *et al.* 2010), the positive and negative qualities of such behaviors, what distinguishes proactive behaviors from, for example, discretionary behaviors (Chartered Institute of Personnel and Development 2002), and how such behaviors should best be measured. There is also still the need for more work which progresses and develops a more integrative understanding of how the different proactive constructs (personality, personal initiative, voice, and taking charge) relate to one another (Thomas *et al.* 2010). What is not in doubt, though, is that individuals do engage in proactive ways to redevelop and reshape their work (Grant *et al.* 2008), and that researchers should now give as much emphasis to investigating these proactive behaviors as they have previously given to investigating reactive ones (Grant 2000).

Prosocial behavior

In reviewing over three decades of debate and discussion that followed their work Oldham and Hackman admit that they "were not alone," and like many other researchers "neglected the social dimensions of work" (2010, p. 467). Now, because social relationships characterize the very nature of contemporary work, "the time is ripe for research to focus squarely on the social aspects of work itself" (Oldham and Hackman 2010, p. 467). Spurred on by the positive psychology movement, researchers are now urged to distinguish between those social characteristics of the job that enable individuals to interact with others, and those prosocial characteristics that permit individuals to

TABLE 3.2 **Job design and proactive behavior**

- It is clear from the challenges facing organizations that in such a demanding environment employees are increasingly required to actively participate in job design, dispelling the idea that managers manage the redesign of jobs and employees are simply passive recipients of such change; hence the importance of cultivating proactive behavior (Grant and Ashford 2008; Grant and Parker 2009; Grant *et al.* 2010).
- Growing out of the work on the proactive personality and personal initiative, proactive behavior is, in essence, taking the initiative to improve or create new conditions (Frese and Fay 2001; Grant 2008b; Grant and Ashford 2008).
- What distinguishes proactive behavior from other forms of motivated behavior is that it is all about thinking and behaving ahead, and engaging in change focused behavior to achieve an impact (Grant and Ashford 2008; Parker *et al.* 2006; Rank *et al.* 2004).
- In thinking about proactive behavior it is important to recognize that such proactivity can come with a downside, producing unanticipated consequences, unwelcome and unappreciated responses from colleagues, stress, and conflict (Belschak *et al.* 2010; Bolino *et al.* 2010).
- There is still much work to be done to better understand proactive behavior and its consequences. Research needs to examine the different roles proactive behavior may play, its positive and negative qualities, what distinguishes this type of behavior from others, and how best it should be measured (Bolino *et al.* 2010; Grant 2000; Grant *et al.* 2008; Thomas *et al.* 2010).

benefit others; in other words, designing jobs that allow individuals to do good (Grant 2008b). Grant argues that we now need to identify not only those job/work characteristics that develop the motivation to do good, but also those that enhance individual abilities to do good, whilst at the same time building our understanding of what it means to do good and make a positive difference. Exploring job/work design through what Grant (2008b) describes as a "prosocial lens" provides researchers with the opportunity to explore how jobs/work can be designed in a way that not just allows individuals to do well, but to also do good as well.

The motivation to engage in prosocial behaviors is all about having a positive impact on others (Grant 2007). So, argued Grant, the time is right to reexamine and reinvigorate research on job design by focusing on the "relational" structure of jobs, and how those structures motivate individuals to make "a prosocial difference by connecting" individuals to the affect their work is having on others (2007, p. 395). Grant (2007) recognized that there was merit in revisiting the largely abandoned notion of "task significance" (Hackman and Oldham 1976), as it was this job characteristic that perhaps held the key and offered clues as to the way people engage with, nurture, and shape relationships with those affected by their work. Grant identified two "relational job characteristics." The first he described as the impact of the job on others, or job significance, ("an awareness that one's actions affect other people"), while the second he described as contact with others ("opportunities to interact and communicate" with those affected by their work). These two characteristics provide the motivational fuel to engage in helping behaviors that have a positive impact on others (Grant 2007, pp. 397–398). Further elaborations and developments to his work led Grant to conclude that emphasizing the relational structure of jobs enhances prosocial behaviors and provides the motivation to make a difference (Grant 2007).

There is, as Grant (2008a, pp. 35–36, 2008b) acknowledges, still much work to be done around the concept of prosocial behaviors, particularly in terms of exploring the link between relational job characteristics and other job characteristics, the way prosocial behaviors develop over time and the temporal nature of these behaviors, those contexts within which prosocial behaviors emerge and flourish, the relationship between prosocial behaviors and intrinsic motivation, whether prosocial behaviors stimulate reciprocal relational effects, the practical implications surrounding intervening in a prosocial way, and the nature of the domain of prosocial behaviors themselves. Grant (2007) also points to the need to explore the "dark side" of prosocial behavior, looking at whether there would be a tendency to exaggerate one's abilities or achievements at the expense of colleagues and clients, whether prosocial behaviors are more susceptible to, and lead to, forms of social control, and whether individuals may find it difficult to maintain prosocial behaviors, leading to unanticipated behavioral consequences, depleted resources, and trade-offs.

What is quite clear is that contemporary job design interventions cannot ignore the importance of exploring the relational nature of jobs; giving to these social aspects of the job the same emphasis as has traditionally been given to enriching the task aspects of the job. Understanding more about those job characteristics that initiate prosocial behaviors provides an "expanded understanding" (Grant 2008a, p. 36) of job design. Such a focus reflects the argument mooted by Grant and colleagues when "putting job design in context in the twenty-first century." They suggest that by continuing to redevelop, remodel, and broaden job design theories by aligning them with the "ever-changing world of work," job design maintains its place as a "major area" of investigation (2010, p. 154), and one that presents a viable framework for expressing contemporary work experiences.

Job design: The way ahead?

We began this section on work by arguing that job design theories offered researchers and practitioners a context for understanding and enhancing work experiences. This is still true. Over the last decade there has been a renewed interest in job design, a reinvigorated enthusiasm and sense of energy to "redesign" job design, a reemergence of the significance of the social context in job design research, a redeployment of empirical resources towards expanding and broadening the range of job characteristics, motivational states, and outcomes, and a realignment of all these innovations into one single goal: to bring job design research into the twenty-first century and establish it as a unique expression of contemporary work experiences.

However, there is still much to be done. Future research will, in continuing the innovative changes that have already been made to job design models, need to consider what Parker and her colleagues describe as "process matters." These include, for example, exploring

TABLE 3.3 **Job design and prosocial behavior**

- Changes to the way work is organized, and the emphasis placed on the importance of social relationships, means that job design now needs to focus on the social aspects of work, an area that has received little attention from job design researchers (Grant 2008b; Oldham and Hackman 2010).
- The time is now right for researchers to give as much attention to redesigning jobs that permit individuals to benefit from others as they have to those social aspects of the job that enable individuals to interact with others (Grant 2007).
- Investigating job design through a prosocial lens offers researchers an opportunity to explore how jobs can be designed to allow individuals not just to do well but to also do good – having a positive impact on others (Grant 2008b).
- The impetus that motivates individuals to engage in prosocial behaviors comes from the need to understand the consequences of one's actions on others and the opportunities to communicate and interrelate with those affected by such actions (Grant 2007).
- There is a downside that needs to be considered when investigating prosocial behaviors, including the unanticipated consequences of prosocial behaviors, its role as a form of social control, and whether it energizes individuals to overstate their abilities and achievements (Grant 2007).
- There is still much work to be done, with researchers exploring how prosocial behaviors can be developed, the contexts under which prosocial behaviors emerge, the nature of prosocial behaviors and the practical implications that come from behaving in a prosocial way (Grant 2007, 2008a, b; Grant *et al.* 2010).

how prepared organizations are for work redesign: whether there has been a history of work design changes, the outcomes of past changes, the impact of past attempts on employees, the extent to which other organizational functions are aligned to proposed redesign changes, the degree to which design changes can be separated from other changes that are occurring, and the level of managerial support and employee involvement in developing redesign changes (2001, pp. 431–432).

Other operational issues include, for example, how, when a number of simultaneous changes are made to a job, the individual effects of such changes on redesign goals are determined, whether redesign is just not possible for some jobs, whether organizations use appropriate instruments and methods when identifying redesign opportunities or are more "organic" in their approach and the consequences different approaches have on design outcomes, and in order to achieve a level of redesign change the impact that "trade-offs" may have on outcomes (Morgeson and Humphrey 2006, pp. 1334–1335). Other areas for research include, for example, the decision-making process associated with job redesign, how decisions are made, and the impact they have on design outcomes, the interactions among different job characteristics and the influence of such interactions on different design outcomes, and the multidimensional nature of job characteristics and the varying effects of these different dimensions (Grant *et al.* 2008, pp. 438–441).

Then there is the often-overlooked question of what is meant by motivated behavior? Identifying proactive and prosocial behaviors is an important step in answering this question. It may be possible to distinguish one from the other, on the basis that proactive behaviors reflect more of a self-actualizing motive (developing oneself), whereas prosocial behaviors are more driven by transcendence needs (developing others). This, of course, can only be decided empirically by continuing to build on our understanding of the architecture of each behavior. However, it still leaves open for debate what distinguishes proactive and prosocial behaviors from organizational citizenship behaviors, discretionary behaviors, engagement behaviors, commitment, and involvement.

There is also more work to be done in order to better understand the relationships between these different behaviors, and whether different job designs have more specific behavioral effects. These directions for future research reflect a field moving forward and the creative tensions that develop between what we know, what we want to know, and how best we can continue to build our knowledge. In this way such tensions simply reflect the hope that "researchers will keep their eyes open to new phenomena that helps to gain a deeper understanding of job design" (Grant *et al.* 2008, p. 444).

Policy makers have also recognized that considerable benefits can be gained from "making more jobs good jobs" (Constable *et al.* 2009, p. 4), and ushered in the idea of a good work agenda that supports the notion of meaningful work, work that is valued by employees and which aims to ensure that for as many as possible work should be "a source of well-being, personal growth, fulfillment, autonomy and meaning" (p. 3). For the "good work" agenda to progress employers must, argue Coats and Lekhi, "refocus their attention on the organization of work, the design of jobs and the performance of management" (2008, p. 12). It is clear that work design is "inextricably bound" to the very fabric of organizational procedures, practices, and systems, attesting to its enduring qualities and significance. Even so, as Oldham and

Hackman argue, it requires not just "fresh thinking," but also thinking about how best we can productively "continue to learn about it" (2010, p. 476).

WELL-BEING

Well-being is central to the successful practice of management (Wright 2006). Nevertheless, managing well-being is no simple task (Grant *et al.* 2007), because it is a "complex construct that concerns both optimal experience" and positive functioning (Ryan and Deci 2001, p. 141). Its roots can be traced to those disciplines that have, over the centuries, concerned themselves with questioning "what is the good life?" with the result that the process of trying to define "the good life" has, as Diener suggests, "come to be called 'subjective well-being' and in colloquial terms is sometimes labeled 'happiness'" (2000, p. 34). So, as a means of understanding the lay meanings people gave to happiness, psychologists proposed, as Kesebir and Diener argue, that this would best be achieved through the term "subjective well-being" (2008, p. 118).

Out of this literature the concept of happiness and well-being emerged, and researchers began to explore the ways in which lives are evaluated positively (Diener 1984). With a history of research spanning well over 50 years (Diener 1984), the more recent growth in studies of subjective well-being reflects, in part, the influence of the positive psychology movement (Diener 2000; Diener *et al.* 1999), the belief that psychology has for too long emphasized the negative over the positive (Lucas *et al.* 1996; Ryan and Deci 2001), failed to recognize the potential that lay in understanding psychological growth (Ryan and Deci 2001), and neglected the study of positive functioning (Ryff 1989). Subjective well-being is therefore "of fundamental importance to the behavioral sciences" because it provides a way of assessing how people evaluate the quality of their lives (Diener *et al.* 2003, p. 405).

Defining well-being

It is clear that when attempting to define subjective well-being a "broad category of phenomena" are involved (Diener *et al.* 1999, p. 277). When reflecting on their well-being individuals make not just broad assessments about their life generally, but also assess different life facets, as well as reacting to events around them (Diener 2000; Diener *et al.* 2003). As a result, subjective well-being includes both emotional-affective as well as cognitive evaluation of life (Diener 2000; Diener *et al.* 2003; Lucas *et al.* 1996). So, subjective well-being has what Diener describes as "three hallmarks" (Diener 1984, p. 543). It is: (a) "subjective" – individuals are "the single best judge of their own happiness" (Kesebir and Diener 2008, p. 118); (b) the subjective focus "allows individuals to judge how their lives are going according to what they themselves find important for happiness" (Alexandrova 2005, p. 302); and (c) it is about the positive, not just the absence of the negative – positive is not merely the opposite of negative (Ryan and Deci 2001), and while different life facets may be assessed it includes a general "global assessment" of life (Diener 1984, p. 544).

While it may not be possible to define subjective well-being to suit everyone, researchers have identified three "separable components of subjective well-being that cohere in understandable ways" (Kesebir and Diener 2008, p. 118). These include: (a) life satisfaction – the global assessments of one's life; (b) the distinction between positive and negative affect and "defining happiness as the difference [balance] between the two" (Ryff 1989; Ryff and Keyes 1995, p. 719); and (c) satisfaction with different life facets (domains) – those closest and "most immediate to peoples' personal lives" are those that have the most influence (Diener 1984, p. 545). Each of the three components should, Diener and his colleagues suggest, be assessed separately (Diener *et al.* 1999).

Factors producing well-being

Identifying the different components of well-being led Diener and his colleagues to consider what factors actually produce subjective well-being and, more particularly, happiness. While research initially focused on "who" is happy (for reviews see Diener 1984; Diener *et al.* 1999), researchers have begun more recently to focus on "when and why people are happy, and on what the processes are that influence subjective well-being" (Diener 2000, p. 40). In pursuing this line of enquiry it has become clear that there would be no simple answers, no single cause, and that the emphasis should be on exploring the "complex interplay" of a range of dispositional, cultural, environmental, and cognitive resources (Diener *et al.* 1999, p. 295). People make their

TABLE 3.4   **Towards a definition of well-being**

- Well-being is a complex construct involving both optimal experience and positive functioning (Ryan and Deci 2001, p. 141). The study of well-being has a long history, has caught the attention of a range of disciplines, and stimulated the imagination of those interested in exploring just what the good life is (Diener 2000; Wright 2006).
- It is from these efforts to try and define the good life that the term subjective well-being has emerged along with its colloquial term – happiness. In arriving at a definition of well-being a broad range of factors need to being taken into account because this is the way individuals go about assessing their lives (Diener 1984, 2000; Diener *et al.* 1999, 2003; Kesebir and Diener 2008).
- Definitions of well-being are built around three criteria – it is subjective as individuals are the best judges of their happiness, that its subjective nature allows individuals to judge their happiness according to what is important for them, and that it is about the positive and not just the absence of the negative (Alexandrova 2005; Diener 1984; Diener *et al.* 2003; Kesebir and Diener 2008; Ryan and Diener 2001).
- Researchers have suggested when attempting to define subjective well-being that it is made up of three separate yet associated components – a global assessment of one's life (life satisfaction), the balance between positive and negative affect, and satisfaction with life different facets (Diener 1984; Diener *et al.* 1999; Kesebir and Diener 2008; Ryff 1989; Ryff and Keyes 1995).
- Identifying these three components led researchers to consider what actually produces well-being and more particular happiness. Over time the research focus has shifted away from "who is happy" to "when and why" people are happy and on those processes that influence subjective well-being (Diener 2000; Keyes *et al.* 2002; Keyes and Lopez 2005).
- It became clear that when focusing on the "when and why" there are no simple answers, no single cause and that research needs to explore the complex interplay of a range of dispositional, cultural, environmental, and cognitive resources (Kesebir and Diener 2008; Ryan and Deci 2001).
- There is still work to be done. This work would include the role of temperament, goals and values, the way individuals adapt and cope, and the interrelationship that emerge between the different components, and the differential effects they may produce (Diener *et al.* 2006; Kesebir and Diener 2008; Peterson *et al.* 2005).
- Individuals make their own decisions as to whether their lives are happy and so researchers have suggested that it is also time to consider alternative views of subjective well-being that focus on positive functioning and how this shapes well-being, on developing an understanding of positive health, and on the social dimension of well-being (Kesebir and Diener 2008; Keyes 1998; Ryan and Deci 2000).

own decisions as to whether their lives are happy, and if a person is happy with life they are almost certainly experiencing the things that are important to them (Diener 2000). From his research Diener and his colleagues argued that the processes underlying subjective well-being include temperament, adaptation, goals, and coping strategies (Diener 2000; Diener *et al.* 1998, 1999; Kesebir and Diener 2008).

Yet for each of these processes there is still work to be done to better understand their role. As Diener (2000) suggests, "temperament" is a powerful predictor of subjective well-being, but what is its relationship to adaptation and more particularly how does it influences the "when and why" of adaptation (p. 40)? Goals and values are also "intimately linked" to well-being, but is moving towards achieving the goal more important than achieving the goal itself (Diener *et al.* 1999), and is knowing when to change or alter goals an important part of the adaptive process (Diener 2000)? When the focus changes from adaptation to the more deliberate process of coping, why do people engage in certain types of coping, why are some coping strategies more effective, and how does coping differ across the different well-being components (Diener *et al.* 1999)? Other issues point to understanding the interrelationships that may exist between these different processes (Diener *et al.* 1999), whether the different processes have differential affects in relation to the well-being components, the role of culture and the environment, and the nature of happiness itself (Kesebir and Diener 2008).

Ryff (1989), together with her colleague (Ryff and Keyes 1995), presents an alternative view of the nature and structure of well-being. Using positive functioning as the theoretical framework to explore the nature of wellness, and to integrate the somewhat neglected perspective of psychological growth into a model of well-being, Ryff (1989) offers a model that represents a more "parsimonious summary" of well-being. When reviewing the structure of psychological well-being, Ryff and Keyes drew attention to the need to better understand what it means to be psychologically well and how positive functioning shapes well-being (1995). From their reviews they identified "six distinct components of positive functioning" as a "theoretical foundation to generate a [more] multidimensional model of well-being" (Ryff and Keyes 1995, p. 720). Taken together these components capture a "breadth of wellness" that includes: (a) self-acceptance (feeling good about oneself and one's past); (b) a sense of continuing personal growth and development; (c) a feeling that there is meaning and purpose to life;

(d) having valued and supportive relations with others; (e) having the resources and capacity to manage one's environment; and (f) a sense of self-determination (p. 720).

While Keyes *et al.* acknowledge that subjective well-being and psychological well-being are related but different, both approaches reflect "humanistic values that elevate the human capacity to examine what makes life good" (2002, p. 1017). Ryff and her colleagues focus their work more towards developing a positive human health agenda (Ryff and Singer 1998a, b): they clearly challenge the idea that happiness is at the core of positive functioning. While not dismissing happiness, they view it more as springing from a life well-lived, in this way drawing attention to the need to distinguish between the causes of "short-term affective well-being" (i.e. happiness) and the more enduring and "demanding realization of one's true potential" (Ryff 1989, p. 1077). We will return to and take up this distinction later in this chapter.

A third view of well-being comes from the work developed by Keyes (1998). Keyes argues that the social challenges people face may be criteria against which individuals evaluate their lives, and so there is a need to measure the social dimensions of well-being. Social well-being is the "appraisal of one's circumstances and functioning in society" (Keyes 1998, p. 122). Keyes goes on to identify five social challenges that "constitute possible dimensions of social wellness" (p. 122). These include (see pp. 122–123): (a) feeling part of the community-belonging (*integration*); (b) understanding and caring about the world you live in and what goes on around you (*coherence*); (c) feeling positive towards others (*acceptance*); (d) feeling that you have something to offer (*contribution*); and (e) feeling confident about the future and the opportunities society provides for all (*actualization*). Keyes and Lopez (2005) suggest that combinations of all three of these approaches to well-being offer opportunities for individuals to flourish.

Finally, there is the self-determination model developed by Ryan and Deci (2000). Their primary concern is also with the well-being of individuals. Their work emphasizes people's growth tendencies and psychological needs, as expressed through a natural proactivity towards self-motivation. Their theory is built around the idea that where an organization's social context is receptive to developing human potential, particularly in relation to the need for competency, autonomy, and relatedness, that context offers a developmental mechanism for growth, performance, and optimal functioning (p. 68). For these authors, the "design of social environments that optimize people's development, performance, and well-being" is a fundamental step in facilitating motivation and commitment (p. 68).

Routes to happiness

The questions "What does it mean to be well?" and "What does it mean to be happy?" seem simple enough. It is clear however, that any attempt to answer these questions must come with the acceptance that happiness is a complex emotion. To understand the journey that ends in a state of happiness, and to explore those components by which it is achieved, researchers must acknowledge that they are part of a debate on the "discourse of happiness" that has continued for at least "the last two and a half millennia" (Kesebir and Diener 2008, p. 118). The richness of that debate, its nature, and the passion with which it has been expressed cannot be captured here. What can be illustrated though is just how eclectic the debate can become when questions such as "Can people be happy?" "Do people want to be happy?" "Should people be happy?" and "How can people be happy?" are raised (Kesebir and Diener 2008), and when it is possible to explore happiness from at least six theoretical positions (Diener 1984). Nevertheless, underlying much of the discussion around well-being are "two relatively distinct, but overlapping perspectives" (Ryan and Deci 2001, p. 142), or orientations, which offer different routes to understanding happiness, it is those that we outline below.

Both routes can be traced back to the early Greek philosophers, and are "as ancient as they are current" with the first broadly expressing *hedonism*, where well-being reflects the states of pleasure or happiness. The second – *eudaimonism* – broadly speaking suggests that well-being goes beyond just happiness, and is found more in the fulfilling or maximizing of individual potential (Ryan and Deci 2001, p. 143), of living a life of meaning or self-realization and personal expressiveness (Waterman 1993). These two perspectives on happiness lead to different approaches to the investigation of well-being, and reflect an "engaging and instructive debate" (Ryan and Deci 2001, p. 146) that surrounds well-being. Subjective well-being (Diener 1984) best conceives of happiness more in a broad hedonistic sense that extends beyond simple pleasure to goal achievements and valued outcomes across a number of life domains. On the other hand, those promoting the psychological approach to well-being (Ryff 1989; Ryff and Keyes 1995) suggest

70

that the subjective approach to well-being is "limited in scope" (Ryan and Deci 2001, p. 146) and fails to emphasize the importance of positive functioning, and so along with the self-determination approach (Ryan and Deci 2001), embraces more of a eudaimonic approach.

The debate continues to ebb and flow, and at times shifts beyond perspectives on happiness to whether, when it comes to measurement, the eudaimonic approach is too prescriptive in its specifying of human potential, whereas, because of its focus, the subjective approach allows the assessment of happiness to flow from the individuals themselves (Alexandrova 2005; Diener *et al.* 2003; Ryan and Deci 2001). However, there does seem to be general agreement that the hedonistic and eudaimonic approaches are "sufficiently close" (Kesebir and Diener 2008), are "related but distinguishable" (Waterman 1993), differing more in terms of how they relate to individual potential and "thus are able to be pursued simultaneously" (Peterson *et al.* 2005, p. 36). Interestingly Peterson and his colleagues offer an approach which suggests that happiness may lie in what they describe as the "pursuit of engagement," built around Csikszentamihalyi's work on flow. These authors argue that it is engaging activities which give this sense of flow, of losing oneself and becoming absorbed in the task. Peterson and his colleagues conclude that "either hedonism or eudemonia can accompany a satisfying life, and so too can engagement" (Peterson *et al.* 2005, p. 36). The discussion will undoubtedly continue as to the different routes to happiness.

Happiness: A complex emotion

Happiness is a complex and at times controversial emotion (Ryan and Deci 2001). Two broad perspectives have emerged – the hedonistic and the eudaimonic. Each offers a different route to understanding happiness and each promotes that route either through the subjective qualities of well-being, or through well-being's psychological properties. Reviewing contemporary research on happiness and human potential, Ryan and Deci point to two periods where there have been "bursts of interest in well-being" (2001, p. 142): the 1960s with its focus on motivation, individual growth, and the development of potential, and, more recently, the rise in importance of the positive psychology movement. It is tempting, when thinking of those two periods, to conclude that the 1960s, with its emphasis on individual satisfaction and the search for the happy productive worker, led researchers more towards subjective well-being and its broadly *hedonistic* qualities.

On the other hand, the recent interest in positive psychology, which embraces a similar interest in human flourishing, but through prosocial behaviors, doing well, and contributing to others pushed researchers more towards psychological well-being and its *eudaimonic* qualities. Whether such associations can be made is, of course, a somewhat speculative endeavor, and no doubt something of a moot point. What needs to be kept in mind is that despite these different perspectives they are "to some degree overlapping," and that it is through the different questions they ask and the way that they "complement each other" that a rich and more extensive understanding of happiness and well-being emerges, which supplies what Ryan and Deci describe as a "nutriment for structured interventions to better the lives of people" (2001, p. 161).

There are still questions about happiness and well-being that need to be explored. A number of these questions are, as Kesebir and Diener point out, "of an empirical nature," and in their view it is only a matter of time before answers begin to emerge. These questions include, for example, identifying the specific "correlates and causes" of the different components to subjective well-being and extending this work to other conceptualizations of well-being (Kesebir and Diener 2008, p. 123). There is also the question as to how, and in what way, the different routes to well-being "shape, conduct and thereby produce more or less happiness" (Peterson *et al.* 2005, p. 37). Peterson and his colleagues go on to suggest that it is also important to understand whether, how, and in what way a satisfying life leads to behaviors that reflect pleasurable, engaging, and meaningful activities. As part of understanding the different routes to happiness it is, Diener and his colleagues argue, "pointless to look for a single cause of happiness," and researchers must be ready to explore whether different strategies are more effective in different environments and for different people, making the complexity of the transaction between the individual and the environment an important focus for empirical study (1999, p. 295). Similarly Alexandrova (2005) raises the question as to whether, and in what way, subjective well-being differs across different life circumstances.

Then there is the issue of the "intensity" with which happiness is experienced, and the role that adaptation plays in shaping such feelings (Diener 2000; Diener *et al.* 2006; Kesebir and Diener 2008). There is, as these authors suggest, a need to explore how people adapt, over what sort of time period, the pace at which adaptation occurs, whether the adaptation process is ever complete, what levels people return to, the sorts of factors (the events and circumstances) that influence adaptation, how much control people have in terms of being able to adapt, and the limits of adaptation in maintaining happiness (2000, pp. 37–38). Finally, there is the interesting moral question of what role research should play, and how far research should explore, what makes people happy and where such happiness can be found (Kesebir and Diener 2008), not forgetting the ethical issues of how this type of information should be used in interventional contexts.

Happiness, and by implication well-being, is "a curious object of science" (Alexandrova 2005, p. 321), because it is an intimate part of ourselves and cannot be adequately studied without taking seriously individual intuition and insights. Nevertheless, despite these difficulties, or because of them, well-being is clearly related to different life domains, and so in the next chapter we begin to explore the role of work and its impact, both positive and negative, on well-being.

CHAPTER 4

RESOURCE DEPLETION

In this chapter we explore the role of work and its impact, both negative and positive, on well-being. We do this through a framework where "resource depletion" is viewed as a significant outcome flowing from the causes of work-stress (Hobfoll 2001). The chapter opens with a discussion of the term "stress," the way it has been defined and how these definitions reflect and shape the way stress research has evolved. It then moves beyond the concept of stress, and argues that since stress implies emotions (Lazarus and Cohen-Charash 2001) it is emotions rather than stress that "should become the language of researchers" (Dewe *et al.* 2010, p. 5). Focusing on emotions not only overcomes the ambiguity that surrounds the troublesome word "stress" but is more likely to capture the reality of the stress experience. We follow this discussion by examining the debate that surrounds the Conservation of Resources Theory (Hobfoll 2001), and from this, initiate a more detailed discussion on the nature of work stressors, their measurement, and how they express the changing landscape of work.

THE TERM "STRESS"

When the term "stress" began to achieve a level of popular currency in the 1950s it was already a term accompanied by a long history (Cooper and Dewe 2004), and so in many respects, as Cassidy so neatly points out, "its discovery in the twentieth century was [perhaps] more of a rediscovery" (1999, p. 6). Yet, even by then, despite the fact that the term had achieved a level of legitimacy as a subject worthy of empirical investigation (Newton 1995), doubts remained, precisely because of its popularity and the attention it was attracting, suggesting that perhaps it was nothing more than a fad (Haward 1960). As we know, the term has survived (Jones and Bright 2001), but because it has become so much a part of everyday conversation its meaning has been so diluted that it is not always entirely clear what it is that is actually being talked about, and just how much it reflects individual experiences. The concern is more with stress "the label," rather than stress "the concept" (Cooper and Dewe 2004; Dewe *et al.* 2010), requiring researchers to be clear about what it is that they are defining and how that definition informs research.

Traditional approaches to defining stress

At the core of definitions of stress is "the relationship between the individual and the environment" (Wainwright and Calman 2002, p. 41). Yet, as Wainwright and Calman go on to suggest, although researchers recognize the importance of both, changing social and political contexts have, over the years, influenced the emphasis that has been given to each. Hence, tracing the different approaches to defining stress helps to explain why, at one time or another, stress has been defined as a stimulus, a response, or an interaction between the two. Understanding the context within which these different definitions were embedded provides each with a "historical as well as an empirical value" (Dewe *et al.* 2010, p. 3), allowing reviewers to capture, through this sense of time and context, why different approaches to defining stress prevailed, what they offered in terms of understanding, how they informed research, their shortcomings, the directions they set for future research, and the contribution they made to practice (Cooper and Dewe 2004; Dewe *et al.* 2010).

Each of these approaches to defining stress, has amassed a considerable body of knowledge and, as our understanding develops, researchers continue to return to such definitions to test their relevance to, and fit with, the contemporary landscape of work. This process of "return and test" is naturally evolutionary and continuous. While it adds incrementally to our understanding of what the different structural components to the stress process are, the question still remains as to the contribution these definitions make to our understanding of the stress process itself. Any evaluation of these more traditional ways of defining stress now lies less in the knowledge and understanding they have provided over the years and more in whether, and in what way, they can now contribute to and support a process-driven theory of stress (Lazarus 1990). While researchers will continue to investigate the changing nature of stressors (stimuli) and strain (responses), research still needs to give as much attention to the sequencing and unfolding of a stressful encounter as it has to simply exploring the interaction between stressors and strains (Kaplan 1996). In relation to the present state of our knowledge, definitions of stress should be offering a better understanding of those process issues that underlie stressful encounters (Dewe *et al.* 2010).

Stress as a transaction

"Process-driven" definitions express stress in *transactional* terms (Lazarus 1966). As Lazarus points out (1999), expressed in this way stress does not simply reside in the individual or in the environment but in the relationship between the two. The power of this approach lies in its focus on understanding the nature of that relationship, those psychological processes that link the individual to the environment, and the manner in which the relationship unfolds (Lazarus 1999). It is drawing attention to those processes that bind the individual to the environment that distinguishes the transactional approach from earlier attempts at defining stress. So, as Lazarus describes, stress follows from "the *relational meaning* that an individual constructs from the person–environment relationship" (2000, p. 665). These relational meanings, which link the individual to the environment, are expressed through a "process of appraisal" (Lazarus 2001a). Focusing on appraisals is promising, as Lazarus suggests, simply because "people are constantly evaluating [appraising] their relationships with the environment with respect to their implications for well-being" (1999, p. 75). In this way, stress arises from a person's appraisal that particular environmental demands are about to tax individual resources, thus threatening well-being (Holroyd and Lazarus 1982).

Lazarus (2001a) draws attention to what he describes as primary and secondary appraisal, making it clear that these descriptors distinguish one type of appraisal from the other not in terms of its timing but in terms of its content (Lazarus 1999), for each, as Lazarus points out, is part of and engaged in a dynamic relationship, where together they shape the nature of a demanding encounter. The first, *primary appraisal*, is concerned with the personal meanings individuals construct from the events themselves. It is where the individual, through these personal meanings, evaluates the significance of "what is at stake" in terms of harm, loss, threat, or challenge (Lazarus 2001b). However, the meanings individuals give to events is further refined through secondary appraisal. *Secondary appraisal* is concerned with "what can I do about it?" It is where the individual appraises the availability of coping resources to deal with or manage the demands (threat, loss, harm, or challenge) of an encounter. It is this emphasis on process, as expressed through primary and secondary appraisal, which offers a causal pathway that not just conveys the transactional nature of a stressful encounter but also an understanding of the adaptive process itself.

Conceptually, stress should now be thought of in transactional terms (Dewe *et al.* 2010). To ignore the explanatory potential of appraisals is to ignore what are critical aspects of the stress process (Dewe 2001; Dewe and Cooper 2007; Dewe *et al.* 2010). While appraisal and the transactional model of Lazarus "has dominated the wider stress literature, its impact has been much less marked in the occupation field" (Jones and Bright 2001, p. 185). Supporters and critics of the transactional approach are generally in agreement in their belief that "organizational stress researchers have much to gain by familiarizing themselves with Lazarus's theoretical and empirical contributions" (Brief and George 1991, p. 15) and that research "will benefit from the careful and thoughtful application of the transaction process model" (Harris 1991, p. 28). On the other hand, disagreements with Lazarus's approach stemming from his emphasis on intra-individual processes and the importance of the subjective work environment (Brief and George 1991; Frese and Zapf, 1999; Schaubroeck 1999), mean that concepts like appraisal and emotions have received a less than complete treatment from work-stress researchers. However, far from questioning the theoretical rigor and empirical significance of Lazarus's approach, most critics conclude that there is room in the work-stress agenda to "actually study *all* of the relevant issues of the stress process" (Frese and Zapf 1999, p. 764) and that work-stress research would be enhanced by "reflecting more carefully on how such [appraisal] processes follow" (Schaubroeck 1999, p. 759).

THE TRANSACTIONAL APPROACH: A WAY FORWARD

The transactional model offers a number of ways forward when considering the relationship between work and well-being. The first stems from its focus on primary appraisal, recognizing not just the explanatory potential that resides in the meanings individuals give to demanding encounters but more that such meanings offer a theoretical framework for exploring both negative *and* positive appraisals, and what distinguishes these types of appraisal from each other. In discussing the idea of appraisals, Lazarus drew attention not just to what he described as "negatively toned" appraisal, such as harm/loss (something that has already occurred) and threat (possible future demand), but also to "positively toned" ones such as challenge. In the case of challenge, Lazarus described it as "somewhat like Selye's eustress in that people who feel challenged enthusiastically pit themselves against obstacles" (Lazarus 1999, p. 76). Later in his writing Lazarus drew attention to another "positively toned" appraisal that he described as "benefit;" identifying the benefits that may accrue from an encounter (Lazarus 2001b). Others suggest that another type of appraisal that may be important stems from "concern over others' problems" (Aldwin 2009, p. 32), reflecting perhaps, the humanistic qualities of Maslow's self-transcendence and the eudaimonic qualities of well-being.

Distinguishing negative from positive appraisals offers other avenues for future research including developing an understanding of the more subtle meanings associated with the different types of appraisals, helping to develop our understanding of the nature and architecture of each, exploring whether a number of appraisals are associated with a particular encounter, how and in what way appraisals change during an encounter, whether some appraisals are more powerful than others, the level of cognitive activity associated with an appraisal, and whether some appraisals are more cognitively complex than others, and the role that appraisals play in relation to coping strategies and the emotions associated with an encounter (Aldwin 2009; Dewe *et al.* 2010; Lazarus 1999, 2001b). The "distinctly different content of each type of appraisal" (Lazarus 1999, p. 78) provides good reason for exploring them separately, but they need also to be considered as part of a complex process, one that now presents a more balanced pathway for understanding the role played in the stress process by both negatively and positively framed appraisals.

Appraisals also play an essential role in the emotions experienced during a stressful encounter. Understanding this link offers a rich source of information about what is happening to a person, one that better captures the qualities of a stressful encounter than simply measuring something called stress, which, as Lazarus argues (1999), is a rather restrictive and somewhat blunt approach to capturing a stress response when compared to the variety of emotions that stress actually produces. As Lazarus (1993b) points out, since stress is essentially about emotional reactions it seems "illogical and counterintuitive" to continue to have "two separate research literatures," one that focuses on stress and the other on emotions, when it is emotions that offer a richer source of what it is that is being experienced (Lazarus and Cohen-Charash 2001, p. 52). As Lazarus and Cohen-Charash go on to make clear, because "stress always implies emotions" (p. 53) and it is the appraisal an individual constructs around a stressful encounter that gives the encounter its emotional quality (Lazarus 2001a), exploring the causal pathway between appraisals and emotions offers a more direct "theoretically rich and important" focus (Park and Folkman 1997, p. 132).

It is clear, as Kasl argues (1983), that the more we focus our research on the stress process the less we have to rely on the troublesome word "stress." Exploring appraisals in the context of emotions is important because particular appraisals may initiate particular emotions. It is important to understand not just the kind of appraisal and the emotion it triggers, but that if appraisals are the emotion-generating process (Lazarus 2001a) then this provides an explicit pathway through which both negative and positive emotions can be explored.

The strength of a transactional view of stress lies in its process-oriented focus, expressed through primary and secondary appraisal. We have emphasized the importance of the causal pathways that flow from the appraisal process as providing a theoretical context and opportunity for exploring both the negative and the positive aspects of personal meanings, coping, and emotions. This emphasis should be viewed as illustrating the explanatory potential that resides in the transactional approach to stress, and not as suggesting that stress research has consistently ignored the positive. We are suggesting nothing other than a balanced approach, and how this can be achieved through a view of stress centered on relational-meaning. When stress is viewed in this meaning-centered way any encounter has the potential of being positive or negative, or both at different times and even perhaps at the same time, as individuals look for the positive in the negative (Tennen and Affleck 2005). Both need now to be explored in an inclusive way as each offers a much-needed perspective that captures the richness of the individual experience. While there may now need to be a "catch up" phase (Folkman and Moskowitz 2003), stress research has historically always pointed to the positive side of stress through the concept of eustress, and it is to this concept that we now turn.

EUSTRESS: THE POSITIVE SIDE OF STRESS

Hans Selye introduced the word stress to describe "the nonspecific response of the body to any demand" (1984, p. 74), but at almost the same time talked about stress as not necessarily something bad. "It all depends," he added, "on how you take it," adding "the stress of exhilarating, creative successful work is beneficial" and the stress reaction, just like energy consumption, may have good or bad effects" (1984, p. 63). Selye went on to differentiate between *distress* – the harmful or unpleasant variety of stress – and *eustress* – the good, pleasant or curative variety (1984). Despite the early use of the term eustress, the controversy surrounding Selye's work (Mason 1971) meant that little was done to develop it beyond "its original presentation" (Nelson and Simmons 2004, p. 275). Nevertheless, the term "eustress" has more than just a historical role to play. It presents researchers, argue Nelson and Simmons (2004), with the challenge, especially when viewed through the lens of positive psychology, to investigate what exactly distinguishes eustress from distress, how the two are related, and how it contributes to well-being at work.

It is not as if, once Selye had coined the term eustress, it was completely ignored by researchers. Edwards and Cooper in their 1988 article reviewing the impact of positive psychological states on health did point to the role of eustress. These authors, while acknowledging that research into the negative aspects of work-stress had "yielded invaluable evidence," stated that this research had also "failed to answer an equally fundamental question: What are the impacts of *positive* psychological states on health?" (p. 1447). Pointing to the different pathways through which eustress directly and indirectly improves health, Edwards and Cooper suggest that while such pathways may currently be somewhat speculative they "nonetheless outline potential processes by which eustress may improve health" (p. 1449). Making it clear that measuring eustress must be via the presence of positive states, rather than simply the absence of the negative, focuses attention, these authors argue, on identifying those factors that facilitate positive psychological functioning and points to the need for researchers to investigate the effects of both stress and eustress on employee health and well-being.

Reintroducing eustress into mainstream research

Nevertheless, there still remained the issue as to how to reintroduce eustress back into mainstream research. There is no doubt, as Nelson and Simmons suggest, that the concept of eustress has much to offer. Its contribution to our understanding of stress is, in many ways, even more important when set within the positive psychology movement that "accentuates the positive aspects of human adaptation and functioning" (2004, p. 267). It also chimes with the idea of "good work," how work practices help create positive workplaces, and how these practices and processes offer "employees a context in which they can excel" (Turner *et al.* 2002, p. 725). It is not just the positive psychology movement that offers support for a more focused and integrative approach to eustress.

There has always been, as Nelson and her colleagues suggest, clear support for such a concept pointing to appraisal as "a cornerstone of research on eustress" (Nelson *et al.* 2008, p. 56). While Lazarus (1966) may not have used the term eustress, Nelson and Simmons (2004) argue that his notion of positive appraisal, where appraising an encounter as a challenge describes focusing on the potential for gain or growth, "is consistent with the notion that eustress is 'good stress'" (p. 277) and with the idea that the concept of stress is multidimensional and capable of producing both positive (eustress) and negative (distress) responses.

The more recent work by Lazarus (2001b) on benefit appraisals, and Lazarus and Cohen-Charash (2001) on "discrete emotions," offers further evidence for persevering, if not with the word eustress, then with the multifaceted notion of stress in both its positive and negative guises. Indeed Simmons and Nelson (2007) make it clear that eustress simply reflects the extent to which an event is appraised as benefiting or enhancing well-being. Reshaping eustress through the process of appraisal serves not just as a means of integrating it into contemporary stress research, but provides a more enduring context for describing how the positive stress experience occurs (Nelson and Simmons 2003).

In order to guide future research, the holistic stress model developed by Nelson and Simmons (2003, 2004) and Simmons and Nelson (2007), integrates the idea of eustress and its positive qualities into its structure through their proposition that the appraisal of any stressor can produce a positive or negative meaning. These authors then go on to describe a number of unique aspects of the model that capture the essence of eustress but through more contemporary indicators, the individual differences that may promote these indicators, and the need to reconsider the nature of coping (Nelson and Simmons 2003, p. 101). Simmons and Nelson in discussing their model argue that emotions "merit a place," because they are "legitimate indicators" of the appraisal process (2007, p. 47), and when considered in terms of approach behaviors their positive nature can be expressed in terms of hope, meaningfulness, manageability, and positive affect (Nelson and Simmons 2003, p. 102). Although each of these emotional indicators of eustress are somewhat distinct, taken together they do, argue Nelson and Simmons (2003), reflect a sense of engagement with work.

These authors go on to add that this group of "eustress indicators" should not be considered the only ones or the most appropriate ones. More research is needed that explores positive psychological work states and how these states differ from or contribute to our understanding of, for example, job satisfaction, involvement, and self efficacy (Nelson and Simmons 2003). They also add "that joy, contentment, love, excitement and happiness may be good indicators to add to [their] Holistic Stress Model" (Simmons and Nelson 2007, p. 48). Nelson and Simmons (2003) then turn their attention to the types of individual differences that may help trigger positive indicators like those mentioned above, suggesting that the role of such individual differences may be to arm individuals with a belief that they can deal with work demands and in that way promote eustress by generating positive appraisals. Nelson and Simmons suggest "five possible [individual difference] candidates" that include optimism, internal locus of control, hardiness, self-reliance, and a sense of coherence (2003, p. 108). Going on to discuss each of these "five candidates" Nelson and Simmons (2003) point to how, through their positive qualities, each may not only provide a resource for managing work demands, but also aid our understanding of the positive process through which work demands are appraised.

A holistic model of eustress

Finally, in line with the positive holistic focus of their model, Nelson and Simmons argue that by extending the concept of eustress to coping, in contrast to the more traditional view where coping is discussed in terms of managing distress, there "must exist a complement" where individuals take pleasure in or "savor" the feelings of eustress (2004, p. 313). In their view (Nelson and Simmons 2004), the idea of savoring the positive of eustress adds to our understanding of coping by suggesting a separate and distinct aspect to coping, where the emphasis is on prolonging the experience so as to relish such positive feelings. Rediscovering the concept of eustress, embedding it within the positive psychology movement, and aligning it with more contemporary positive indicators gives, as we have suggested, a more enduring context, if not for the term itself then for what it means.

It is clear that a more integrated approach is now being demanded of researchers, one that offers a more inclusive approach to understanding the totality and richness of the individual experience. If one route through which this inclusiveness can be achieved is by embedding eustress into more contemporary frameworks, then this is entirely in keeping with developing a more comprehensive understanding of the nature of stress and its relevance to contemporary work issues.

FROM STRESS TO EMOTIONS

That people continue to describe demanding encounters in terms of being stressed ensures the terms place in everyday language. Yet from an empirical point of view the term "stress" has long lost any specific focus and, as many have argued, the term should now simply be used as a rubric, embracing a range of complex meanings and emotions. It is also clear that when we now think of the term "stress" we should think of it more in terms of offering a way of understanding "the stress of the stress process" (Lazarus 1990, p. 4) and those mechanisms that best express the nature of that process. In this way the focus of attention then shifts to those psychological processes that best describe the transactional nature of the relationship between the individual and the environment. This process-oriented approach, working through the processes of appraisal, yields a set of causal pathways that provides researchers with the opportunity to explore the role of discrete emotions that better capture the reality of the demanding experience. By focusing on the process we become less reliant on the term "stress" and more concerned with exploring discrete emotions; emotions both positive and negative that flow more naturally from the processes of appraisal. Researchers will, of course, continue to refine and develop our understanding of those components of the process. Nevertheless, the fact that it is the process that represents the research context ensures that appraisals and emotions become the common language of the researcher, and their causal pathways the mechanism through which good research practice will emerge.

TABLE 4.1   **The evolution and defining of a concept: From stress to emotions – the debate**

Traditional approaches to defining the concept of stress
- Stress as a stimulus (an encounter perceived as a source of stress).
- Stress as a response (a response type indicating stress).
- Stress as an interaction (the interaction between the two).

Shortcomings of these traditional approaches[a]
- The purpose of these definitions has been somewhat taxonomic, providing researchers with a list (range) of stimuli or responses that fall under each heading.
- In providing a range of stimuli-responses little attention is given to the inherent properties of either.
- By arbitrarily limiting the focus to only one component of what is a complex process they say little about the process and more often than not draw attention away from developing any understanding of the stress process.
- They ignore individual differences and those perceptual processes that may underlie the stress process.
- The interaction approach is essentially "structural" and "static" with any consideration of process being inferred from those variables that may moderate the relationship.
- Their value as definitions lies more in the knowledge that they have provided historically than their ability to express the nature of the work experience.

Towards a transactional definition of stress[b]
- Stress involves a stimulus and response *in relation to one another,* and it is the relational nature of this relationship that should become the focus of any definition.
- Understanding stress in relational terms focuses attention on process, particularly those psychological processes that specifically link the individual and the environment.
- The psychological processes that link the individual and the environment are expressed through a process of appraisal simply because individuals are always appraising the environment in terms of what impact it will have on their well-being.
- Appraisals involve a primary appraisal (the meaning given to an event – What does this mean? What is at stake?) and secondary appraisal (What can I do about it?).
- In this way stress, is defined in relational terms and emerges from the appraisal that a particular environmental demand is about to tax individual resources thus threatening well-being (Holroyd and Lazarus 1982).

Issues when defining stress in transactional terms
- The explanatory potential that comes from understanding the appraisal process has received a less than complete treatment. Why? (Dewe 2001; Dewe and Cooper 2007; Dewe *et al.* 2010; Jones and Bright 2001).

(Continued)

TABLE 4.1 **(Continued)**

- Its focus on the intra-individual (appraisal) process raises questions as to whether by emphasizing an individual level approach attention is shifted away from identifying those encounters that are more likely to threaten the well-being of most workers (Brief and George 1991).
- Focusing on how individuals appraise and give meaning to demanding encounters raises questions as to how such findings would be generalized to all workers (Brief and George 1991; Harris 1991; Schaubroeck 1999).
- Focusing on the appraisal process raises the issue of just what such an approach offers management in practical and interventional terms (Brief and George 1991; Frese and Zapf 1999; Harris 1991; Schaubroeck 1999).
- Nevertheless, despite these issues there is a general feeling that our understanding of the stress process would be advanced by investigating the role appraisals play in it (Brief and George 1991; Frese and Zapf 1999; Harris 1991; Schaubroeck 1999).

Abandoning stress and thinking more in terms of emotions
- If we are to better understand the nature of a stressful encounter then research could do well to focus on appraisals as the level of analysis. Why? (Dewe 2001; Dewe and Cooper 2007; Dewe *et al.* 2010).
- Because the emotional nature of a stressful encounter is based on the process of appraisal – appraisals are essential to understanding the emotional consequences of a stressful encounter (Lazarus 1991, 1999, 2001b).
- Appraisals offer a direct and theoretically important pathway for understanding the emotional process – they act as a trigger and a bridge, providing a causal pathway for understanding how one feels in a stressful encounter (Lazarus 2001b; Lazarus and Cohen-Charash 2001).
- Understanding that emotions flow from the appraisal of a stressful encounter means that attention can shift away from using the rather blunt term "stress" to explicitly exploring emotions (Lazarus 1999).
- In this way, rather than always grappling with what we mean by "being under stress," the focus can now move to exploring discrete emotions – in this way capturing a more differentiated and nuanced understanding of the consequences of a stressful encounter (Lazarus 1993b, 1999, 2001b; Lazarus and Cohen-Charash 2001).
- By focusing our attention on emotions a more balanced approach can emerge, where both the role of positive and negative emotions are explored and their properties better understood (Lazarus 2001b; Folkman 2011; Park and Folkman 1997).
- It is stress the "label" rather than stress the "concept" that now needs to be abandoned and through the use of transaction theory with its emphasis on appraisals and emotions becomes the way in which we begin to better understand the stress process (Dewe *et al.* 2010).

Notes: [a](e.g. Cox 1978; Cooper *et al.* 2001); [b](e.g. Lazarus 1990, 1993a, b, 1999, 2001b).

An interlude with Conservation of Resources Theory

Writing in 2011, Hobfoll pointed to the Conservation of Resources Theory (COR) as being one of two leading theories of stress (the other being the seminal work of Lazarus (1966)). The authority of COR theory lies in the central role it gives to both resource loss *and* resource gain, and how "an understanding of both is critical to how people respond to stress" (p. 128). COR theory (Hobfoll 1989, 2001, 2011) builds on the belief that individuals are motivated to obtain, retain, foster, and protect those key resources that they value, and that what is "threatening to them is the potential or actual loss of those valued resources" (1989, p. 516). Resources are described as "those objects, personal characteristics, conditions, or energies that are valued by the individual in their own right or valued because they serve as a means to attain or protect valued resources" (Hobfoll 2001, p. 339). Resources, then, as Hobfoll (1989) goes on to explain, are essential to understanding stress. Hobfoll (2011) outlines a number of principles that capture the essence of his theory.

These principles stem from the critical importance of resource loss as the primary component in the stress process (Hobfoll 2001). In this way, stress is defined as a response to the environment when resources are lost or threatened, or where there has been a failure to gain resources (Hobfoll 1989). Hobfoll (2011, p. 133) goes on to emphasize that resource loss generates more loss, that individuals must invest in resources to protect against resource loss, that resources are typically linked to one another, and that individuals with more resources are less vulnerable to resource loss, view threats differently, and have a greater capacity to engage in resource gain. Having a surplus pool of resources is, as Frydenberg (2002) suggests, more likely to be associated with eustress, and investing in resources signals proactive behaviors and emphasizes the significance of fostering and accumulating resources that can be put to best use.

The power of Hobfoll's COR theory lies in the way it draws attention to and emphasizes the importance of both resource loss and resource gain, and in this way broadens and enhances our understanding of stress. However, developing such a vigorous and compelling contribution to stress research (Quick and Gavin 2001) does not come without debate. Stress researchers have long debated the subjective–objective nature of stress (Aldwin 2009). It is arguing that because resources are real, objective, and observable there is less of a need to emphasize the primacy of appraisal in the stress process, that has led to Hobfoll

(2001, 2011) and Lazarus (2001a, b) exchanging views. While arguing that the "personal subjective component" of appraisal "has received too much weighting" at the expense of its other more objective and socially derived components (Hobfoll 2001, p. 359), Hobfoll neverthe-less sets out when each will be of greater importance in COR theory, and perhaps offers a "theoretical rapprochement" (Thompson and Cooper 2001), by suggesting that as each operates on a continuum then in any encounter neither can be ignored (Hobfoll 2001).

Hobfoll's laudable aim to broaden the focus of stress research and move it more towards exploring those objective components that capture the "reality" of the stress experience left Lazarus (2001a) unconvinced. Yet as other commentators point out, if the objective and subjective can be seen as correlated styles of thinking and responding, then there are opportunities for theoretical coalescence (Thompson and Cooper 2001). If so, then the differences between the theories of Hobfoll and Lazarus should be viewed more in terms of emphasis, and therefore more a matter of degree than principle (Schwarzer 2001; Schwarzer and Taubert 2002).

It is clear that COR theory's resource-based approach to stress has stim-ulated and motivated researchers to explore further the role of resources in stress research. Commentators, recognizing the significance of a resource-based focus, have suggested that while resource loss is central to Hobfoll's theory, resource gain might be an equally powerful concept, especially when considered from a developmental point of view (Freund and Riediger 2001). Linking resources to individual development and functioning helps not only to define resources in terms of their potential for achieving goals, but has an added value in that it directs attention to exploring "what I do" issues, in terms of successfully managing avail-able resources ("what I have") (Freund and Riediger 2001). "Individual development" is also a theme taken up by Schwarzer (2001) in his commentary on COR theory. Schwarzer positions "resource gains" in terms of individual strivings and argues that the building up of resources reflects a "forward time perspective" capturing the essence of proactive coping and broadening our understanding of coping strategies.

Similarly, Quick and Gavin (2001) suggest that a better understand-ing of resource loss and resource gain emphasizes the importance of these when developing intervention strategies, as they draw attention to both health promotion and stress prevention. To capture the full potential of COR theory work needs to continue to explore what dif-ferentiates one type of resource from another, when, and under what type of circumstances, something becomes a resource, how long some-thing remains a resource, and when depleted how are they reenergized, what the particular nature of the interaction between resources is, and what the processes are that link resources and well-being. We use this "resource loss–resource gain" approach as a framework for first explor-ing work stressors and then different approaches to resource gain.

RESOURCE DEPLETION – WORK STRESSORS

Defining stress in terms of a stimulus has provided a rich history of those demanding work situations that are perceived by individuals as about to tax their resources, thus threatening well-being (Holroyd and Lazarus 1982). We begin this section on work stressors by taking a historical perspective to provide the context for understanding how researchers approached the task of identifying different categories of work stressors. By pointing to how changing social, economic, and work conditions shape work stressors, we then use these changes to identify new work stressors, explore how they alter the nature of existing stressors, and raise questions about the measurement of work stressors and their associated health consequences.

Early approaches to identifying work stressors

Investigations into identifying demanding work situations stem from the seminal work of Kahn and his colleagues (Kahn *et al.* 1964). Stimu-lating their work was an all too familiar environment, where rapid expansion of industry and increasing importance of "large scale organizations in shaping individual and social life," "encouraged and accelerated technological change," demanded increases in efficiency, the search for new markets, and the need for a new generation of management techniques that carefully prescribed levels of individual performance and conformity "under conditions of ceaseless and accel-erating change" (pp. 4–6). By identifying role ambiguity, role conflict, and role overload Kahn and his colleagues introduced researchers to what they described as the "costly ideology of bureaucratic conform-ity" (Kahn *et al.* 1964, p. 6). These costs, as Kahn and his colleagues described, are something more than irritations or frustrations. They are costs that lead directly to reductions in satisfaction, a growing sense of futility, high levels of tension, a lowering of self-confidence, emotional turmoil, and a loss of identity. These three types of role stressors identified by Kahn and his colleagues established the first in an ever-expanding search for work stressors (Dewe *et al.* 2010). Even so, half a century later these three role stressors still remain at the centre of much research into the causes of work-stress.

Since the work of Kahn and his colleagues, and prompted by a need to better understand the well-being of working people, researchers have begun to give more attention to the job as a source of stress, and the different ways that work stressors could be categorized. McGrath (1976) was one of the first researchers to suggest a framework for categorizing potential sources of work-stress. In addition to the role requirements of the job, McGrath suggested that work stressors could be further categorized into those that were task-based, intrinsic to the behavior setting, arising from the physical environment, arising from the social environment, and those "within the person system" (p. 1369). McGrath conceded that no one category is completely separate from the other, and that individuals will differ in how they appraise and respond to a given stressor. Even at this very early stage, McGrath was already pointing to the way in which the term stress was being used in a pejorative sense. Researchers, as McGrath warned, need to be aware of the impact that such a value-laden term would have on research, especially in terms of the way findings are interpreted. We mustn't, he added, become "caught in our own semantic trap" (p. 1393). To reinforce this point, McGrath questioned what the outcome would have been if instead of "stress" we had used the label "challenge."

The seminal work of Beehr and Newman (1978) and Cooper and Marshall (1976) in the 1970s continued to raise the focus and extend the range of work stressor categories. Using a design to "facetize a complex set of phenomena along lines that seem most natural" Beehr and Newman (1978, p. 674) identified four broad facets of work stressor which they described as job demands and task characteristics, role demands or expectations, organizational characteristics and conditions, and organization's external demands and conditions. These four facets covered 37 potential sources of work stressors. While pointing to the health and well-being consequences that accompanied these work stressors, Beehr and Newman also pointed to the value-laden nature of the term "stress," noting that they had not excluded "the possibility of beneficial effects of stress" (1978, p. 670) on health.

These authors concluded that if researchers were to look at aspects of work using a stress–health perspective, then this would not only broaden our knowledge about job stress, but also provide results that may be "most interesting and worthwhile" (p. 696). The Beehr and Newman review became one of the most frequently cited articles of the 1970s. Two decades later, when reflecting on why this may be so, Beehr (1998) pointed to the timeliness of the review, the explicit directive the authors gave researchers to focus on the health and well-being of the individual, its fit with the themes emerging from the quality of working life movement, and the fact that it gave researchers a "readymade" framework for researching a range of different relationships. Work-stress research has, Beehr acknowledges, made many advances since 1978 "but it is still unfinished business" (1998, p. 843).

The work of Cooper and Marshall (1976) examined the work-stress literature in an effort to explicitly link environmental and individual stressors with "physical and mental disease or illness" (p. 13). They identified six categories of stressors. These they described as: intrinsic to the job, role in the organization, career development, relationships at work, organizational structure, and climate and extra-organizational sources of stress. Across these categories they identified 24 potentially different stressors. Their aim was to get organizations, practitioners, and researchers to work together on these stressors in the hope that such endeavors would make significant contributions "not only to the social, managerial, and medical sciences but to the physical and mental well-being of men and women at work" (p. 25). It is possible to identify common categories of work stressors from the research of those reviewed. Stressors, however, as this brief historical interlude suggests, emerge from the dynamics of an ever-changing social, economic, and working environment. We now turn to exploring how the impact of these different forces helps us to understand the evolving nature of work stressors.

The evolving nature of work stressors

Organizations are not immune to change, or the social, economic, and political turmoil that brings with it wave after wave of government initiatives, accompanied by complex legislation, changing management styles, economic imperatives that accelerate social, individual and community costs, changing employee expectations and values, and an increasingly diverse workforce. These sorts of changes are

90

accompanied by demands being placed on organizations to actively engage in practices that foster environmental sustainability, fair-trade and social responsibility, ethical leadership, flexible working patterns, and cost-effective strategies and techniques that intensify the nature of work and its emotional qualities, the role and significance of technology and technological development, and the need to operate in an increasingly competitive global market (Dewe *et al.* 2010). These changes shape work stressors and present a context for better understanding their continuously evolving nature. As the characteristics and architecture of even the most traditional and frequently researched stressors change, so must our understanding of that change keep pace so that we can identify new stressors, reconsider the nature of existing stressors, explore what this means for how stressors are measured, and explore their consequences for health and well-being.

In his 1988 review of work stressors, Burke acknowledged the way in which stressors change over time. The late 1970s and early 1980s witnessed, argued Burke, economic slowdown characterized by financial constraint, a greater need for fiscal responsibility, the rationalizing of production, outsourcing and closures, and a "mood of austerity" that accompanied all managerial decisions (p. 94). As a consequence of these economic conditions Burke (1988) pointed to four "newly emerging" sources of work stressors that had begun to attract increased research attention. These were mergers and acquisitions, organizational retrenchment and decline, future job ambiguity and insecurity, and organizational locking-in, where employees feel "boxed-in" with almost no opportunity to move from their present job (pp. 94–98). Burke (1988) went on to note that these four stressors are related, since they each reflect the effects of the economic recession, all require organizations to engage in strict budgetary controls, and each present significant issues in terms of individual and organizational interventions. It would not, Burke suggested, be an exaggeration to conclude that "stress has become a central topic in the field of organizational behavior" (Burke 1988, p. 106).

A decade later we welcomed in the new millennium, and sources of work stressors continued to attract "considerable empirical attention and public fascination" (Barling *et al.* 2005, p. 3). By this time, despite a decade of economic buoyancy and growth, the costs of such prosperity were beginning to take their toll through long hours, performance-related management techniques, lean organizational practices, continuous improvement requirements, competency-based initiatives, multiskill requirements, changing work patterns, complex interpersonal relationships, continuous technological change and development, and work–home social costs.

The downturn in economic activity in 2008–2009, the banking crisis described as "possibly the largest financial crisis of its kind in human history" (Hayman 2008, p. 1), and cuts in government spending all added to a stark reality where organizations, individuals, and society expressed alarm at the rising costs of stress expressed in terms of absenteeism, presenteeism, and turnover (Cooper and Dewe 2008; Dewe *et al.* 2010), witnessed greater levels of job insecurity, work intensity, and interpersonal conflicts (Chandola 2010), needed to recognize and acknowledge the scale of mental ill health problems at work (Sainsbury Centre for Mental Health 2007), and accept that if interventions are to succeed, then organizations must look both within and without for help in developing a partnership approach to develop best practice, and to build expertise necessary to manage work-stress and well-being (Black 2008).

Shaping the future: Contemporary work stressors

What emerges from these economic, social, and political changes and their impact on the organization of work and working relationships is the tensions they create, which shape the nature of future work stressors, and their impact on employee health and well-being. Under the heading of contemporary work stressors Sulsky and Smith (2005, pp. 122–124) pointed to, in addition to the changing nature of work–family and career stressors, increased automation and computerization, electronic performance monitoring (including unobtrusive electronic inspection and surveillance; see Coovert *et al.* 2005), downsizing, job loss, and the accompanying survivor stressor. To these can be added job instability and the continued concerns about, and potential threats to, job continuity (Cheng and Chan 2008), employment relations, and new forms of employment contracts.

This is what Chandola describes as "precarious contracts such as temporary, on-call and part-time contracts" (2010, p. 34), work intensity, work schedules (Totterdell 2005), the demanding emotional qualities of work (Dewe *et al.* 2010), and organizational politics (Ferris *et al.* 2005; Harris and Kacmar 2005), violence, aggression, bullying, harassment and discrimination (Chandola 2010; Rospenda and Richman 2005;

Schat and Kelloway 2005), work–life balance (Chandola 2010) and conflict (Bellavia and Frone 2005), fairness and organizational justice (Cropanzano *et al*. 2005), and terrorism (Inness and Barling 2005).

As already inferred, even the more established and readily researched work role stressors are not immune from societal changes. The changing nature of role stressors is nicely captured in the work of Hellgren and his colleagues (Hellgren *et al*. 2008). These authors point to the changing nature of work and employment, particularly the transition to a service economy, and explore how, against this backdrop, work roles are changing. Noting "that working life is still in a process of change," in that it is now more likely to be characterized by mental rather than physical demands, three themes emerge from their work that express changes to working roles: (a) the requirement for continual competency development; (b) difficulties in determining whether the work has been completed; and (c) difficulties in judging the quality of work (p. 61).

Expanding on these three themes, the authors point to such issues as: (a) that the responsibility for determining whether their competencies are aligned with their jobs is now more likely to be left up to the individual; (b) that individuals cannot always predict whether their competencies are the ones that will be demanded in future tasks; (c) that tasks frequently have no well-defined completion points or criteria for considering the work completed especially when colleagues and clients may have different views; and (d) that individuals are more likely to have to assume responsibility for appraising the quality of their own work, particularly when working independently of other colleagues (pp. 50–51). These authors conclude that it is important for researchers, when considering both new and classical stressors, to consider then in terms of how today's employees experience work.

Stressors: Some measurement challenges

Social, economic, and political forces will continue to create environmental conditions from which new work stressors will emerge and existing stressors change. The evolving nature of work stressors, as Beehr (1998) rightly suggests, makes work-stress a never-ending business. It also means that researchers need to consistently review whether work-stressor measures are actually measuring what we think they are (Cooper and Dewe 2004). By asking whose reality is it that is being

TABLE 4.2 **Work stressors: Their evolution**

The 1960s
Characterized by the increasing importance of large-scale organizations in shaping individual and organizational life – "the costly ideology of bureaucratic conformity" (Kahn *et al.* 1964, pp. 4–6).
Work stressors[a]
• Role ambiguity
• Role conflict
• Role overload

The 1970s and 1980s
The late 1970s and early 1980s saw the beginning of economic slowdown, a greater need for fiscal responsibility, outsourcing and closures, and a "mood of austerity" (Burke 1988, p. 94).
Additional work stressors
• Intrinsic aspects of the job
• Career development
• Relationships at work
• Organizational structure
• Organizational climate
• Extra-organizational issues
• Mergers and acquisitions
• Job insecurity
• Organizational retrenchment

The 1990s and forward
Despite a decade of economic optimism the costs of such prosperity were beginning to take their toll reflected in constant organizational and technological change, intense competition, home–work social costs, and a banking crisis with servere economic consequences (Dewe et al. 2010).
Additional work stressors
• Increased automation and computerization
• Electronic performance monitoring
• Unobtrusive electronic inspection
• Downsizing
• Job loss
• Job instability
• New employment relationships
• Work intensity
• Emotional demands of work
• Workplace violence, harassment, aggression, and bullying
• Work–life balance
• Fairness, equity, and discrimination

Note: [a]The lists of stressors were developed from a range of sources including for example: Barling *et al.* 2005; Beehr and Newman 1978; Burke 1988; Chandola 2010; Cheng and Chan 2008; Cooper and Marshall 1976; Coovert *et al.* 2005; Kahn *et al.* 1964; McGrath 1976; Sulsky and Smith 2005.

measured, and what meaning does it have for those completing the measure, we ensure that measures which have long been available and constantly used are now evaluated as much in terms of their relevance as they are in terms of their reliability (Dewe *et al.* 2010). The level of turbulence and change must mean that stressor measures are prone to an "inherent bias" (Glowinkowski and Cooper 1985) that over-emphasizes some stressor events, ignores others, and fails to reflect the evolving nature of the stressor itself.

By focusing on relevance, stressor measures are seen more in terms of their ability to describe an experience than to actually define it. As we have argued before (Dewe *et al.* 2010), uncritically accepting the "a priori labeling of a stressor as always reflecting the same events" (p. 18), or as having the same meaning, or providing a comprehensive description of the experience, fails to capture the evolving nature of the stressor and the influence of environmental forces. Persisting with a stressor measure simply because it exhibits sound psychometric properties may not, in fact, be advancing our understanding of what it is that is being experienced or the nature of the stressor itself.

In practice this means that researchers should pay particular attention to the events being measured, their relevance, and whether they reflect the working lives of those being researched (Cooper *et al.* 2001). That is, are they grounded in day-to-day work experiences and are they informed by "a bottom-up approach that is able to capture local concerns and context" (Mackay *et al.* 2004, p. 101). Measures, if they are to capture the intensity of the stressor experience, need now to incorporate metrics which capture issues like duration, frequency, and demand (Trenberth and Dewe 2006). Because of the multidimensional nature of many work stressors, and the complex nature of such relationships, it is as important to understand "within-stressor" relationships as it is to understand the relationships between different stressors, since these offers a richer pathway for understanding how different stressor items and the stressors themselves combine to influence what is being experienced at work (Trenberth and Dewe 2006).

By rethinking the pattern of relationships within and between stressors, the extent and reasons for such relationships must raise "interesting questions" (Daniels 2006, p. 284). Indeed, the explanatory potential residing in understanding the patterns from which mean scores are derived highlights the fact that "absolute levels of work stressors may be no reason to believe that individuals are experiencing the same thing" (Dewe and Brook 2000, p. 4). Then there is the question of whether the relationship between different work stressors and strain is more specific than generally assumed. Researchers may now need to give more careful thought to the relationship between stressors and strain since, as Spector and Jex suggest from their review, "different stressors may evoke qualitatively different emotional responses" (1998, p. 364).

In addition to these "operational issues" relating to work-stress or measurement, three other conceptual issues are important. These are the role of appraisal in stressor measurement, whether stressors are always a bad thing (Beehr and Grebner 2009), and stressor measurement and interventions. When a distinction is drawn between the meanings individuals give to events and the nature of the events themselves it is clear that these meanings or appraisals offer a powerful pathway to understanding the stressors–strain relationship. Lazarus's (2001a) transaction theory makes it clear that the appraisal which individuals make triggers the emotional experience, and so to ignore this pathway and the role appraisal plays in it is to ignore one of the most powerful constructs we have for better understanding the transactional nature of stress. It is clear that researchers should now give as much attention to understanding the nature of such appraisals, and their role in the stress transaction, as they have to developing an understanding of the different categories of stressors themselves.

Beehr and Grebner explore whether stressors are always a bad thing, and point to three issues in respect of work stressors. These include whether in some encounters, while stressors lead to strain, there are aspects of that encounter that are valued positively by the person, whether stressors can lead to good outcomes as well as strains, and whether under some conditions stressors produce little if any strain (2009, p. 20). While these authors point to how definitions of stress have conditioned us to think in terms of bad outcomes, they argue for more research that explores how often success or other good outcomes are "tied to the experience of stress," saying that "there can be a positive psychology even in relation to occupational stress" (p. 30). Finally, stressor measurement cannot be divorced from intervention strategies. If stressor measurement fails to capture the nature of the experience, and establish the context within which strain may occur, then this can only place an almost impossible burden on those designing stress interventions and on the benefits that can emerge in terms of employee health and well-being.

TABLE 4.3   **Work stressors: Measurement issues**

The challenges
- The evolving nature of work stressors makes reviewing how they are measured a constant requirement (Beehr 1998).
- Researchers need to constantly review whether our measures of work stressors are actually measuring what we think they are, whose reality is being measured, and what meaning and significance they have for those filling out such measures (Cooper and Dewe 2004; Dewe *et al.* 2010; Glowinkowski and Cooper 1985).
- Because of the level of turbulence and change, researchers need to ensure that they are not over-emphasizing some work stressors, ignoring others, and failing to reflect the evolving nature of the work stressor itself (Dewe *et al.* 2010; Glowinkowski and Cooper 1985).
- Researchers should acknowledge and accept that work-stressor measures need to be seen more in terms of their ability to describe rather than their ability to define, in this way recognizing that established measures do not always provide a comprehensive description of the experience or the evolving nature of the stressor itself (Cooper *et al.* 2001; Dewe *et al.* 2010).
- Researchers may need to recognize that emphasizing reliability over relevance does not advance our understanding of what is being experienced or the nature of the stressor itself (Cooper and Dewe 2004).

Measurement issues
- Particular attention needs to be paid to the events being measured, their relevance, and whether they reflect the reality of the work experience (Cooper *et al.* 2001; Mackay *et al.* 2004).
- If measures are going to capture the intensity of the experience then more attention needs to be given to the metric being used and what it is capturing (Cooper *et al.* 2001).
- Because of the complexity of work stressors and their multidimensional nature it needs to be remembered that while respondents may have the same scale score this does not mean that they are experiencing the same thing. More attention needs to be given to "within-stressor relationships" the relationships between different stressor events and the way scale scores are derived (Cooper *et al.* 2001; Dewe and Brook 2000).
- Attention should also be paid to relationships between different stressors and the consequences of experiencing one on the experiencing of another (Cooper *et al.* 2001; Trenberth and Dewe 2006).
- More attention needs also to be given to whether different stressors trigger their own unique responses and so the stressor–response relationship may be more specific than generally assumed (Cooper *et al.* 2001; Daniels 2006; Spector and Jex 1998).
- Measurement practice also means that researchers need to acknowledge the difference between the "objective" nature of a stressor event and its meaning (appraisal). Ignoring the way stressors are appraised is to ignore one of the most potent causal pathways available to researchers (Dewe *et al.* 2010; Lazarus 2001a).
- Researchers may also need to consider the positive side of stressors and those aspects of a stressor that may be valued (Beehr and Grebner 2009; Lazarus and Cohen-Charash 2002; Nelson and Simmons 2004).

OVERVIEW

In this section we set out to explore how, over time, researchers identified and classified those work events which had the potential to deplete individual resources. These events, described as work stressors, are defined in terms of those work situations that are perceived by individuals as about to tax their resources, and thus threaten well-being (Holroyd and Lazarus 1982). Our aim here has been to show how social, economic, and political forces shape the nature of work stressors, ensuring researchers consider in addition how, through the tumult of change, new stressors emerge that express the character of work, how we work and how we engage at work in pursuit of organizational and individual goals, and how traditionally classified stressors also evolve over time. While our review did not always explicitly point to the "resource-depleting" qualities of the different categories of work stressors, those doing the reviewing did, couching their work in terms of the physical, psychological, and behavioral consequences of such encounters. In order to better understand these consequences, and their relationship to work stressors, we have argued that once more researchers should return to, and refocus on, how work stressors are measured, considering not just important operational issues that emerge from how stressors evolve, but the relationships, patterns, and profiles that can emerge within and between stressors, their multidimensional nature, the meanings associated with, and how the different stressors are appraised, the specific effects of different stressors including whether stressors lead to good outcomes, and how, in designing any type of stress intervention, good stressor measurement is crucial.

CHAPTER 5

RESOURCE ACCUMULATION

This chapter partners the previous chapter on resource depletion, and considers resources from the point of view of a process that emphasizes investing in resource-conservation strategies (Hobfoll 2001). These are designed, in the face of work demands, to protect, foster, build, and maintain a reserve that contributes to personal development, individual functioning and capability, health, and well-being. Hobfoll (2001), through his COR theory, points to the way people strive to invest in and accumulate resources that protect against the possibility of loss. The value associated with these resources lies in their ability to strengthen personal characteristics, provide a sense of energy, offer self-protection, help achieve goals, and restore well-being.

We begin our exploration of resource accumulation by first returning to the concept of well-being, and explore, using the framework offered by Warr (1990, 1994, 2007), what it is about work that makes people happy or unhappy. We then move to Fredrickson's (1998) work on positive emotions, their adaptive significance, and how these emotions, through their ability to "broaden and build," offer opportunities to develop lasting individual resources. Continuing with this theme of positive human functioning we explore the concept of positive psychological capital (Avey *et al.* 2009; Luthans *et al.* 2007a), and how this acts as a positive resource that enhances motivational capabilities, identifies individual strengths, and develops psychological capacities (Luthans *et al.* 2007a). From the work of Luthans and his colleagues, we then examine in more detail the resource-building concept of resilience (Masten 2001; Masten and Reed 2005; Sutcliffe and Vogus 2003). We conclude this section on resource accumulation by touching on positive health (Seligman 2008), and positive growth, thriving, and flourishing (Fredrickson and Losada 2005).

HAPPINESS–UNHAPPINESS AT WORK: THE VITAMIN MODEL

Warr (2007) begins his writings on work, happiness, and unhappiness by drawing attention to the definitional complexity surrounding the term "happiness" and how researchers have, more often than not, preferred instead to use the term "well-being." Pointing to the two aspects of happiness, happiness as subjective well-being (*hedonism*) and happiness as self-validation (*eudaimonic*), Warr goes on to add that happiness as well-being needs also to be considered, not just in terms of its energised (e.g. fun, excitement, enthusiasm) and tranquil forms (e.g. peace of mind, comfort), but also whether it is being used as a broad overall term (context-free), or as a more narrow context-specific (e.g. work), or facet-specific (e.g. particular job aspects) term.

Acknowledging that research has focused almost entirely on happiness as well-being because of the difficulties surrounding exactly how happiness as self-validation should best be operationalized, Warr goes on to suggest a positive relationship between the two, and says that there "may [even] be a hierarchical or sequential element in the two experiences" (2007, p. 12). However, the complexity surrounding an emotion like happiness remains, because, as Warr (2007, p. 13) points out, individuals may experience at much the same time different forms of happiness. Happiness, as Warr notes (2007, pp. 14–15), differs depending on the comparisons being made, the time period being compared, and understanding that happiness is necessarily going to depend not just on the source that is being investigated, but also on the individual's interaction with it.

The power of Warr's (2007) work comes when he turns his attention to the relationship between work and happiness–unhappiness. In confronting the question of why some people are happier than others, Warr structures his argument around two perspectives: *"environment-centered"* and *"person-centered"* (p. 15), complicated at times because of the interaction between the two. Turning to the environment-centered perspective, Warr (1987) first identified what he described as the "needed nine" sources of happiness or unhappiness that applied across any kind of setting, and which differentiated one setting from another depending on their presence or absence.

These nine comprise: opportunities for personal influence, skill use, goal generation, variety, environmental clarity, social networks, money, physical security, and a valued role (Warr and Clapperton 2010, p. 72). Transferring these to a work setting, Warr added another three: supportive supervision, good career outlook, and fair treatment.

These "top twelve" work sources are "the ones that really matter for happiness or unhappiness" (Warr and Clapperton 2010, p. 10). Why is happiness important? The empirical evidence suggests that happiness is critical to successful adaptation and positive mental health, and that "happy individuals appear more likely to be flourishing people both inwardly and outwardly" (Lyubomirsky *et al*. 2005, p. 112). So, how do these "top twelve" work sources, as outlined by Warr (2007), contribute to happiness and its resource enhancing qualities?

Sources of happiness at work

Warr makes it clear that there is no one "correct" number of work sources. His framework of twelve were selected as being "pragmatically appropriate" (2007, p. 82) out of the many that flow from the considerable research evidence and as the "ones that most affect" happiness or unhappiness (Warr and Clapperton 2010, p. 71). Warr goes on to add that the number of these sources will differ from job to job, and that not all of these sources will be significant across all settings. The importance of the different sources will also depend on individual needs and values; a theme we will return to later in this section. In describing the association between these twelve environmental features and happiness–unhappiness, Warr (2007) suggests that the best way is to liken the relationship to "the effect of vitamins on physical health" (p. 92) where, like vitamins, moderate levels are generally good for you, but only up to a certain point. It may be, suggests Warr (2007), that in general terms the absence of these sources may produce unhappiness, but, beyond a certain point, for some at least, their presence does not produce greater levels of happiness.

So, the impact of these twelve work features can be summed up as: their absence will, it seems, produce unhappiness or other negative feelings, moderate levels are generally desirable and produce happiness or other positive feelings, but beyond that level there is a "tipping point" (Warr and Clapperton 2010, p. 73), where too much of a work feature either creates demands that reduce happiness and damage well-being, or happiness stays more or less the same as further increases fail to produce "additional benefits [because] you've already reached a plateau of what is 'enough'" (Warr and Clapperton 2010, p. 95). Warr (2007, pp. 107–108) adds one more detail by suggesting that of the twelve job features, as the first six (opportunities for personal influence, skill use, goal generation, variety, environmental clarity, and social networks) become more demanding they become potentially more harmful (e.g. produce negative feelings), because at such levels they are likely to be more than individuals want from their job. In the case of the remaining six features (money, physical security, a valued role, supportive supervision, good career outlook, and fair treatment), Warr (2007) argues that once a threshold has been reached these have a fairly constant effect on happiness, because increases beyond that threshold point don't add much or make much difference to happiness. Again low levels in any of the twelve make people unhappy, whereas low-to-threshold levels tend to produce happiness or other positive feelings.

Happiness at work and individual differences

However, the chances of being happy at work are not just dependent on individual job features, but also "come from you" (Warr and Clapperton 2010, p. 109), so it is necessary to consider how, in conjunction with job features, personality, values, and motives influence happiness–unhappiness at work. While the evidence points to the content of the job having a greater impact on well-being than perhaps individual dif-ferences, "there is," as Warr and Clapperton point out, "no getting away from the fact that your own characteristics also make a contribution" (2010, pp. 110; 114; 122). These authors draw attention to a number of themes when it comes to individual characteristics and happiness. The first suggests that there is a consistency in people's happiness, and even when unhappiness occurs people appear to have a "baseline level of happiness" which they return to over time. Another suggests that, although such relationships are complex, generally speaking happiness is associated to some degree with personality traits like extroversion, agreeableness, and conscientiousness, and less so with neuroticism. A third theme suggests that happiness also depends on the sorts of comparisons each of us make in terms of, for example, whether or not we are better off than others, what we want versus what we are getting versus how important all this is to us, what it is we are looking for, and what we are used to.

Our outline of the work–happiness relationship cannot capture the depth of detail, the complexity of argument, or the scope of research reviewed that represents Warr's work. Our overview does allow us, however, to draw attention to a number of issues when considering the resource enhancing properties of work and happiness. The first concerns the complexity of an emotion like happiness, and how future research needs to continue to explore the nature of happiness, the different ways it may be expressed, and how it may vary from context to context. Similarly, when the different work features are considered, it is also important to continue to explore the nature and architecture of those features, what it is about those features that produces feelings of happiness, whether different features produce different forms of happiness, and, of course, whether happy employees are productive employees. It is interesting to note in respect of the last point that the "extent of support for the happy–productive worker thesis may depend on what is meant by happiness" (Zelenski *et al*. 2008, p. 535).

Work and happiness: A complex relationship

The complexity of the work–happiness relationship needs also to be understood in terms of the impact of personality, values, and motives. If, as the research suggests, individuals have "tipping points," where happiness dissolves into unhappiness or damages well-being, then future research needs to continue to explore when such a point is reached, what is it about that point that causes happiness to tip, what are the consequences of such a tip not just in terms of the emotions that emerge but how long such feelings remain, and what individuals do to cope with such feelings. Research into tipping points cannot of course be considered in isolation and needs to be explored in relation to the stability of happiness over time. Reviews of the research suggest that (Warr and Clapperton 2010) even though happiness levels do vary up and down, individuals have a baseline or "set point" of happiness–unhappiness to which they return.

Future research may wish to further explore whether this means that there are limits to what can be done to improve happiness over time (Warr 2007; Warr and Clapperton 2010), whether happiness set points are "fixed, stable over time, and immune to influence or control" (Lyubomirsky *et al*. 2005, p. 116), the "intentional activity" individuals actually engage in or factors they look for in, for example, work that increase happiness, whether those activities produce the desired effect (Lyubomirsky *et al*. 2005), and just how far happiness can be

HAPPINESS – THE TERM

- There is a complexity surrounding the term "happiness" with researchers often preferring the term well-being (Warr 1990, 1994, 2007; Warr and Clapperton 2010).

- Happiness as well-being needs to be considered in terms of its energized (excitement, enthusiasm) and tranquil (peace of mind, comfort) forms (Warr 2007, p. 20), but also;

- As a broad overall term (context-free), or as more context-specific (e.g. work), or as facet-specific (e.g. particular job aspect) (Warr 2007, p. 29).

HAPPINESS AT WORK (CONTEXT AND FACET SPECIFIC)

- Two perspectives are needed – *environment-centered* and *person-centered* (Warr 2007, p. 15), although it is complicated because of the interaction between the two.

ENVIRONMENT-CENTERED

Different job-facet sources of happiness (see Warr and Clapperton 2010, p. 72):

- If absent will produce unhappiness or other negative feelings (Warr and Clapperton 2010, pp. 73, 104).

- Moderate levels are generally desirable and produce happiness or other positive feelings but;

- there is a "tipping point" where too much of a job facet either (a) creates demands that reduce happiness; or (b) happiness stays more or less the same because of having already reached a plateau of what is enough (see Warr and Clapperton 2010, pp. 73; 93).

PERSON-CENTERED

Individual characteristics (Warr and Clapperton 2010, p. 114) and happiness – a number of themes:

- There is a consistency in people's happiness where people appear to have a baseline level of happiness that over time they return to (Warr and Clapperton 2010, p. 111).

- Happiness is generally associated with personality traits like extroversion, agreeableness, and conscientiousness, and less so with neuroticism (Warr and Clapperton 2010, pp. 114–119).

- Happiness seems also to be influenced in terms of the comparisons individuals make as to whether they are better off than others, what they want versus what they are getting, the importance of this, and what it is that is being looked for and what they are used to (Warr and Clapperton 2010, p. 122).

FIGURE 5.1 **Happiness at work: A structure based on the work of Warr**

FUTURE DIRECTIONS FOR HAPPINESS RESEARCH

- Happiness is a complex emotion, so future research needs to explore the nature of happiness, the different ways it may be expressed, and how it may vary from context to context (Warr 2007; Warr and Clapperton 2010).

- Similarly, in relation to those job facets that produce happiness, the need is to explore what it is about those facets that produces feelings of happiness, whether different facets produce different forms of happiness, and whether happy employees are productive employees (Zelenski *et al.* 2008).

- If, as the research suggests, individuals have "tipping points" in relation to happiness then future research needs to explore when such a point is reached, what it is about that point that causes happiness to tip and what are the consequences of such a tip (Warr and Clapperton 2010).

- Future research may also like to explore whether there are limits to what can be done to improve happiness over time, the way individuals actually seek happiness, and just how far happiness can be taught (Lyubomirsky *et al.* 2005; Warr 2007; Warr and Clapperton 2010).

- It is also important to continue to examine the role different personality traits play in terms of individual happiness and the way individuals use social comparisons to evaluate their happiness (Warr and Clapperton 2010).

FIGURE 5.1 **(Continued)**

"nurtured, acquired, or directly taught" (Lyubomirsky 2001, p. 245). It is also important to continue to explore the role that different personality attributes play in terms of individual happiness, as well as the sorts of social comparisons individuals make when evaluating their happiness levels (Warr and Clapperton 2010).

Exploring the relationship between work and happiness, as Warr (2007) has done, clearly resonates with the work of those who argue for an agenda where the focus is on "good work" that is meaningful and a source of well-being, individual growth, and fulfilment (Coats and Lekhi 2008; Constable *et al.* 2009; Overell 2008), and those who argue for rethinking and broadening job design research to better understand how job characteristics provide meaningful opportunities for proactive behaviour (Parker *et al.* 2010). In line with these themes, others have argued that when exploring orientations towards happiness, we should not overlook the pursuit of engagement (Peterson *et al.* 2005) or work engagement as a type of employee well-being (Schaufeli *et al.* 2008). *Engagement* is defined as "a positive, fulfilling, work-related state of mind that is characterized by vigor, dedication and absorption" (Schaufeli *et al.* 2002, p. 74).

Bakker *et al.*'s review (2011a) outlines ten key questions that should shape the agenda for future research into work engagement. It is clear that the debate surrounding the conceptualization of work engagement will continue (Schaufeli and Salanova 2011), as will the need to explore it within a broader work context (George 2011). Our understanding of its relationship will need to develop across a range of other areas of work behavior, particularly those circumstances underlying how, when, and why engagement influences job performance (Parker and Griffin 2011), and the need to extend our understanding of its positive and negative consequences in a more balance way (Halbesleben 2011). Nevertheless, as Bakker, Albrecht and Leiter conclude, "now is not only a good time to study engagement but also to 'do' engagement" (2011b, p. 85). Progressing research on engagement can only add to our understanding of its role as one route to happiness. However, what is demanded of us now is to focus our attention on just how complex concepts like happiness and well-being confront the different approaches to conceptualizing both these concepts in a way that reinforces the need to consider how best such approaches and the complexity that surrounds them can be captured thereby requiring us to consider more innovative and creative methods that signal the way we wish to move forward.

EMOTIONS AT WORK

It may come as somewhat of a surprise to learn that although organizational research is now well and truly in the grip of an "affective revolution" (Barsade and Gibson 2007), with reviewers proclaiming that now is an "exciting time" (Elfenbein 2007) for those interested in exploring "emotions at work," this has not always been the case. Research into the role of emotions in the workplace went from "rich beginnings" through, until recently, a relatively lean period where, almost without exception, investigations narrowed to simply focus "almost exclusively" on job satisfaction (Brief and Weiss 2002, p. 281). Even by the early 1990s academics were still commenting that to review the research on emotions at work you actually had to have research that you could review, leading them to suggest that despite the importance of such an area "there is little research that speaks directly to the issue of work and emotions" (Pekrun and Frese 1992, p. 153).

Even so, Pekrun and Frese still provided a comprehensive review and although they concluded that there was "not as much as one would like [there] to be" (p. 191), they still managed to identify and discuss a range of positive and negative work-related emotions, providing a taxonomy for understanding them, and linking them to various job characteristics. Others shared these sentiments and they, too, expressed their concerns, suggesting that although "the experience of work is saturated with emotions" (Ashforth and Humphrey 1995, p. 97), there was "clearly a need for more research on emotions in the workplace" (Fox and Spector 2002, p. 167). Research had in many ways simply neglected this aspect of organizational life. So, how can we explain these lean years of research and why now there is this "dramatic shift in momentum in affect research" (Barsade *et al*. 2003, p. 33)?

Understanding emotions at work

Researchers are clear as to the relevance of understanding emotions at work, citing such reasons as the centrality of work to one's emotional life, health, and well-being, the influence emotions have in transforming organizational culture and individual development (Pekrun and Frese 1992), the manner in which they influence motivation, leadership, and group dynamics (Ashforth and Humphrey 1995), how they affect other critical organizational outcomes such as decision making, creativity, prosocial behavior, and negotiations (Barsade and Gibson 2007), and how they influence coping and adaptation. Researchers are also very clear that, despite understanding the importance and relevance of emotions to the workplace, research into their influence has been limited because there is a perceived awkwardness that such research may disturb the rather orderly way in which organizations work, hence the need to regulate them (Ashforth and Humphrey 1995; Ashforth and Kreiner 2002), with the consequence, perhaps, that any research that has gone forward has been narrowed to exploring job satisfaction (Weiss 2002), or because of the urgency to understand their effects research has limited its focus to simply investigating negative emotions (Fredrickson 2000b). Each of these different views will be briefly examined.

As Ashforth and Humphrey (1995) suggest, organizations have a very limited view of socially acceptable emotions, and generally work to regulate the expression of strong emotions. Given this view, it is understandable that organizations prefer to emphasize rationality at the expense of emotionality, as if each is at opposite ends of the same continuum. As a result, organizations engage in a number of activities to limit and regulate the influence of emotions in the workplace, turning what has the potential to be "the extraordinary into the ordinary" (Ashforth and Kreiner 2002, p. 231), overlooking the dysfunctional affects that such regulation may have (Ashforth and Humphrey 1995), and failing to distinguish between different types of emotions, particularly those positive emotions that are less threatening and more likely to express work behaviors that enhance individual performance (Ashforth and Kreiner 2002; Frederickson 2001).

What are the ways in which organizations regulate emotions? These include: (see Ashforth and Humphrey 1995, pp. 104–117; Ashforth and Kreiner 2002, p. 216) (a) *neutralizing*, where more threatening, undesirable emotions are prevented from occurring; (b) *buffering*, deliberately separating emotional expression from workplace performance; (c) *prescribing*, outlining and specifying the ways emotions may be expressed; and (d) *normalizing*, where the emotion is reframed so as to make it more socially acceptable. These different mechanisms overlap, are more operationally complex than outlined above, and reflect the fact that because emotions are an intimate part of the ebb and flow of organizational life they simply cannot always be regulated (Ashford and Humphrey 1995; Ashforth and Kreiner 2002). The answer lies, as Ashforth and Humphrey suggest, in researchers and managers alike recognizing "the functional complementary of emotionality and rationality" (p. 120) and not in simply accepting uncritically the view that "the best way to manage emotions in the workplace is not to have any" (Elfenbein 2007, p. 316).

JOB SATISFACTION: A SURROGATE MEASURE OF EMOTIONS?

Perhaps as a consequence of organizational attempts to regulate emotions, researchers have turned their attention not just to the issue of "emotional labor," where employers require employees to display desired emotions (Zapf 2002; Zapf and Holz 2006), but also to the use of job satisfaction as a measure of emotions. It is clear that in its leaner years, the study of emotions in the workplace was limited to a narrow focus on a few relatively general and stable states dominated somewhat by job satisfaction, but also including constructs like stress and mood (Ashforth and Humphrey 1995). It is also clear that job satisfaction has been, and is, probably the preferred measure of affect for many organizations. But the concept itself is not without its issues, including a long period before researchers even bothered turning to and exploring exactly what it was that job satisfaction measures were measuring, accepting that what was needed was for job satisfaction to be defined independently of any measurement tool, thereby challenging the long-held mantra that whatever job satisfaction is, it is simply what my measure is measuring (Weiss 2002). Locke's (1976) definition, where job satisfaction emerged as an emotional response to a set of value judgments individuals make about their job, led to the concept being viewed as an affective state.

However, as academics turned their attention to the nature and meaning of job satisfaction, debate soon occurred as to whether it should be defined as an attitude (Weiss 2002), whether there is a cognitive component to it, how influenced it is by dispositional factors (Ashforth and Humphrey 1995), and whether the literature on job satisfaction continues to confuse "overall evaluative judgments about jobs, affective experiences at work and beliefs about jobs" (Weiss 2002, p. 177). Despite its continual use, job satisfaction remains a troublesome concept, has been used uncritically, and certainly requires more research to explore and distinguish between its use as an attitude or affect variable, its cognitive versus affective dimensions, dispositional influences, the process that best describes it (Ashforth and Humphrey 1995), and the need to more carefully distinguish and separate out evaluations, beliefs, and affective experiences (Weiss 2002). Only by engaging with these issues, and more importantly, continuing to clarify what we mean by job satisfaction, and what it now means in terms of twenty-first-century work, will we begin to offer to organizations a concept that merits its continued use.

Because of the centrality of job satisfaction to working life, it is likely that for many researchers the concept of job satisfaction had assumed the mantle, and became the representation of emotionality in working life. Since the 1960s, the search by occupational psychologists for what motivates working people (what is it that energizes and sustains behavior) continued to reinforce the primacy of job satisfaction as a measure of emotion, and led to job satisfaction being considered as the natural outcome when considering the "happy productive worker." Yet, at best, the emotional qualities of job satisfaction reflect a more enduring feeling about the job, overshadowing the significance and expression of more "immediate emotions," and once again highlighting that when it comes to understanding workplace emotions "there is much more work to be done" (Fox and Spector 2002, p. 167; 171).

Even when researchers step beyond job satisfaction, there still appears to be a feeling that the research focus continues to settle on relatively generalized and often negative states like stress. For many commentators, continuing to focus on these more general affective states simply fails to recognize the explanatory potential that may emerge from more carefully differentiating between emotions, and the opportunity to better understand the role of everyday emotions in organizational life (Barsade *et al.* 2003; Brief and Weiss 2002). If, as Brief and Weiss (2002) suggest, workplaces are more likely to produce a range of more specific emotions, then researchers need now to broaden their focus so as to capture the emotional richness of the work experience.

DISCRETE EMOTIONS

Clearly, as Barsade and her colleagues argue, researchers have recognized that focusing mainly on job satisfaction reflected a rather narrow approach, and have initiated a richer and broader focus on how emotions influence organizational life. How did this change come about? A number of changes in perspective may have helped to make this an "exciting time" for researchers interested in the emotional aspects of working life (Elfenbein 2007, p. 316). These changes would include the arrival of the positive psychology movement, with its emphasis on individual strengths (Seligman and Csikszentmihalyi 2000), the recognition that research on emotions needs to become increasingly more "differentiated and nuanced" (Barsade *et al.* 2003, p. 11), requiring that greater attention be given to understanding the role of discrete emotions in working life, the acknowledgment that Lazarus's (1999) transactional theory with its emphasis on appraisal offers a theoretical pathway for understanding the emotional process but has been "underappreciated for its power to shed light on phenomena central to organizations" (Elfenbein 2007, p. 323), and the progress and advances continually being made in psychology in terms of construct development and measurement (Barsade *et al.* 2003). We briefly expand on some of these changes.

The mission of positive psychology is to explore those individual strengths that maximize human potential. While this mission has been incredibly effective in forcing researchers to engage in a more open and serious dialogue about positive emotions (Fredrickson 2000b), its effectiveness may equally lie in not just introducing researchers to, and expanding their knowledge about the resource-building qualities and range of such emotions, but in convincing them that such emotions are as worth cultivating as negative ones. Researchers, while acknowledging that positive emotions have been investigated less frequently than negative ones, have, of course, identified different positive emotions and developed frameworks that carefully distinguish between them (Barsade and Gibson 2007; Brief and Weiss 2002; Pekrun and Frese 1992). Reviewing and identifying lists of positive emotions may well have helped researchers to recognize that such emotions cannot simply be subsumed into a more general structure of affective states (Brief and Weiss 2002). Research would be better directed towards investigating discrete emotions, differentiating one from the other, and exploring those antecedent factors from which such emotions flow (Barsade *et al.* 2003).

Discrete emotions: Identification and measurement

Discrete emotions are "the coin of the realm," argue Lazarus and Cohen-Charash (2001, p. 45), when it comes to understanding how employees cope with organizational life. These authors point to the need to adopt a discrete-category approach to emotions, as each emotion offers a different way to understand how individuals deal with organizational life. While they identify such positive emotions as, for example, happiness, joy, pride, gratitude, and compassion, the importance of these emotions lies less in being part of a list and more in terms of their distinctive characteristics, their antecedents, and their consequences (Lazarus and Cohen-Charash 2001, p. 49). Even more important perhaps, is the theoretical pathway that Lazarus (2001b) offers which captures the tone of the emotional process. Lazarus (2001b), as we have discussed earlier, makes it clear that it is the way in which individuals appraise and give meaning to a work encounter that operates as a trigger; a bridge that facilitates the emotional response. Positive appraisals initiate positive emotions, and it is this appraisal process that provides a direct and conceptually "rich and important" (Park and Folkman 1997, p. 132) causal pathway for the study of discrete emotions at work.

Researchers have long grappled with the issue of where current methodologies are taking us, and what alternative methods could provide. Research into positive emotions is not immune from this discussion. It is clear that psychologists need to capture the richness of the emotional process. The use of questionnaires offers a conventional, practical, and convenient opportunity for data collection, but their utility is at times sorely tested when trying to capture meaning, expression, and the rich texture of experience (Fineman 2004). The question of whose reality is being measured, and how that reality is expressed, is one that frequently confronts researchers across many areas of organizational psychology. Creative ways forward that are ecologically sensitive have been explored and operationalized: one example of such creativity is the *emotional narrative* (Lazarus 1999), where the emotion is captured using a storytelling approach which is rich in meaning, allowing "the fine grain nuances" of the experience to emerge, a procedure that is "abundant in insight, plausibility and texture" (Fineman 2004, pp. 733; 736). Another approach is what Barsade and her colleagues describe as tracking affective patterns of everyday emotions, using experience-sampling methodology that involves daily sampling of affective experiences (2003, p. 30). All these influences – positive psychology, discrete emotions, appraisal theory, and creative measures – are part of the changing face of organizational psychological research, and offer a context for exploring in more detail the role of positive emotions and their resource accumulation qualities.

If, as Fineman (2004) suggests, emotion is now regarded as the missing piece in our understanding of working life, then perhaps it is time to explore what we mean by emotion. It is clear from even the most cursory review that to pin down, let alone measure, what we mean by emotion is fraught with difficulties (Fineman 2004). Even though we think we know emotions when we see them (Elfenbein 2007), there is still considerable variation in how they are defined, with no generally agreed definition (Ashforth and Humphrey 1995). Nevertheless, a number of themes emerge from the discussion which point us towards an understanding of the term. It seems reviewers agree that affect is "an umbrella term encompassing a broad range of feelings" one of which is emotion (Barsade and Gibson 2007, p. 38). So, emotions are best viewed as a subset of affect.

Two other themes emerge to express what the central features of an emotion are, and reflect its core meaning. These themes include that emotion "is a reaction to a stimulus and has a range of consequences" (Elfenbein 2007, p. 317), and that emotion is "simply a subjective feeling state" (Ashforth and Humphrey 1995, p. 99). These features provide a broad framework for exploring not just the nature of those feeling states, but their intensity, duration, meaning, and significance. So, emotions are "typically about some personally meaningful circumstance," frequently brief in duration and often thought of as "fitting into discrete emotional families" (Fredrickson 2001, p. 218).

Reviewers acknowledge that the number and description of "discrete emotional families" is still robustly debated (Barsade and Gibson 2007). However, if discrete emotions are telling us a story about the nature of working life then our aim should be, as Lazarus and Cohen-Charash (2001) suggest, to work towards understanding which emotions are important, their distinguishing features, their cause and their consequence. In working towards this aim what helps to distinguish one emotion from another (i.e. their focus (positive–negative), their intensity (activation–quiescence)), will simply reflect and flow from the context within which they are expressed (p. 49). Although "any list is arguable" (Lazarus and Cohen-Charash 2001, p. 49), such a list could include for example joy, love, anger, fear, shame, guilt, jealousy, sadness disgust, anxiety, fright, envy, happiness, pride, relief, hope, gratitude, and compassion (Ashford and Humphrey 1995; Barsade and Gibson 2007; Lazarus and Cohen-Charash 2001).

Before turning our attention to the role of positive emotions, one last point needs to be reiterated. Given the complexity that surrounds the nature of emotions, researchers are warned to approach the measurement of emotions "with care" (Fineman 2004), recognizing that reconstructing feelings through scales has limits as to the type of knowledge it can produce and is but one approach. As already emphasized, other more creative approaches may now be needed in order to capture the essential richness of what is being felt, experienced, and expressed, and although such approaches may not have the utility and simplicity of scales, they are more "likely to be" rich in the insights they offer, subtle in the textures of the experience they produce, and sensitive to the nuances of the context itself (Fineman 2004, p. 736).

POSITIVE EMOTIONS

Even though the study of emotions at work has entered its exciting phase, studies on positive emotions still remain "few and far between" (Fredrickson 1998, p. 300). Typically, the focus for most researchers is still directed towards exploring the consequences of negative emotions, sidelining, somewhat unintentionally perhaps, the role and importance positive emotions play in the workplace. Understanding the reasons why positive emotions have been marginalized, argues Fredrickson (1998, 2000b, 2001, 2003b, 2005), helps researchers better understand the value that resides in investigating them. Perhaps the most pressing reason as to why positive emotions have been sidelined is the immediacy that accompanies the need to understand and resolve those problems that distress many working people.

But could it also be, suggests Fredrickson, that positive emotions are "a little harder to study," because there are fewer of them, it is more difficult at times to distinguish between them, and that it shouldn't be assumed that by "shoehorning" them in, they can be understood through a framework that is specifically designed to understand negative emotions (Fredrickson 1998, 2003b, pp. 330–331, 2005). Because positive emotions are a natural part of human experience, yet are discrete and different in form from negative emotions, to understand their distinctiveness and to "liberate them" a different model for understanding them is needed (Fredrickson 1998).

Against this backdrop, and to provide insights into "why it is good to feel good" (Fredrickson 2003b, p. 330), Fredrickson proposed her "broaden and build" theory of positive emotions because, as she wanted to make clear, "positive emotions appear to *broaden* people's momentary thought–action repertoires and *build* their enduring personal resources" (Fredrickson 2003a, p. 166). By the time the positive psychology movement began to gain momentum it was clear that positive emotions had a unique role to play in their mission, because they, like the positive psychology movement, tell the story about how people flourish and so the "take home message[must be]that positive emotions are worth cultivating" (Fredrickson 2001, p. 218). To capture the essence of Fredrickson's theory, we need first to step back and revisit the nature of emotions. Emotions flow, as we have discussed, from the way individuals appraise and give meaning to an encounter. The triggered emotion is then linked to some sort of specific action-tendency (Fredrickson 2001). Although this process is meant to apply across all emotions, its application is clearly linked to negative emotions, with the consequence that irrespective of the type of emotion, all emotions are now by implication and "by definition associated with specific action tendencies" (Fredrickson 2000b, p. 3).

Positive emotions: Plotting a new course

Fredrickson's argument is with the idea that all emotions are by implication and definition associated with specific action-tendencies. To understand the value of positive emotions it was necessary, Fredrickson argues, to "plot a new course" built around the proposition that whereas negative emotions "narrow people's ideas about possible actions, positive emotions do the opposite" (2009, p. 21). In order to accommodate positive emotions researchers now need, she argues, when considering how positive emotions function, to move away from the narrowing ideology to a more all encompassing term that captures how positive emotions broaden, open, and expand people's awareness to a greater range of thoughts and actions, making them "more receptive and more creative" (Fredrickson 2009, p. 21). This term she described as *"thought action-repertoires"* (Fredrickson 1998, 2001, 2003b; Fredrickson and Branigan 2005). Why?

"Specific action-tendencies," Fredrickson argued, are associated with negative emotions, because they reflect evolutionary physical reactions which *narrow* actions down to those concerned with life preservation. These types of action-tendencies do not easily relate to, or fit comfortably with, the function of positive emotions, because for these emotions their effect is too general to be prescribed or called specific, they are more likely to trigger changes in cognitive activity, and their focus is more directed towards enhancing individual growth than resolving life-threatening encounters (see Fredrickson 1998, 2000b, 2001, 2003b, 2005).

So instead of trying to squeeze positive emotions into a model designed to explain negative emotions, Fredrickson's model is in contrast one where the emphasis is on the "more inclusive" concept of momentary thought–action repertoires (Fredrickson and Branigan 2005, p. 314) that embraces a much broader range of flexible, creative, and generative thoughts and behaviors (Fredrickson and Losada 2005). Fredrickson's model also contrasts with the immediate adaptive action-tendencies required by negative emotions, by stating that "the benefits of broadening thought–action repertoires emerge over time," illustrating the second distinctive feature of her model where "broadening builds enduring personal resources" (Fredrickson and Losada 2005, p. 679).

The empirical support for Fredrickson's broadening and building effects of positive emotions spans almost two decades. Most notably the evidence suggests that positive emotions produce thought patterns that are creative, integrative, open to information, efficient, "increase people's preferences for variety and broaden their array of acceptable behavioral options" (Frederickson 2003a, p. 168). The evidence also points to positive emotions having a "unique capacity" to undo lingering negative emotions, increase and develop people's coping strategies when facing difficulties, generate "upward spirals" where the positive builds on the positive to produce enduring resources that promote resilience, enhance well-being, and increase the likelihood that people will feel good in the future (Fredrickson 2000b, 2003a, pp. 168–171).

Research also points to the specificity of the relationship between "positive emotions and personality" with the evidence suggesting that positive emotions "can be meaningfully differentiated at least" in their association with the big five personality measures (Shiota *et al.* 2006, p. 68). The research evidence also suggests that positive emotions contribute to a more acute sense of self, which helps to smooth relationships, develop an appreciation of others, build a greater sense of social closeness, and sustain relationships (Waugh and Fredrickson 2006). There is also emerging evidence to suggest that those with deeply held positive emotions who embrace the benefits that emerge from a stressful encounter "are more likely to experience more advantageous physiological outcomes" (Moskowitz and Epel 2006, p. 88). This continually growing body of evidence reinforces Fredrickson's view that positive emotions need to be taken seriously (2000b), and provides support for her original proposition that positive emotions are good for you (Fredrickson 1998).

Positive emotions: More work to be done

Nevertheless, there is, as Fredrickson admits, still more work to be done. This would include exploring strategies that cultivate positive emotions, identifying those personality traits like, for example, optimism, hopefulness, and happiness, that predispose people to find positive meanings, and exploring the mechanisms by which upward spirals enhance well-being (Fredrickson 2000b). Reviewers of Fredrickson's work support her theoretical ideas, offering ways as to how the work can be progressed. They suggest ways forward that include expanding the range of possible positive emotions so as to determine, not just their distinctive contribution to broadening and building, but how they relate to each other in such an enterprise (Haidt 2000; Myers 2000). Exploring, in addition to the intrapersonal aspects of positive emotions, their social underpinnings as well (King 2000), and defining more precisely the concept of broadening so as to avoid the danger of an all-inclusive concept, where any positive activity becomes by implication broadening (Lyubomirsky 2000).

TABLE 5.1 **Emotions at work: The debate**

Why we need to understand emotions at work
- The centrality of work to one's emotional life and well-being (Ashford and Humphrey 1995; Fox and Spector 2002; Pekrun and Frese 1992).
- The transforming influence they have on organizational culture and individual development (Pekrun and Frese 1992).
- The manner in which they influence critical organizational outcomes (Ashford and Humphrey 1995; Barsade and Gibson 2007).
- The way they influence coping and adaptation (Lazarus 1999, 2001b; Lazarus and Cohen-Charash 2001).

The organizational view of emotions
- Organizations have a narrow view of emotions and their social acceptability (Ashford and Humphrey 1995).
- There is a perceived awkwardness that researching emotions at work may disturb the orderly way organizations work (Ashford and Humphrey 1995; Ashford and Kreiner 2002).
- The consequence of this narrow view is that research has been limited to exploring job satisfaction or simply focusing on negative emotions (Ashford and Humphrey 1995).
- Organizations are more likely then to engage in activities to regulate emotions (Ashford and Humphrey 1995; Elfenbein 2007).

Emotions at work: Towards a richer and broader focus
- Job satisfaction has become a surrogate measure of emotions at work, obscuring the explanatory potential that may lie in more carefully differentiating between different emotions (Barsade *et al.* 2003; Barsade and Gibson 2007).
- Research on emotions at work needs to become more "differentiated and nuanced," with greater attention being given to understanding the role of discrete emotions (Barsade *et al.* 2003, p. 11; Brief and Weiss 2002; Lazarus and Cohen-Charash 2001).
- Research needs now to focus on the causal pathways through which emotions are expressed at work, the measurement strategies needed to capture the richness of different emotions, and, more particularly the role and significance of positive emotions in organizational life (Elfenbein 2007; Fineman 2004; Fredrickson 2000b; Lazarus 1999).

Lyubomirsky (2000, pp. 2–4) also raises the question of whether negative emotions may have broadening qualities, whether positive emotions have the potential to narrow thinking, whether all positive emotions are equal, whether more attention needs now to be given to understanding the role of time, and whether, as Rathunde (2000) proposes, the narrowing of negative emotions may also have a creative aspect to it. This dialogue, as Fredrickson (2000a) acknowledges, is essential if our understanding of positive emotions is to be advanced. To move such dialogue along Fredrickson urges all researchers to "join in" and develop research programs that focus on positive emotions (Fredrickson 2000a, p. 1), reinforcing her belief that positive emotions rigorously and properly investigated "may turn out to be" the foundation on which human flourishing is built (Fredrickson 2006, p. 57). The significance of Fredrickson's work surely lies in the fact that her broaden and build theory provides a powerful conceptual framework for exploring the role of positive emotions, and offers researchers the opportunity to focus on the positive and in doing so identify pathways towards individual fulfillment, enhanced well-being, and optimal functioning.

POSITIVE PSYCHOLOGICAL CAPITAL

As we discussed in Chapter 1, Luthans discovered in the positive psychology movement what it was that he had been looking for to reenergize his thinking, and to turn his "new-found enthusiasm," his positivity as he described it, towards exploring how positive psychology could be applied to organizational behavior (Luthans 2002a, p. 697). Luthans' view was that now was the time to take a more proactive positive developmental stance, to initiate a shift in emphasis, and to draw on the research traditions of organizational behavior to develop a theory driven approach to exploring people's strengths and psychological capabilities. This approach he described as *positive organizational behavior* (Luthans 2002a, b). If, as Luthans (2002a) argues, positive organizational behavior is to offer something different then "the question becomes" what psychological capabilities best express this approach. From his research came the answer: positive psychological capital. So, why positive psychological capital?

Positive psychology played its part in providing the stimulus. Conservation of resources theory (Hobfoll 2001) also played a role with its emphasis on fostering and accumulating resources. Luthans and his colleagues (Luthans *et al.* 2004; Luthans and Youssef 2007) also saw positive psychological capital as a better way of capturing the more contemporary view of competitive advantage, where a greater emphasis was now being placed on individual competencies, resource based strategies, and competing through people. To Luthans and his colleagues, traditional views on where an organizations competitive advantage lay did not capture what they described as "the other layer;

the psychological capacity of the people in an organization" (*Gallup Management Journal* 2007, p. 3). If, as these authors went on to argue, organizations are to achieve sustainable competitive advantage, then, while traditional economic capital captured "what you have," human capital "what you know," and social capital "who you know," positive psychological capital offered a way of not only moving these ideas forward to capture "who you are," but took them further by coupling "who you are" with a developmental focus that emphasized "who you are becoming" (Luthans *et al.* 2004, 2007a, p. 20).

Positive psychological capital: Its components

Luthans and his colleagues described positive psychological capital as a higher-order term. As such the term expressed those individual qualities "that contribute to a motivational propensity to accomplish tasks and goals" (Luthans *et al.* 2007b, p. 548). Just as traditional forms of capital are made up of different facets, so also is positive psychological capital. The individual qualities that best express the nature of this sort of capital, and which binds them together to express the higher order term are self-efficacy, hope, optimism, and resilience (p. 542). It is the collective motivational tendencies that flow from these four positive components that capture the spirit of positive psychological capital (Luthans *et al.* 2007a). Why these four? In order to distinguish them from other positive approaches that don't always meet standards of methodological rigor each met the inclusion criteria required by positive organizational behavior of "being positive, unique, measurable, developable and performance related" (Luthans and Youssef 2004, p. 153). Each is also "state-like," making them open to development through interventions and management (Luthans *et al.* 2007a; Luthans and Youssef 2007). Each also, when combined, had a "synergistic effect" (Luthans *et al.* 2006) leading to the belief that the developmental, motivational and capacity outcomes of the whole may well be greater than the sum of their constituent parts (Luthans *et al.* 2007a).

For each of the four components Luthans and his colleagues draw on an extensive body of research and theory that illustrates how each contributes to the conceptual underpinnings of positive psychological capital (Luthans *et al.* 2007a; Luthans and Youssef 2004; Youssef and Luthans 2007). Broadly, self-efficacy is described as a confidence in ones abilities, hope in terms of a sense to achieve, optimism in terms of a positive explanatory style, and resilience in terms of an ability to bounce back from adversity (Luthans *et al.* 2007a, pp. 17–18; Luthans and Youssef 2004). While there has been some discussion as to the conceptual overlap between the different components, each it seems adds value (Page and Donohue 2004), even though their distinctiveness is at times subtle. However, what does emerge from the research is that there is strong support for the idea of a synergy between the four components, as the overall measure of positive psychological capital appears to be a better predictor of outcomes like performance and job satisfaction than the individual components (Luthans *et al.* 2007a, b).

There is no doubt that there is a considerable body of research supporting the significance of positive psychological capital, and its relationship to organizational outcome measures (Luthans *et al.* 2007a). Luthans and his colleagues acknowledge the pitfalls and challenges that scales measuring positive psychological capital present, and whilst continuing to refine their measure recognize that future research may be best served by using more of a multimeasure approach (Luthans *et al.* 2007a). These researchers also recognize that the four components were never intended to represent an exhaustive list, but were selected because they meet the scientific criteria required by a positive organizational behavior approach, have a real sense of relevance that better reflects an organizations competitive advantage, and can more readily be managed and developed (Luthans and Youssef 2004).

The reason why it is important to consider other psychological capacities (e.g. creativity, wisdom, well-being, flow, humor, authenticity; p. 18) is not just because, argue Luthans and his colleagues, it deepens our understanding of the nature of psychological capital, but because it also aids our understanding of other positive constructs and enriches the contribution that can be made to those whose working lives we study (Luthans *et al.* 2007a). The last word should be left to Luthans: "the key here is that we have to show impact, and that's what we're trying to do. We are not trying to make a buzzword out of this. We're trying to show that there's science to this and, it has impact" (*Gallup Management Journal* 2007, p. 3).

FROM HARDINESS TO RESILIENCE

Resilience is a core feature of positive psychological capital, worth exploring in its own right. However, because there are multiple pathways to resilience, and because the "hardy personality" has been identified as one of these pathways (Bonanno 2004), it is important that we first turn our attention to the concept of hardiness. There are a number of reasons for doing this; hardiness functions as a "resistance resource" in buffering the effects of stressful events (Kobasa 1979; Kobasa *et al.* 1982), hardiness enhances resilience (Maddi 2005), and hardiness has, for the last 30 years, been a key word in the language of positive psychology and needs to be added and recognized as a necessary component of that movement (Maddi 2006).

The idea of hardiness has its roots in existential thinking; thinking that has at its core the contention that a "person can take hold of her or his own life and shape it through an active process of decision making (Kobasa and Maddi 1977, p. 244). This emphasis on having the courage to make the most out of life was "instrumental in building the conceptualization of hardiness" (Maddi 2006, p. 162). This thinking led researchers to the question of whether those who, when encountering stressful conditions failed to fall ill, have a different personality structure from those who did (Kobasa 1979; Kobasa *et al.* 1982). The answer was that this personality difference was best expressed through the term "hardiness" (Kobasa 1979).

Hardiness: Its characteristics

A hardy person, or hardiness, consists of three characteristics: (a) *control*, the belief that through effort one can positively influence outcomes; (b) *commitment*, the belief that one can find meaning and purpose in what one is doing; and (c) *challenge*, the belief that through change one can continue to grow, develop, and learn from all life experiences, whether positive or negative (Bonanno 2004; Kobasa 1979, p. 3; Maddi and Hightower 1999, p. 96). It is these three characteristics that should keep individuals healthy in the face of stressful encounters (Kobasa *et al.* 1982). These "3Cs," as Maddi explains, give individuals the courage and motivation to engage in the hard work that necessarily turns "stressful circumstances from potential disasters into growth opportunities instead" (2006, p. 160).

These "3Cs" have strong ties to positive mental health (Maddi and Khoshaba 1994), and all three are necessary to fully express hardiness (Maddi 2002; 2006). There is, in some of the writing on hardiness, a hint that perhaps it is now time to add a fourth term, or "C," *closeness*; a form of hardy social support where there is a giving, receiving, and sharing of help and encouragement (Kobasa 2003; Maddi 1999a). Reviews covering 30 years of empirical work on hardiness show clear support for its predictive power (Maddi 2006), suggesting that it is perhaps "one of the best dispositional predictors of well-being" and is " consistently associated with stress mitigating variables" (Eschleman *et al.* 2010, pp. 303–304).

There are strong positive messages associated with the hardy personality. Hardiness signals a high level of proactivity, where hardy individuals don't wait for things to happen but deliberately choose their future (Kobasa 1979; Maddi 2002), recognizing that turning away from challenging events limits their chances to grow and develop (Maddi and Hightower 1999). Hardiness predisposes individuals towards actively engaging with the situation in order to solve the problem (Maddi 1999b), and offers a structure that generates positive appraisals and a motivation to accomplish difficult things (Maddi 2002). Hardiness is something that is learnt, and can be developed through training (Maddi 2002). Organizations can also contribute to this development by building a culture that captures the ideals of the hardy personality through such values as cooperation, credibility, and creativity (Maddi *et al.* 1999).

Nevertheless, there is, as the different researchers agree, still work to be done. Work needs to continue using a comparative analytic mode to explore how hardiness differs from other variables as a pathway to resilience (Maddi 2005), in addition to continuing to explore how hardiness differs when compared to other personal strength variables (Maddi 1999b). Because of its emphasis on development, growth, and learning, there is a need to continue to consider practical issues, such as when to conduct hardiness assessments, the utility of multimethod training programs (Maddi 2002), the way in which hardy individuals use different coping strategies and how best to evaluate their effectiveness (Maddi 1999b), the issues surrounding using hardiness as "a quick index for mental health" (Maddi and Khoshaba 1994, p. 265), and how best, in a constantly changing and demanding workplace, organizations learn to recognize that developing a culture which expresses hardiness values is as relevant to the organization and its ability to flourish and survive as it is to their individual employees (Maddi 1999a).

Resilience: The concept and its definition

While there may be different pathways towards achieving resilience (Bonanno 2004), resilience as a concept is clearly associated with terms like hardiness, resourcefulness, and mental toughness. While used interchangeably, resilience is something more than just being a "hot topic," or a new buzzword. The concept of resilience is backed by four decades of research, where researchers have engaged in "an intriguing area of enquiry" (Richardson 2002, p. 307) that investigated those individual resources which allow growth in the face of adversity. It is from this work that the term "resilience" emerged as the most utilitarian way to describe such individuals (Masten and Reed 2005). The idea of individuals achieving and developing in the face of adversity clearly resonates with the ideals of the positive psychology movement, and helps to account for its current popularity both as a term and as a concept, because it is "a prime example of what is right and good about people" (Luthans *et al.* 2006, p. 28).

Reviewers continue to point to the positive connotations associated with a term like resilience (Masten and Reed 2005; Sutcliffe and Vogus 2003), and go on to suggest that resilience research has helped to "rekindle positive psychology," because of its focus on "successful individual functioning" (Masten 2001, p. 235). Resilience also sits comfortably with the work on positive emotions, because positive emotions may operate in a way than reinforces and strengthens resilience by providing "access to a reservoir of positive resources" (Ong *et al.* 2006, p. 731), building effective coping resources, and allowing more cognitive flexibility (Tugade and Fredrickson 2006) which "prompts individuals to pursue novel and creative thoughts and actions" (Tugade and Fredrickson 2004, p. 331). Investigating resilience is "worthy of scholarly attention" as it offers new perspectives and insights into how people flourish, how they cope with constantly changing and challenging work situations, and how such a capacity can be developed (Sutcliffe and Vogus 2003, p. 99).

When it comes to defining resilience, Coutu makes it clear that although there is a great deal we can learn about resilience, "it is a subject none of us will ever understand fully" (2002, p. 46), helping to explain why, perhaps, there are still inconsistencies in how it is defined and operationalized (Sutcliffe and Vogus 2003), and why its meaning has attracted much debate and at times controversy (Masten and Reed 2005). Definitions of resilience have, like resilience research itself, developed through a number of phases, where resilience has been defined in terms of individual characteristics or qualities, the utilization of individual qualities in coping with adversity, and as an embodiment of individual forces, capacities, energies, and strengths

(Luthans *et al.* 2006; Richardson 2002; Sutcliffe and Vogus 2003; Wilkes 2002). Definitions frequently express all of these different phases, and while it may "not do justice to the subject to [try] to sum it up succinctly" (Neenan 2009, p. 16), our understanding of resilience may best be developed by exploring not just what it is, but also what it is not, and the themes that embrace different definitional approaches.

The spirit of resilience is often captured in definitions which draw on the theme of "bouncing back" or "rebounding." Luthans, for example, in what he describes as a good fit with positive organizational behavior (Luthans 2002a), defines resilience in these terms and describes it as the "developable psychological capacity to rebound, or bounce back from adversity, conflict, failure or even positive events, progress and increased responsibility (Luthans *et al.* 2006, p. 28), as do Tugade and Fredrickson, who view it as "being characterized by the ability to bounce back from negative emotional experiences and by flexible adaptation to the changing demands of stressful experiences" (2004, p. 320). While an important component, it would be a mistake to focus simply on the idea of "bouncing back" as each of these definitions offers a more complex reality. Tugade and Fredrickson, for example, view their definition more in terms of expressing a "frame of mind" that is characterized by the proactive enactment of "positive emotionality" (2004, p. 320), while Luthans (2002a) and his colleagues (2006) emphasize through their definition the need to recognize its state-like properties and thus the developmental potential that can be positively and proactively unleashed.

Resilience: Further definitional approaches

Other definitions take up the theme of positive adaptation and define resilience in terms of "positive adjustment under challenging conditions" (Sutcliffe and Vogus 2003, p. 95) or "good outcomes in spite of serious threats to adaptation or development" (Masten 2001, p. 228). Again, there is a more complex side to these definitions. Sutcliffe and Vogus, for example, point particularly to the developmental perspective embodied in their definition, a perspective that implies the presence of a capacity to learn so as to build a resource where individuals "in the process of responding, strengthens [their] capabilities to make future adjustments" (2003, p. 97). For Masten (2001) the underlying theme that accompanies her definition is the need to understand the process that ends with a good outcome. To Masten, resilience is inferred from judgments as to how well a person is doing under threatening circumstances.

What, for her, needs more debate and empirical investigation is just how to establish the criteria for evaluating what is a "good outcome," who should define what those criteria are, what emphasis the context plays when establishing such criteria, and by whose standards such judgments are being made (Masten 2001; Masten and Reed 2005). Outlining a number of ways forward, Masten stresses the need for more debate around these issues by simply pointing to the fact that resilience is not some magical characteristic but stems from "everyday ordinary" processes – and because of this quality of the "power of the ordinary" researchers must now "address some tough questions about how naturally occurring resilience works" (Masten and Reed 2005, p. 86).

Reflecting on resilience as representing an "ability to maintain a stable equilibrium" (Bonanno 2004, p. 20) provides Bonanno with the opportunity to suggest that unless we embrace a broader view of responding to stress, we will continue to underestimate and even misunderstand the ability to flourish under extremely harrowing situations (2004, 2008). Bonanno outlines his argument (2004, pp. 20; 22; 25) by suggesting that if we are to develop our understanding, we must: (a) recognize that resilience differs from recovery in the sense that resilient individuals when faced with adverse events appear to maintain "relatively stable levels" of healthy functioning in addition to exhibiting a capacity for growth and positive emotions; (b) accept that in the face of distressing events resilience is not something rare "but relatively common" and should be viewed less in pathological terms and more as "rather healthy adjustment"; and (c) be aware that there are many and at times unexpected pathways to resilience. Building on the evidence associated with these arguments, Bonanno concludes that resilience, if it is to be understood, then this must be by adopting a broader view of health and illness that offers "a fresh look at the various ways people adapt and even flourish" in the face of adversity (2004, p. 27).

In many ways the comprehensive work done by Neenan, together with his colleague Windy Dryden (see Neenan 2009), captures what is involved when attempting to define resilience. To these authors, definitions should attempt to include the range of possible responses (e.g., cognitive, behavioral, emotional), and the characteristics of the situation being faced (e.g. acute, chronic, unusual, commonplace). Then, against this context, the qualities of resilience should themselves

TABLE 5.2 **Defining and understanding resilience**

Why bother?
- It is clearly important to understand more about how individuals mobilize resources in the face of adversity (Bonanno 2004).
- Using the term "resilience" as the best way to capture the idea of individuals achieving and developing in the face of adversity has a long research history and it is now time to take this research into the workplace (Luthans *et al.* 2006; Masten and Reed 2005).
- The idea of resilience clearly resonates with the ideas of positive psychology and investigating resilience offers new perspectives and insights into how individuals flourish, how they cope with the constant challenges of work, and how this capacity can be developed (Masten 2001; Tugade and Fredrickson 2004; Sutcliffe and Vogus 2003).

What is resilience – two predominant themes?
- **The theme of "bouncing back"**
  Resilience is often defined in terms of a capacity to bounce back from adversity (Luthans *et al.* 2006).
- **The theme of "positive adjustment – maintaining a stable equilibrium"**
  Resilience is often defined as positive adjustment, positive adaptation, or maintaining a stable equilibrium in the face of adversity (Bonanno 2004; Sutcliffe and Vogus 2003).

Resilience – a complex reality
- Need to go beyond these two themes to capture the complexity of resilience.
- Resilience expresses a "state of mind" characterized by proactive actions (Luthans *et al.* 2006; Sutcliffe and Vogus 2003).
- It reflects a state-like property and thus implies a capacity to learn how to build and develop resources when responding to adversity (Luthans *et al.* 2006, 2007a; Sutcliffe and Vogus 2003).
- There is a need to understand the process of resilience and how good outcomes are achieved (Fredrickson 1998; Luthans *et al.* 2006; Masten 2001; Masten and Reed 2005).
- Resilience is something different from just recovery since resilience individuals maintain a level of healthy functioning throughout the adverse event (Bonanno 2004, 2008).
- Resilience is something that can be learnt and what is learnt acts as a resource for the future (Luthans *et al.* 2006; Luthans *et al.* 2007a).
- Through the process of learning resilience becomes "an attitude you adopt" – at the core of resilience is attitude (Neenan 2009).

be identified, these would include, for example: (a) that it can be learnt; (b) that it is something "within the grasp of everyone"; (c) that it embraces the idea of moving forward through learning from the experience; (d) that what is learnt builds capacity and acts as a

126

resource for the future; and (e) that the most important aid to learning and developing from the experience is "the attitude you adopt" – it is attitude which "is the heart of resilience." (p. 17).

Taking resilience into the workplace

As Luthans and his colleagues point out, taking resilience into the workplace "has considerable appeal," because of the challenges and demands facing organizations and those working in them (Luthans *et al.* 2007a, p. 122). When the question is raised as to how resilience can make a difference, the answer requires that researchers need to identify not just risk factors, but those features of the environment that support the development of resilience (Masten 2001; Masten and Reed 2005; Luthans *et al.* 2007a). These features would include not just identifying assets, resources, and protective factors, those individual and situational characteristics/qualities that sustain positive adaptation, but exploring as well the processes through which such factors work to enhance and develop facets of positive adaptation (Masten and Reed 2005, pp. 76–77).

Drawing on the themes that emerge from their review, Sutcliffe and Vogus (2003) point to at least two "building blocks" from which individual resilience develops. The first they describe as the availability of quality resources through which individuals can develop their competence, and the second is where individuals experience opportunities that add to their capacity to grow and succeed. In a work setting this means, argue Sutcliffe and Vogus, being able, for example, to exercise in their work, judgment, discretion, control, decision latitude, and to be able to develop through training, skills, knowledge, and abilities all of which "develops a sense of efficacy and competence" providing individuals with a resource that enables then to better respond successfully to challenging situations (p. 100).

The role of resilience at work has also been comprehensively explored by Luthans and his colleagues (Luthans *et al.* 2006, 2007a). In developing the concept of positive psychological capital their work emphasized that because of the challenges facing working people, resilience offers a proactive pathway to "sustainable positive gains," a resource that goes beyond simply surviving to thriving, flourishing, improved performance, with a potential for increasing job satisfaction, and enhancing commitment, and an attribute that among its range of qualities offers the capacity to reflect and grow from adversity (Luthans *et al.* 2007a, p. 123). Resilience is, as these authors emphasize, "an overlooked opportunity for human resource development" (Luthans *et al.* 2006, p. 31). To reinforce this point, they make it clear that those organizations which work towards developing resilience in their employees will, over time, be more adaptive and successful in meeting the challenges that they face. Luthans and his colleagues offer two approaches to developing resilience in the workplace.

Developing resilience in the workplace

The first they describe in proactive terms where, building on the framework offered by Masten and Reed (2005), they recommend three strategies that "help structure the organization to anticipate and facilitate the resiliency of employees" (Luthans *et al.* 2006, p. 32). This requires the development of strategies that focus on (a) *risks* (identifying stress and positively intervening); (b) *assets* (building and improving individual and organizational resources); and (c) *process* (developing adaptational effectiveness). In short, managing risk by turning a threat into an opportunity, investing in the potential of employees, and influencing the way employees give meaning to and learn from experiences (Luthans *et al.* 2006, p. 32, 2007a, p. 116).

The second approach they describe in reactive terms, but make it clear that describing it in this way is not to suggest that it reflects something negative, but more that it simply expresses how individuals generally respond to negative or positive events (Luthans *et al.* 2006). What lies behind this strategy is that individuals need to be reminded "to think positively and find meaning when negative events occur" (2006, p. 32). At its heart lies the idea that reactive ways can be found that build and foster resilience, and that these ways are, in themselves, important pathways to resilience. Luthans (2006) and his colleagues go on to illustrate how these pathways to resilience can be built by using positive emotions (Fredrickson 1998) and through the use of strategies like, for example, self-enhancement, attribution, and hardiness (Bonanno 2004). In developing human resource strategies to build resilience, in keeping with the idea of balance, both proactive and reactive strategies are necessary, while individuals and organizations may not always be able to control external factors they can do their "best to anticipate the future" (Luthans *et al.* 2006, p. 32).

Resilience: Future research

There are, as Sutcliffe and Vogus (2003) point out, two essential elements to understanding resilience: threatening, adverse, or stressful conditions, and positive adaptation in the face of such adversity. Taken together, these two conditions provide a useful starting point and a framework against which future research may wish to be judged. Considerable research already accompanies the concept of resilience, but the domestic and global challenges facing organizations, the demands of new forms of technology, and the cries for ethical, social, economic, and political reform, all provide a context for understanding why the study of resilience has come to express the world that we live in. The relevance of resilience to our times, and the need to guard against it simply becoming "an overused and meaningless construct" (Sutcliffe and Vogus 2003, p. 108), must now be the mantra that continues to drives research.

While Neenan and his colleague Windy Dryden (see Neenan 2009) identify some of the structural issues characterizing threatening and challenging situations in their definition of resilience,, there is work to be done to understand how such characteristics are appraised and interpreted (Sutcliffe and Vogus 2003), what it is about such characteristics and appraisals that enhance development and learning versus those that inhibit it (Masten 2001), and how positive adaptation should be judged when set against the threats and challenges of the situation. Masten and Reed (2005) have also drawn attention to how good outcomes and positive adaptation should be judged. They point to the ongoing debate as to whether such outcomes or adaptations should include not just external factors but internal (e.g. well-being, emotional health) ones as well, not forgetting, of course, the points raised above as to who should define what those criteria are, and by whose standards such judgments are being made (Masten 2001; Masten and Reed 2005, pp. 75–76). The nature of good outcomes has also been raised by Luthans and his colleagues (2006, p. 39) in relation to work situations, leading these authors to suggest that future research may wish to explore further the nature of the relationship between resilience, satisfaction, and commitment, whether organizational leadership and/or organizational culture mediate such relationships, and the way in which resilience relates to physical and mental well-being.

While learning is a critical component of resilience, Sutcliffe and Vogus raise issues which suggest that future research may like to explore whether "learning can be maladaptive or at least misleading," and whether such learning produces what they describe as "competency traps" that blinker the need to identify new competencies (2003, p. 109). There is also the question of whether resilient people cope differently and, if so, what types of coping strategies distinguish these people from those who appear to be less resilient. Finally, there is the issue of whether enough attention has been given to not just identifying resilient qualities and how those qualities may develop, but how people "use aversive events as a springboard for further growth and development" (Linley and Joseph 2005, pp. 262–263); the notion of posttraumatic growth or stress-related growth.

While the debate continues as to how growth has been articulated in the context of resilience, as will discussions as to the role and relevance of growth in assessment and intervention (Tedeschi and Kilmer 2005), the plea is "not to sell the argument short" and to adopt a more holistic approach when considering resilience that includes the idea of "adversarial growth" (2005, p. 263). What remains clear though, is that as our understanding of the resilience process develops, then so to must the evidence of how from the everyday ebb and flow of organizational life emerge resources which "promote competence, restore efficacy and encourage growth" (Sutcliffe and Vogus 2003, p. 110).

POSITIVE RESOURCES

The positive psychology movement, with its emphasis on optimal human functioning, captured the attention of researchers and opened the door for "the study of work organizations in which people can be well and do well" (Peterson *et al.* 2009, p. 161). Couple this emphasis with the call for a "good work agenda" that highlights the importance of "meaningful work" and it is understandable why researchers have, over the last decade, shifted their attention more towards identifying and exploring a range of less traditional, but no less important, positive dispositional factors that lead to satisfaction and well-being. We touch on three of these – zest, thriving, and flourishing. Each has an immediate relevance to work, but each also captures a sense that a new direction is emerging, where old boundaries have been exposed as being too limiting, and where concepts once thought too outrageous or too unconventional for researchers to explore now emerge at the centre of what work should all be about, and through which individuals can learn more about their strengths and how through their strengths well-being can be achieved.

Zest

Zest is defined in terms of approaching life "with anticipation, energy, and excitement" (Petersen *et al.* 2009, p. 162), and, in terms of work, converts into satisfaction, commitment, and achieving. When exploring the work resources necessary to promote zest, Petersen and his colleagues draw attention to the importance of working relationships, and argue that the goal for organizations should be to provide opportunities that create "energizing relationships," within an understanding of the potential that resides in "a psychology [or even a culture] of energy" (2009, p. 169). Thriving at work is not just another conversational convenience, it is a state that is not only linked to positive health but provides individuals with a sense of just how much they are achieving and developing by evaluating "what they are doing and how they are doing it" (Spreitzer *et al.* 2005, p. 537).

Thriving

Thriving is defined as a "psychological state in which individuals experience both a sense of vitality and a sense of learning at work" (Spreitzer *et al.* 2005, p. 538). Spreitzer and her colleagues considered those factors that allow individuals to thrive at work, turned first to the job context and those embedded job features that encourage discretion when making decisions, allow information to be shared, and build an environment of thrust. These factors, they argue, not only produce purposeful and motivated behaviors, but through these behaviors individuals "actively cultivate resources in the doing of work to fuel more thriving," it is the generation of these purposeful behaviors that represents, for these authors, "the engine of thriving" (2005, p. 540). Recognizing that more work needs to be done led Spreitzer and her colleagues to argue for more research that explores the relationship between embedded work factors and thriving, thriving and health, whether thriving can occur at a more collective level, and how thriving is sustained over the longer term (2005, p. 546).

Flourishing

Continuing to review and develop his ideas led Seligman (2011) to rethink what positive psychology is, what its elements are, and what its goals should be. It was the belief that positive psychology should now be less about focusing on people's happiness and more about their ability to flourish that transformed Seligman's view. The word "happiness," as Seligman remarked in an interview, had always troubled him "partly because it was scientifically unwieldy and meant a lot of different things to different people, and also because it's subjective" (McVeigh 2011, p. 19). Building our understanding of positive psychology solely around the idea of happiness "under explains," as Seligman (2011) argues, its nature because it overlooks other important elements. Calling for a more expansive theory led Seligman towards the concept of well-being, and so the goal of positive psychology is by contrast "plural and importantly different; it is to increase the amount of flourishing in [one's] own life" (Seligman 2011, p. 26).

If *flourishing* introduces a new way of thinking about positive psychology then what are the criteria for flourishing? The criteria are stringent argues Seligman (2011, p. 24), and include positive emotions (including happiness), engagement, and meaning, plus positive relationships and achievements. No one element on its own defines flourishing but each contributes to it. The first three come from "authentic happiness theory" with the remaining two elements adding to the expression of flourishing. Each of these five elements also has three properties: each contributes to well-being, each is pursued for its own sake, and each can be defined and measured independently (p. 16). While Seligman "expects a vigorous debate and a great refinement about how exactly to measure the elements of well-being" (2011, p. 240), these two paragraphs cannot capture the detail, richness, and captivating way in which Seligman describes his ideas. The force that drives his ideas forward rests not just in how well-being through flourishing helps people get the best out of themselves, but in doing so how they give back to others the opportunity to do the same.

SOME FINAL COMMENTS

This chapter on resource accumulation is meant to provide an overview of some of the resources that are designed to protect, foster, build, and maintain individuals in the face of work-related stressors. The chapter, as we indicated, should be read and considered in relation to the previous chapter on resource depletion. The two chapters together offer a balanced approach, where the issue is not just on eliminating the negative, but explicitly emphasizing the positive and providing those work features through which individuals can accumulate resources. In this way this chapter is not just about resources that help individuals manage, but those through which individuals can grow, develop, and maximize their potential. Much of what has been discussed in this chapter clearly resonates with job design, the importance of meaningful work, and the principles of the "good work" agenda. It is also clear that many of the ways in which work can contribute to the building of resources need more attention in terms of the type of resource being discussed, how that resource differentiates itself from other resources, the behaviors associated with the resource, and those aspects of work that contribute to the generation and maintenance of such resources.

It is also clear from the topics covered that much can be learnt from paying more attention to discrete emotions. This involves not just recognizing their theoretical significance, but the need to better understand their nature, architecture, and structure, the ways in which they may be used and displayed, and what this means in terms of them being a positive or negative force. It is also worthwhile continuing to build and advance our understanding of the role of psychological capital, particularly since it reinforces the notion of "what it is you can become." Here, too, there is a need to understand not just the role of those resources that contribute to this type of capital, but what distinguishes one resource from the other, and how best the synergies between the different resources can be explored.

Finally, as positive psychology provides the theoretical context for exploring a range of resources that may once have been regarded as too unconventional to even acknowledge, it is important that researchers now establish what the distinctive qualities of such resources are, what distinguishes and defines such a resource from other similar resources or resources more generally, and the way that work may have to be designed to release their potential. It is clear that just as researchers are identifying new, and legitimizing old and perhaps more empirically controversial resources, so too will they need to match these resources with new, creative, and perhaps controversial methods that provide the knowledge necessary so that such research may fulfill the aspirations of all those involved in contributing to the quality of working lives.

CHAPTER 6

COPING AND STRESS INTERVENTIONS

At the turn of the century Lazarus described the volume of research on coping as "awesome" (Lazarus 1999, p. 118). In the decade that followed his remarks no one would find reasons to disagree with his comment, or think that the pace of research into coping has slowed. Coping is of "intrinsic interest" to all of us. How each of us copes with the ebb and flow of everyday life is, as Aldwin suggests, of "immediate personal relevance" (2000, p. 73). This continued "preoccupation" with coping may have been heightened over the last decade by the sheer force of social, economic, and organizational change and the turbulence and upheaval in roles, values, responsibilities, and relationships that accompanied it (Aldwin 2009). Yet despite this "boundless enthusiasm for coping research" (Somerfield and McCrae 2000, p. 620) coping still remains increasingly complex (Snyder 2001) and investigating it is not without its difficulties (Aldwin 2000). The debate continues as to the progress that has been made (Coyne and Racioppo 2000), and whether as researchers we set our goals too high (Burke 2002).

In the second part of this chapter, we shift the focus from the individual to the organization, and explore organizational interventions. We first explore the costs of stress, work, and mental ill health generally, the levels and types of organizational interventions and the evidence that supports them. Finally, we explore positive psychology and its influence in reshaping organizational interventions.

There is a growing confidence running through coping research (Lazarus 2000) that new creative ways are being vigorously pursued which provide the field with a sense of realism as to what can be achieved and a maturity as to how the richness of the coping process can be explored (Dewe and Cooper 2007; Dewe *et al.* 2010). In the first part of this chapter our concern is with the way in which coping has been defined, the way that coping strategies have been classified, how coping effectiveness has been explored, and the measurement issues involved in taking our understanding forward. As in previous chapters we explore each of these issues by again applying the notion of balance, and what this means when seeking to understand the nature of the coping process.

DEFINING COPING

It should come as no surprise that defining coping is not without debate and, at times, controversy. This should not, however, be seen as a failure in getting to grips with the concept, but more a sign that as our knowledge of coping develops, so too does the intensity of the debate regarding where the boundaries of what actually constitutes coping lie. The most commonly used, but not always agreed, definition of coping "consists of cognitive and behavioral efforts to manage specific external and/or internal demands that are appraised as taxing or exceeding the resources of the person" (Folkman and Lazarus 1991, p. 210). There are a number of key features that emerge when coping is defined in this way. It is process-oriented (what a person is actually thinking and doing in a particular encounter) and relational. That is, it refers to a particular relationship between the individual and the environment, where individual resources are taxed or exceeded (Folkman 1982). The power of this definitional approach lies in the fact that the relationship between the individual and the environment is "defined by the way it is *appraised* by the individual" (Folkman 1982, p. 97), the emphasis it places on the availability of adequate coping resources, and that coping must involve "effort" when managing a stressful encounter. This definition can be simplified, argues Lazarus, "although with a loss of some information – by saying merely that coping consists of cognitive and behavioral efforts to manage psychological stress" (1993a, p. 237).

What constitutes coping: The debate

Coping is a "value laden" term frequently associated with the idea of managing a situation successfully (Beehr and McGrath 1996, p. 66). To introduce balance into the argument about what constitutes coping,

Lazarus points to three themes that underwrite his process approach (Lazarus 1993b, 1999, 2001b; Lazarus and Folkman 1991).

- The first is that "what is most needed in coping measurement" is for coping thoughts and actions to be described in detail (Lazarus 1993a, p. 236).
- Second, and most importantly in this context, is that there is no universally effective or ineffective coping strategy. Coping "must be measured separately from its outcomes" (1999, p. 111). Effectiveness must, Lazarus reiterates, be considered independently; no one strategy should be considered inherently better than any other (1991). It is not always evident from the coping strategy itself, nor from the way it is being used, (Dewe *et al.* 2010), nor how such a judgment is made (Snyder 1999), how effective it is. Effectiveness is, as Lazarus makes clear, inherently contextual, depending, both in the short and long term, on the person, the nature of the situation, the appraisal made, and the stage reached in any encounter (1999, 2001b).
- The third underlying theme is that there are two "major functions of coping;" problem-focused and emotion-focused (Lazarus 1993b, 1999, 2001b).

As we will discuss later, researchers should not allow themselves to "slip into the language of distinct types as if it is easy" to determine what focus a strategy has, whether the same strategy functions differently from encounter to encounter, and whether the same strategy fulfils a number of functions (Lazarus 2001a, p. 48). The temptation to see the two functions as sufficiently distinctive and competing is, as Lazarus states, "a mistake" (2001a, p. 49), and the idea that problem-focused coping "is better" than emotion-focused coping is a value-driven belief, ignores the subtleties of the coping process, and runs counter to the empirical evidence. (Lazarus 1993b). The idea, as Aldwin suggests, is not to assume that coping strategies can be ranked into a "hierarchy of adaptiveness"; taking an empirical approach allows researchers to investigate under what conditions strategies are used and whether "they do or do not promote positive adaptation (2009, p. 116).

Viewed through a transaction lens, Lazarus's definition contextualizes coping within a framework that emphasizes how that process unfolds. While acknowledging the explanatory potential that comes with the transactional, process-oriented focus, and the role of appraisal in linking the individual to the environment, researchers view Lazarus's definition as being somewhat limiting in its approach (Coyne and Gottlieb 1996; Snyder 2001), because it necessarily restricts coping strategies to those that involve effort (Snyder 2001), and those that are purposely initiated in the context of a stressful encounter (Coyne and Gottlieb 1996), and thereby excludes those everyday adaptive behaviors that help individuals to simply get along (Aldwin 2000), those that reflect habits and routines (Costa *et al.* 1996), and those that are thought of as management skills (Aldwin 2000).

As Lazarus and Folkman (1984, 1991) explain, the need is to distinguish between intentional and unintentional acts, and so when using that criterion "not all adaptive processes are coping" (1991, p. 199), and, therefore, while many behaviors may be adaptive they are simply not coping. Recognizing the difficulties that may surround terms like "intention" and "effort" (Snyder 2001), the question still remains, as Costa and his colleagues point out, as to how you make such a distinction when "coping fades imperceptibly into ordinary adaptation" (1996, p. 47). While coping may be a particular type of adaptation (Lazarus and Folkman 1991), it remains, argue Coyne and Gottlieb, "a serious omission" if certain reliable stress management behaviors are "no longer to be considered coping" (1996, pp. 962–963). If they are not coping, then, as Coyne and Gottlieb (1996) question, what are they to be considered as? The debate continues.

Reviewers have also drawn attention to whether coping is always a conscious process (Coyne and Gottlieb 1996; Snyder 2001). What is clear from the debate is that "all or nothing" (Snyder 1999, 2001) arguments around the role of consciousness in coping need to be avoided. Rather, reviewers have adopted more of a middle-ground approach, where it is generally agreed that while some coping activities grow out of a body of experience that requires little in the way of deliberate reasoning (Coyne and Gottlieb 1996) it is more likely to be the case that most coping responses flow from a level of awareness (Snyder 1999). In this case the challenge facing researchers lies not just in reaching some agreement as to what constitutes a level of awareness but also in how that state should be measured (Dewe and Cooper 2007).

The more general debate as to whether coping should be defined more broadly will best be served by acknowledging the complexity of what it is we are dealing with and accepting that if we are going to advance our understanding of coping then we cannot decouple that understanding from conventional measurement practices (Dewe and

Cooper 2007; Dewe *et al.* 2010). The responsibility that now rests with researchers is that there must be a willingness to break away from the convenience of established measurement practices if, when it comes to coping, we are to establish where the boundaries of such behaviors lie.

CLASSIFYING COPING STRATEGIES

Whether or not the classification of coping strategies is seen as a primary research goal, it is generally the first issue all researchers confront when initiating their data analysis. Researchers have used both theory-driven and empirically driven methods to classify coping strategies. Yet, there still remains the challenge for coping researchers of arriving at some commonly agreed schema, "so that findings across studies can be discussed meaningfully" (Folkman and Moskowitz 2004, p. 751). Three themes emerge from the literature when considering the classifying of coping strategies. These themes – focus, mode, and time – provide a useful framework for exploring different approaches to classifying coping strategies, how such schemes have evolved and developed, how they reflect social and economic change, and how they deal with the need to balance the negative and the positive.

The way that coping strategies are classified is fundamental to the way in which we understand their use, the role they play, and the value placed on them. Such schemas do not come without difficulties, and are only as good as the measures we use and the interpretations that flow from such measures. Measurement and interpretation are at the heart of how our knowledge develops. Both issues have been the focus of considerable debate. So, we follow our discussion on classifying coping strategies with one that explores the debate which surrounds the measurement of coping and the interpretation of results. Our aim in exploring these two issues is to provide a context for considering how they have influenced the direction of coping research and our understanding of the coping process. We then move to address the thorny issues of coping effectiveness.

Classifying coping: The theme of focus

Classifying coping strategies in terms of their focus had its beginnings in the work of Folkman and Lazarus (1984). As discussed previously, these researchers identified two "major theory-based functions of coping": problem-focused and emotion-focused. This classification provided a "broad brush approach" for researchers when confronting the many types of coping (Folkman and Moskowitz 2004, p. 751). When thinking about this classification Folkman argued that it is important to note that neither strategy should be thought of as inherently better or worse than the other, that each can support or inhibit the other, and that the intensity with which each is used depends on how the encounter is appraised (Folkman 1982, p. 99). The problem-focused/emotion-focused model became the benchmark from which other researchers took their cue. As different schemas were proposed, support and debate ebbed and flowed as to the number of categories, the features that distinguished one category from another, their complexity, their description, and their goodness of fit with the Lazarus and Folkman model. From this volume of work it is possible to identify a number of trends. While it may be too soon to suggest that, taken together, these trends represent some form of consensus as to the number of coping categories, they at least suggest the direction research is taking in order to achieve such an agreement.

These trends point to a need to consider, in addition to the problem-focused/emotion-focused categories, two additional categories: meaning-focused coping and relationship–social coping. These, Folkman suggests, represent "major gaps in the original formulation" (2011, p. 454). Meaning-focused coping grew out of the need to accommodate the way individuals reappraise the meaning of a stressful encounter (Folkman and Moskowitz 2007). It is where individuals "search for meaning once a situation has been appraised as stressful" (Park and Folkman 1997, p. 122). The "theoretically rich" role that meaning plays in stress research (Park and Folkman 1997, p. 132) has led other researchers to explore benefit-reminding coping (Tennen and Affleck 2005), where individuals remind themselves of benefits that emerge from a stressful encounter, and sense-making coping, where individuals attempt to make sense of stressful encounters (Davis *et al.* 1998). Meaning-focused coping has the potential to sustain, provide respite, and restore individual resources (Folkman and Moskowitz 2007). Similarly, Folkman and Moskowitz point to "the meaning and purpose" (2004, p. 759) that comes through religious coping, with Folkman (2011) pointing to this type of coping as adding another dimension to the original model (Lazarus and Folkman 1984).

Although coping research emphasizes the importance of context, because of its more individualistic orientation, social aspects of coping have been somewhat short-changed (Folkman and Moskowitz 2004). As Berg and her colleagues point out, since "terms such as interpersonal, communal, relationship-focused and collaborative coping have all been used to characterize interpersonal aspects of coping" it is now time to broaden our work beyond the more conventional views of social support (Berg *et al.* 2008, p. 505). At the heart of relationship coping lies the idea that social relations can be developed and used as a positive force through such activities as collaborating, sharing resources, giving advice, and working together to solve issues (Berg *et al.* 2008). It also involves the idea of coping that reflects the communal aspects of the social context and how they influence coping behaviors (Folkman and Moskowitz 2004), the idea of co-rumination where thoughts and feelings are shared (Helgeson 2011), and the need to better understand the roles of empathy, engagement, and congruence (Folkman 2011).

Whether coping researchers are closer to reaching some sort of consensus, that is, whether these trends, coupled with the original Lazarus and Folkman (1984) model, suggest four categories – problem-focused, emotion-focused, relationship-focused, and meaning-focused coping – that help "the synthesis of findings across studies" (Folkman and Moskowitz 2004, p. 752), remains a moot point, as does how we arrive at a synthesis without obscuring the richness and complexity of the coping process (Folkman and Moskowitz 2004).

Classifying coping: The theme of mode

Different schemas for classifying coping strategies will continue to be developed, as will the debate that surrounds then. We will rejoin the discussion surrounding classifying coping strategies later in this section when we explore the idea of proactive coping. However, classifying coping strategies is not all about assigning strategies to different descriptors, although it is, of course, fairly fundamental to the process. It is also about the two other themes that emerge out of the classification debate – mode and time – and it is to these themes that we now turn.

When it comes to building a comprehensive picture of coping, Latack and Havlovic argue that we need to consider coping not just in terms of its focus, but also in terms of "the mechanism or mode the person uses during the coping process" (1992, p. 491). General descriptions of coping that emphasize focus are "insufficiently specific" to capture the mode of coping that is being used. This "second conceptual dimension" of coping would include, for example, distinguishing between three types of coping modes: cognitive versus behavioral, proactive/control versus escapist/avoidance, and social versus solitary (Latack and Havlovic 1992, pp. 492–493). Latack and Havlovic acknowledge that as our knowledge accumulates so may the number of modes, but, for these authors, if we are to establish a greater sense of meaning in coping research then this line of enquiry should be pursued.

When discussing the treatment of coping Lazarus also made clear that classifying coping strategies needed to be considered alongside the issue of mode. He described "four main coping modes," each capable of being directed to the self or the environment and each concerned with past, present, or future appraisals. These four modes are: information-seeking, direct action, inhibition of action, and intrapsychic processes (1998, p. 205). To capture the "full ground" of these modes of coping, Lazarus emphasized, would require developing new measurement techniques that capture how a person thinks and acts in a stressful encounter (1998, p. 207).

Bringing the themes of focus and mode together is represented in the work of Stanton *et al.* (2000). Concern about how emotion-focused coping was usually discussed in terms of its dysfunctional avoidance mode led these authors to recommend that attention be redirected towards its approach-oriented adaptive mode. In this way the adaptive potential of emotion-focused coping is captured through actively pursuing and acknowledging positive emotional expression and the way emotions can be positively processed (Stanton *et al.* 2005). Exploring the different modes of coping highlights the idea that coping can be future oriented and proactive, and so brings us to the third theme when it comes to developing our understanding of coping: time.

Classifying coping: The theme of time

Coping, as Schwarzer points out, "depends, among other things, on the time perspective of demands and the subjective certainty of events" (2004, p. 347). He goes on to argue that the concept of time can be used to distinguish between four types of coping. These Schwarzer describes as: (a) *reactive*, dealing with a stressful encounter that has happened; (b) *anticipatory*, dealing with a looming demand; (c) *preventive*, building resources for the future; and (d) *proactive*, building general resources that facilitate the attainment of demanding goals and promote personal growth (2001, pp. 348–349). Traditional views of coping tend, argues Greenglass (2002), to migrate towards reactive coping. While anticipatory, preventive, and proactive coping are all future-oriented, there is still debate as to where the boundary lies between them, since all seem to have a proactive capacity building element (Dewe *et al.* 2010).

Ways to distinguish one from the other may be on the basis of what motivates its use (Schwarzer and Taubert 2002), whether there are different types of proactivity (Aspinwall and Taylor 1997), or whether, irrespective of the timing, all coping strategies can be used positively to produce individual growth and development (Dewe 2008). Because of their future orientation, researchers may, as Folkman suggests, question "whether you can have coping without stress" (2011, p. 455) signaling, that perhaps it is now time to reconsider how coping is defined (Coyne and Gottlieb 1996).

Nevertheless, it is proactive coping that now represents a new way forward for coping research (Folkman and Moskowitz 2004). A number of factors have contributed to the growing interest in this form of coping. They include a long interest in the idea of proactive coping (Aspinwall and Taylor 1997), greater attention being given to the role of appraisal, and more particularly positive appraisals (Lazarus 2001a), the focus on discrete emotions and the power of positive emotions (Fredrickson 1998), the distinction between resource accumulation and resource depletion (Hobfoll 2001), and of course the rise of the positive psychology movement (Seligman and Csikszentmihalyi 2000). At the core of proactive coping is the idea of improving one's quality of life (Greenglass 2002). Proactive coping is forward-looking, concerned with resource accumulation that aids personal growth and achievements (Schwarzer 2001), it is all about positive appraisals (Aspinwall and Taylor 1997), it prepares and forewarns (Aspinwall and Taylor 1997), it emphasizes goal management rather than the management of risk (Greenglass 2002; Schwarzer 2001, 2004), it creates performance opportunities that are personally meaningful, valued, and provide purpose (Schwarzer 2004), it has the capacity to develop an awareness of potential stressors (Aspinwall 2011), and has as its motivation the belief that through change there is an opportunity for considerable personal development (Greenglass 2002). As Folkman concludes, proactive coping must be considered as "an important addition to the stress and coping model" (2011, p. 455).

TABLE 6.1 **Classifying coping strategies: A themed approach**

The theme of focus (Folkman 2011; Folkman and Lazarus 1984)
- **Problem-focused** (addressing the problem).
- **Emotion-focused** (managing the emotion).
- **Meaning-focused** (searching for meaning – sense making).
- **Relationship-focused** (the development of social relations).

The theme of mode (Latack and Havlovic 1992; Lazarus 1998; Stanton et al. 2000)
- **Cognitive** (mental strategies and self-talk).
- **Behavioral** (taking action, doing something).
- **Control** (taking charge).
- **Escape** (effort to put it out of mind).
- **Social** (seeking out help).
- **Solitary** (doing things alone).

The theme of time (Greenglass 2002; Schwarzer 2001; 2004)
- **Reactive** (dealing with what has happened).
- **Anticipatory** (preparing in anticipation of an event).
- **Preventive** (building resources for the future).
- **Proactive** (building resources for growth and achievement).

Notes:
(a) None of the themes are mutually exclusive; coping is initiated in response to appraisals and each mode helps to identify important differences in coping.
(b) Cognitive and behavioral modes can themselves be further classified into control, escape, social, and solitary (Latack and Havlovic 1992).
(c) The theme of time could be further considered in terms of what motivates the use of a coping strategy (Schwarzer and Taubert 2002) or on the basis of type of proactivity (Aspinwall and Taylor 1997).

COPING CHECKLISTS AND ANALYSIS

Research and debate will continue to surround the classification of coping strategies. Researchers will, as part of this debate, continue to pursue the issues of mode and time so that a more meaningful discussion of coping and its dimensions can take place. What does seem to emerge, when researchers consider coping in terms of its focus, is that coping can be expressed in terms of five foci: problem-focus, emotion-focus, meaning focus, relationship-focus, and proactive-focus. Nevertheless, despite these developments, it is clear that when the different coping strategies are considered within the context of a stressful encounter the task of classifying them is not always straightforward (Dewe and Cooper 2007; Dewe *et al.* 2010). These difficulties can be explained in terms of two challenges that face researchers when engaging in coping research: operational and interpretive (Dewe *et al.* 2010). Operational challenges are concerned with how best to measure coping, the limitations imposed when using checklists and the search for richer more qualitative measures, whereas interpretive challenges are concerned with what it is that our results are telling us and what meaning can be derived from coping scores.

Operational challenges

When it comes to operational challenges, disagreements reach "their greatest intensity when self-report coping questionnaires or checklists become the focus of attention" (Dewe *et al.* 2010, p. 32). The utility of such instruments is not in question. They offer a convenient, adaptable, and efficient means of data collection. What is in question is that, although widely used, they are criticized as being "limited both in their descriptive and in their explanatory power" (Oakland and Ostell 1996, p. 151), raising concerns that they have weighted the field down with self-evident findings (Coyne 1997), leaving some reviewers to suggest that the problems facing coping researchers "cannot be solved by developing better checklists" (Coyne and Gottlieb 1996, p. 961) and culminating in the feeling that we are now seeing a convenience factor creep in, making many researchers less inclined to search for alternative measurement solutions (Coyne and Gottlieb 1996), less sensitive to when it is appropriate to use such instruments (Lazarus 1995), and less likely to agree that checklists will be only as good as our motivation to improve them (Folkman 1992), leaving some reviewers suggesting that this state of affairs can only be solved by "radically refashioning coping research" (Coyne and Racioppo 2000, p. 659).

However, as Lazarus (2000) points out, the view that there is an over-reliance on coping checklists fails to recognize that, increasingly, researchers are exploring new and innovative ways to capture the richness and complexity of the coping process. Rather than think of coping checklists as the only way forward, there is broad sympathy among researchers for the view that coping checklists should have been viewed more as "a first step" (Coyne 1997, p. 153), and that there is a continual need to search for alternative ecologically sensitive approaches, accepting that "in-depth, idiographic techniques that attempt to map the psychological terrain" (Snyder 1999, p. 327) of coping now need to become a more significant part of our measurement repertoire. In coping research there has always been an undercurrent of interest in alternative measures. The use of qualitative measures to capture the nature of the coping process now lies at the heart of many reviews (e.g. Dewe and Cooper 2007; Lazarus 1997, 2000; Somerfield and McCrae 2000) with researchers pointing to the benefits that follow the use of "within-person, process-oriented" approaches which include emotional narratives (Lazarus 1999), and daily process designs (Tennen *et al.* 2000).

Nevertheless, researchers continue to use coping checklists, and the issues surrounding their use, although they have been discussed many times, remain sufficiently salient to rehearse, albeit briefly, one more time (see Coyne and Gottlieb 1996; Dewe *et al.* 2010; Folkman and Moskowitz 2004; Somerfield 1997a, b). Folkman and Moskowitz, for example, suggest that researchers need to consider the length of the checklist in order to cover a sufficient range of coping strategies, response keys that are difficult to interpret, ambiguities that emerge from the way items are expressed, the difficulties surrounding recall, and confusing strategies with outcomes and emotions (2004, p. 749). Synthesizing the views of others, Dewe and Cooper point to the need to consider the specificity of the instructions, the way items are derived, the way they are worded, and the appropriateness of the scoring key (2007, pp. 167–173). Finally Coyne and Gottlieb (1996, p. 961) suggest that when researchers design checklists, they need to be more sensitive to the ambiguities that they may create in the minds of respondents whilst completing them, the relevance of items to respondents, and the variations in the way different items may be interpreted. As Folkman and Moskowitz suggest, when it comes to coping measurement "the art" lies in selecting measures that best reflect, and are appropriate to, what it is the researcher is questioning, and so "sometimes the best solution may involve several approaches" (2004, p. 751).

Interpretive challenges

It is clear that "a rich history of comment and criticism" accompanies the development and design of coping checklists (Dewe *et al.* 2010, p. 39). Yet operational issues cannot be separated from interpretive issues, as each go hand in hand, and so, it is important that when preparing their data for analysis researchers consider the impact this has on its interpretation. As before (Dewe and Cooper 2007; Dewe *et al.*

2010) we draw attention to two issues: the data-reduction features of factor analysis and the interpretation of factor scores. The benefits of using a technique like factor analysis to produce coping groups that have, as Folkman (1992) suggests, a theoretical and pragmatic reliability, is well recognized. While the issues that follow are not a call to abandon such a technique, they are a signal that until we know more about how coping strategies are used, relate to one another, and the roles they play, it is probably best to adopt a more cautious approach when applying factor analysis procedures (Aldwin 2000).

Because of the unique nature of coping data, in the sense that how coping strategies are used doesn't always follow the conventional rules of covariation since using one strategy can inhibit the use of another, particular attention needs to be paid to the issue of factor loadings (Aldwin 2009; Billings and Moos 1984; Dewe *et al.* 2010; Folkman and Moskowitz 2004). Keeping or dispensing with a coping item on the basis of its factor loading, or its failure to load, or it loading across factors, ignores the variety and number of functions that a coping item may fulfill, raising questions about the comprehensiveness of a factor (Folkman 1992), the importance of an item as a coping strategy (Aldwin 2009), the different ways in which it may be used (Stone and Kennedy-Moore 1992), and the interpretation that can be placed on factor scores (Coyne and Gottlieb 1996).

The issues surrounding covariance also help to explain the low reliabilities that often accompany coping scales (Dewe *et al.* 2010) and highlight the importance of the context, as factor structures change across encounters and over time (Aldwin 2009). Deriving factors also raises the question of their interdependence. As coping strategies are used in combination and "seem to travel together" (Folkman and Moskowitz 2004, p. 753), by setting artificial boundaries based on the idea of a presumed statistical independence between factors we fail to capture the nature of the coping process and in this case highlight the difficulty of determining from such a factor structure the range of ways a person may be thinking and acting in a particular encounter.

When it comes to interpreting mean scores, the first difficulty emerges from the criticism that as coping items are "often vaguely worded" and therefore "thin descriptions of coping" (Coyne and Gottlieb 1996, p. 976) interpreting them must be associated with a level of ambiguity as to how different items are actually being used. When coping items are aggregated into mean scores, while two people may have exactly the same score the way they coped may be completely different. Perhaps the pattern of scores becomes a more useful mechanism for analysis than the actual mean score itself. It is clear that by creating mean scores "the likelihood is that crucial aspects of timing, sequencing and appropriateness will be lost" (Coyne and Racioppo 2000, p. 657). Score patterns may help to shed light on what strategies are being used, how they combine, perhaps even how they may be used, and the role they are playing in relation to other strategies within the same pattern (Dewe 2003).

Recognizing that coping patterns will cross factors reinforces the need to consider the limits we are placing on interpretation by treating factors as if each can best be understood independently of others. As Suls and David conclude, "little is known about how coping behaviors are used in combination" even though they are "probably rarely used in isolation" (1996, p. 1000). We are not calling for the abandonment of mean scores. What we are doing is simply drawing attention to the fact that in coping research scores may not operate in a linear-additive fashion (Dewe *et al.* 2010) as they "lump together the idiosyncratic experiences of participants" (Suls and David 1996, p. 998). Raising these issues should not act as a deterrent, but more as a motivation to consider carefully "what it is a mean score can tell us particularly if our goal is to understand the relationship between different coping items and the manner, sequence and the way in which they are used" (Dewe 2001, p. 84).

COPING EFFECTIVENESS

In their review article Somerfield and McCrae raise the issues of "what is meant by effective coping, "what is ineffective coping," and "by what criteria" should it be judged (2000, p. 622). While researchers have, of course, tackled these issues, the theory in relation to under-standing coping effectiveness is regarded as modest (Lazarus 2000), the findings variable (Dewe *et al.* 2010), and the problem described as "one of the most vexing issues of research and theory on coping, namely, what is meant by effective coping and how to measure it" (Lazarus 2000, p. 672). Theory in relation to coping effectiveness is built around two approaches (Folkman and Moskowitz 2000). The first approach considers coping effectiveness in terms of outcomes. This approach views outcomes as those goals that are significant to the individual and relevant and appropriate to the encounter. However, such an approach obscures a number of "important complexities" when it comes to considering outcomes. These include: when an outcome is reached, what constitutes effective resolution, how is it judged, who is making that judgment, expectations as to whether an outcome can be achieved, and the ways outcomes change as the process unfolds (Folkman and Moskowitz 2004, pp. 753–755).

This means that it is now time for researchers to take a more critical approach when it comes to selecting outcomes. While determining the appropriateness of an outcome may not be easy, it is clear that future research should not be driven by the tradition where outcomes are rather casually selected because they fall, one way or another, under the rather blunt rubric of stress (Dewe *et al.* 2010). The second approach considers the "goodness of fit" between the nature of the encounter and coping. In this approach the better the fit the more effective the coping. This approach is not without difficulties either. It requires researchers to recognize and accept the fundamental role of appraisal, the nature of the context and its supportive or inhibiting factors when initiating coping, the impact of individual differences, who is best to judge the "fit" that has been achieved, and just how that "fit" is perceived in terms of effectiveness (Dewe and Cooper 2007).

What is meant by coping effectiveness?

Before turning to discussing in more detail some of the contextual and individual difference issues that surround determining coping effectiveness, we look first at what we mean by effectiveness. Researchers have explored the idea of effectiveness in terms of whether an encounter was satisfactorily resolved (Long 1993), or the extent to which different coping strategies were helpful in reducing stress (Bar-Tal and Spitzer 1994), or by asking confidants of respondents to indicate their thoughts on how well the respondent was able to cope with the encounter (Bhagat *et al.* 1991), or by raising the issue of who is it that is best placed to evaluate whether coping has been effective or not (Folkman and Moskowitz 2004), or by arguing that effectiveness be examined more specifically in relation to the goals that individuals are trying to achieve and in this way try to get closer to understanding what an appropriate outcome is (Aldwin 2009), recognizing that outcomes may be more complex and that individuals "may trade off gains in one area for losses in another" (Aldwin 2009, p. 193).

In exploring future directions for coping research Folkman raises the question: How do we know when coping has an effect? To answer this question Folkman suggests two approaches: to explore "how changes in coping are related to changes in outcomes," and to map "plausible pathways through which coping can affect outcomes" (2011, p. 458). There is also a need, as Aldwin argues, to explore the "qualitative manner" (2000, p. 158) in which a coping strategy is used, as the same strategy can be used in different ways by different people. So, the different ways in which coping strategies may be effective is yet another issue that needs exploring (Dewe and Cooper 2007), bringing researchers to the point where the focus is directly on exploring what we actually mean by effectiveness: what do people actually talk about when they discuss or evaluate the effectiveness of their coping? It must now be time to move away from researching effectiveness by simply drawing inferences from coping relationships, to arrive at a more detailed description of what effectiveness means to those engaged in a stressful encounter. Until we have this understanding we will continue to attempt to give meaning to coping relationships where no meaning can be ascertained; certainly not in terms of what constitutes effectiveness anyway.

Individual differences and coping effectiveness

Coping is a process "embedded in a context" (Zeidner and Saklofske 1996, p. 507), and cannot be understood without reference to individual differences (Suls *et al.* 1996), so understanding coping effectiveness requires an understanding of these two issues. In building up a more detailed knowledge about the context O'Brien and DeLongis (1996, p. 780) argue that we need to move beyond the way stressful encounters are categorized and consider the demands that such an encounter imposes on those coping with it. Differentiating between achievement demands (agentic) and affiliation demands (communal), these authors suggest that each requires a different type of coping, and so, if we are to better understand effectiveness, it is essential to distinguish between encounters in this way.

Taking a similar position, Suls and David (1996, pp. 1001–1002) argue that encounters can be considered in terms of whether they are strong (clear expectations as to how one should act) or weak (no clear expectation as to what behavioral standard is required). Suls and David argue that this distinction provides the basis for understanding why some strategies are not just more appropriate to a context, but more or less effective as well. It is clear that coping will inevitably be judged in terms of the context within which it occurs. Without an understanding of contextual issues, then, as Zeidner and Saklofske suggest, we have "only half the story" (1996, p. 509). What is also clear is that the context is intimately linked to how the individual appraises it. So, our understanding of the coping process can only be advanced if in the future we give as much attention to the meanings individuals give to events, as we have to the nature of the events themselves.

Individual differences add a further complexity when considering coping effectiveness. While reviewing the relationship between personality and coping O'Brien and DeLongis argue that while personality, as measured by the big five, had "important associations with coping responses," more work needs to be done to explore the interaction between personality, context, and coping (1996, p. 775). Nevertheless, O'Brien and DeLongis point to how personality may influence the order in which coping strategies are tried, how coping efforts are coordinated, particularly in relation to others, how persistent individuals are in continuing with a particular pattern of coping, how the role and influence of personality may change as the coping process unfolds, and how personality influences appraisals, goals, values, and expectations (1996, p. 808).

Others suggest that when it comes to personality there is a need to distinguish between using a strategy and a person's competence in using that strategy, noting that "there is a significant difference between using a strategy and using it well" (Suls and David 1996, p. 1001), that it is important to distinguish between coping choice and coping effectiveness, as individuals may be predisposed to using different kinds of coping, and that some "strategies are more useful for certain kinds of people" (Suls *et al.* 1996, p. 726), that personality may influence how flexible individuals are in the way they use coping strategies (Folkman and Moskowitz 2004, p. 756), and that as the stressful encounter unfolds feedback may "either strengthen existing personality processes or set into motion others" (Aldwin 2009, p. 113).

Overview

Coping is fundamental to our understanding of the stress process. Its significance may explain why researchers appear to have moved in haste to try and understand how coping works, before settling on exactly how coping should be measured. While the debate remains open as to how best to measure coping, it is clear that researchers are now being urged to consider how coping has been defined and how it may now need to be broadened to embrace the notion of anticipatory coping and the emphasis now being placed on proactive coping. What is inescapable, though, is that if we are going to continue to make advances in coping research, then the search for new, creative, and person-centered measures needs to become part of all researchers' repertoire of skills. Similarly, as the focus of research necessarily shifts from analysis (exploring relationships between different parts of the process) to synthesis (understanding the process as a whole) then this will demand "scientific tasks [that] are sufficiently distinctive to require different lines of thought and research methods" (Lazarus 2000, p. 668).

Measurement must also be coupled with meaning, and, because the role of meaning is at the heart of coping research, giving meaning to relationships and exploring the role of meaning within those relationships must lead research to pay particular attention to the role of appraisal as the hub of meaning in any stressful encounter, the intimacy with which appraisals link the individual to the context, and its explanatory potential in providing an organizing concept around which future research may wish to develop (Dewe *et al.* 2010). Coping research is not all about intractable measurement problems. The creative tensions that stem from such problems indicate that the field is maturing, that innovative and creative ways forward are already being identified which capture the richness and complexity of the coping process. Much remains to be done but new paths are being developed that provide considerable encouragement about what the future holds.

STRESS INTERVENTIONS

This chapter's focus has primarily been on individual coping and the debate that surrounds not just our understanding of the coping process, but how best to move the field forward. Running parallel to this work there is a well-developed body of knowledge on organizational interventions (Antoniou and Cooper 2005; Cooper and Cartwright 1994; Kinder *et al.* 2008; Kompier and Cooper 1999; Murphy *et al.* 1995; Quick *et al.* 1997; Quick and Tetrick 2003), a recognized structure for identifying the levels at which different interventions take place (e.g. Dewe *et al.* 2010), and the emergence of clear agreed standards of good management practice when confronting work-related stress (Cousins *et al.* 2004; Mackay *et al.* 2004).

However, despite the progress that has been made, there is still an underlying feeling that the lack of effective interventions remains a concern (Brough *et al.* 2009) and that we still do not understand enough about how and why interventions work, those processes linking interventions to desired outcomes, the appropriateness of interventions, and the advantages of using multimethod approaches that better integrate process and outcome evaluations (Nielsen *et al.* 2010, p. 219). To put these concerns into context, we begin by exploring the extent of the work-stress problem and mental ill health generally, the costs to individuals and organizations, the evidence as to the effectiveness of work-stress interventions, the need to take evidence-based practices forward, and the influence of positive psychology in reshaping organizational interventions.

Stress and mental ill health at work

Data from the Health and Safety Executive (HSE) (Sweeney 2010) estimated that in the United Kingdom for the 2009/2010 year an estimated 1.3 million working people suffered from ill health that they thought was work-related. Of those 435,000 (29.1 percent) reported suffering from stress, depression, or anxiety; the second most commonly reported illness type after musculoskeletal disorders. Interestingly, over the last ten years the incidence rate for stress, depression, and anxiety has remained at a similar level, whereas over the same period the rate for musculoskeletal disorders has significantly lowered. The Centre for Mental Health put the organizational costs for sickness absence, presenteeism, and staff turnover in the United Kingdom at £25.9 billion per year; around 3.6 percent of the national pay bill, with the cost per employee averaging £1035 per year (Parsonage 2010). The invisible costs of presenteeism are illustrated in Table 6.2. These illnesses accounted for 9.8 million days lost for the same period. The Centre's research also points to around one in six in the workforce being affected by depression, anxiety, or another mental health condition, that mental ill health problems are almost as common in the workplace as they are anywhere else, that less than 20 percent of mental ill health problems in the workforce are work-related and, more telling,

TABLE 6.2 **Sickness presenteeism**

	Health "Good"	Health "Not good"
No absences	Healthy and present – 35%	Unhealthy and present "Sickness Presentees" – 28%
Some absences	Healthy and not always present – 13%	Unhealthy and not always present – 24%

N = 39,000 employees from general working population (United Kingdom).
With permission: Robertson, I., and Cooper, C. (2011). *Wellbeing: Productivity and happiness at work*. Palgrave Macmillan: Basingstoke, p. 19.

the level and costs of mental ill health problems in the workforce are widely underestimated (Parsonage 2010).

Data from the HSE psychosocial working conditions survey (Packman and Webster 2009) showed that the numbers describing their jobs as extremely or very stressful has risen slowly over the last five years, but then settled at around 16 percent or approximating four million workers. Despite all these facts and figures the underlying impression is that work-related stress and mental ill health problems more generally still don't receive the attention they should. Data from the Shaw Trust survey (2006) showed that around a third of respondents, when asked to think about what specific disorders they would associate with the term mental ill health, couldn't give an answer, although most who did answer suggested stress or depression. Similarly, when asked to estimate the extent of mental ill health problems at work only 17 percent of those sampled got it right to any accurate degree. Yet, it also clear from the Shaw Trust data that organizations "want to do the right thing" (p. 3), feel a little hesitant and somewhat ill-equipped as to how best to deal with such problems, need more support and help to deal with them, and feel "that a great deal of talent is excluded from organizations as a results of this lack of support" (p. 3). The overall impression from their findings is that they represent a "cry for help" from organizations as to how best to tackle mental ill health issues at work (Shaw Trust 2006, p. 3).

Stress interventions: What does the evidence say?

Work at both the policy level (Black 2008; Foresight Mental Capital and Wellbeing Project 2008) and at the organizational level (Chartered

Institute Personnel and Development 2011) recognizes the importance of linking together health, work, and well-being policies, investing in well-being strategies, developing and promoting positive managerial behavior, developing paths to a healthy workplace, and acknowledging the need for clear management standards and practice. So, when it comes to work-stress interventions, what does the evidence say? It is clear that workplaces can do much to enhance individual worker's health and well-being (Black 2008) and that good work is good business. It is also clear that there is a "strong evidence base showing that work is generally good for physical and mental health and well-being (Waddell and Burton 2006, p. 38). Reviewing the evidence on the effectiveness of workplace interventions for common health problems led Hill *et al.* to draw a number of conclusions from their findings, which they hoped would "inform future research priorities and input to the development of evidence-based guidelines for the management of health at work" (2007, p. 1). Their key findings can be summarized in terms of three themes: consultation, comprehensiveness, and practice (2007, p. 1–2).

When the theme of consultation is considered, the evidence that emerges from their review is that interventions which involved some form of worker–management partnership and or consultation improved results (Hill *et al.* 2007). Good communications, cooperation, and agreed goals among all members of the partnership, including extended members, such as occupational health providers and primary care professionals, can result in faster recovery, less reoccurrence of ill health, and less time out of work (p. 1). The evidence that supported the theme of comprehensiveness suggested that interventions should go beyond just health issues and cover attitudes and beliefs as well, in addition to addressing in a complementary way individual and organizational issues (p. 1).

Finally, under the theme of practice, Hill and his colleagues suggest that management initiatives are more often than not "based on convention rather than evidence," and that to ensure the quality of interventions much can be gained by examining a broader type of evidence, across a wider range of health, medical, and occupational health areas (2007, pp. 2–3). Such a review, as the authors point out, needs to work around a number of difficulties and so it is not surprising that in their conclusions they suggest that "as a starting point" there is a need for better-quality evaluation evidence, and evidence that ranges across a wider spectrum, then, they argue, attention needs to be directed towards how the evidence is interpreted for a wider audience and which intervention works best. (pp. 62–63).

In an effort to provide "evidence-based answers" to the mental health causes of work absence Seymour and Grove (2005, p. 2) concluded from their review that there was "moderate" evidence that stress-management interventions covering a range of complementary approaches "have at best a modest or short-term impact" on individual stress (p. 21), "moderate evidence" supporting the effectiveness of interventions that offered a range of methods (p. 22), and "limited evidence" that individual rather than organizational approaches produced better results, although there was "limited evidence" that organizational level approaches can also "be effective in reducing common mental health problems" (p. 3). Like others, these authors also point to the need, in the future, to build an evidence base in the United Kingdom, to learn more about how multimethod interventions work, to do more work on interventions based on employment practices and management styles, more research on retention and rehabilitation, and more research on those interventions that use particularly promising techniques (2005, pp. 39–40).

Evidence-based practice: some challenges

These reviews reinforce the importance of the role of the manager in dealing with stressful situations (Rolfe *et al.* 2006). At the same time, the reviews point to the need for organizations to work in partnership with a range of different health professionals, so that all those involved develop a better understanding of the relationship between work and health (Sainsbury Centre for Mental Health 2007). This emphasis on partnership undoubtedly reflects the feeling that what organizational psychology has failed to do is "promote a synergy between science and practice" (Thayer *et al.* 2011, p. 32). Inevitably, any discussion about the gap between practice and research raises questions as to just how evidence-based a discipline we are and what we can do to help those who manage organizations become more evidence-based (Briner and Rousseau 2011a). A feel for the arguments that accompany any discussion on evidence based research and practice can be found in a special edition on the subject in *Industrial and Organizational Psychology* (Briner and Rousseau 2011a).

In a comprehensive and detailed analysis, Briner and Rousseau in their lead article argue, that organizational psychology "cannot yet claim to be fully evidence-based [although] uniquely qualified" to develop the techniques and procedures demanded of such an approach (2011a, p. 20). To encourage organizations and managers to become more evidence-based in their decision making, Briner and Rousseau suggest providing managers with systematic reviews designed to help them decide whether or not to invest in intervention programs, offering to act as "knowledge brokers" to analyze and interpret their data to help them maximize its potential, and offering to work in a facilitation role for those organizations and their managers who wish to develop evidence-based management (2011a, p. 20). At the heart of their argument, though, is the fundamental importance of systematic reviews because, as Briner and Rousseau argue, they are crucial in progressing evidence-based practice and so this endeavor must become "an essential part" of an organizational psychologist's toolkit (2011a, p. 18).

Commentators don't dispute the importance of an evidence-based approach and its role in crossing the research–practice divide. What is disputed is how we get there, without on the way impacting on the "methodologically diverse in our field," by "dismissing interesting, creative, and promising alternatives that don't quite fit" an approach where systematic reviews are heralded as the best way forward (Cassell 2011, p. 25). Other commentators also follow this line, suggesting that the best way forward may be to adapt and blend the tools that we have with the expertise that we have built up, rather than placing all our emphasis on one particular technique (Hodgkinson 2011). Others suggest that we have the evidence, but need to understand why we don't seem to use it or care to use it (Thayer *et al.* 2011), that we can learn from other areas of psychology (Catano 2011), that we need to broaden our view of what constitutes evidence (Cronin and Klimoski 2011), and just exactly what it is we mean by evidence and how we go about collecting it (Boatman and Sinar 2011).

All these commentators would agree that if we are to move towards evidence-based research and practice then we mustn't avoid debating the issues. As, Briner and Rousseau conclude, by doing so we "may not be there yet but we may now be a little closer" (2011b, p. 76). Such a debate, as Nielson and her colleagues suggest, is "challenging" because its aim is to initiate further research and "promising" because what is debated has considerable practical potential to substantially improve the health and well-being of employees (2010, p. 230).

THE INFLUENCE OF POSITIVE PSYCHOLOGY

In their seminal article on positive psychology Seligman and Csikszentmihalyi make three points which lie at the heart of positive psychology: "that it is about identifying and nurturing an individual's strongest qualities – what they own and what they are best at"; that "it is not just fixing what is broken; it is nurturing what is best"; and that as a discipline it needs to embrace and emphasize what *is* and what *could be* (2000, pp. 6–7). It is against these values that interventions should also now be judged. Positive interventions, as Seligman goes on to explain, are built on the premise that human strengths "buffer against" stress and mental ill health problems and that by "identifying, amplifying, and concentrating on these strengths in people at risk, we will do effective prevention" (2005, p. 5). Positive psychology has now reached a stage where it is time to apply the knowledge of the positive to "real world contexts" (Linley and Joseph 2004b, p. xv). Positive psychology embodies much of what is already being done by practitioners. Much of what is being done has never really been captured in terms of a name, nor has it been recognized as part of "a new perspective for professional practice" (Linley and Joseph 2004a, p. 3). Linley and Joseph argue that applying positive psychology to practice offers a "collective identity and common language" that transcends old boundaries and offers ways of working that are "genuinely integrative and applicable across settings" (2004a, p. 4).

Work on positive interventions has captured the attention of many researchers. A range of issues have been explored, including using coaching and positive psychology to promote a flourishing workforce (Grant and Spence 2010; Kauffman and Scoular 2004), introducing mindfulness to the workplace to promote more effective use of individual and organizational resources (Marianetti and Passmore 2010), building and developing strengths which allow individuals to gain far more from this positive focus (Hodges and Asplund 2010; Hodges and Clifton 2004), and using the language of positive psychology to build a positive workplace through a program of facilitated learning opportunities (Davis 2010).

The values of positive psychology have also been used to shed light on, and develop insights into, our understanding of the course of health and illness, illustrating how work spanning positive psychology and health psychology is "manifold, robust and extremely fruitful" (Taylor and Sherman 2004, p. 315). Still other applications broaden our understanding of emotions and the cultivation of positive emotions to optimize health and well-being (Fredrickson 2000b), our understanding of mental health by thinking of it in terms of a continuum from languishing to flourishing in life, in this way emphasizing the idea of the "mentally healthy" (Keyes 2002, p. 208), and our understanding of health by broadening our meaning of health that goes beyond the absence of illness to the idea that health is fundamentally positive, requiring interventions and indeed research methods that differ from those associated with more traditional views (Fleury 1998; Seligman 2008).

OVERVIEW

Organizations that offer stress-management programs also appear to be indicators of "good places to work," as it seems that they help to encourage employee well-being and are frequently associated with other programs that facilitate worker health and well-being (Nigam *et al.* 2003, p. 345). What also emerges from the literature is the need for balance; a more integrative approach that captures the nature of the workplace, where the "limits of one approach can be compensated by the strengths of another" and the recognition that ultimately each is trying to achieve the same goal of making work a place where employees can flourish, grow, and develop (Biron *et al.* 2011, p. 947). Integration goes beyond just the positive and the negative. It involves "building strong links between the academic and the practitioner communities" as they would be "immensely valuable" when applying positive psychology to the workplace (Davis 2010, p. 297).

Integration extends into the organization as well, requiring a shift in thinking by Human Resources, an emphasis on authentic leadership, and managers having to learn new roles that involve "being mindful, realizing strengths and celebrating good work" (Garcea *et al.* 2010, p. 329). Garcia and her colleagues take the argument one stage further, by suggesting that positive psychology is acting as a force for change, with organizations becoming the driving force and implementer of that change (Garcia *et al.* 2010). Like other ideas we have discussed, stress interventions and the role they play in developing health and well-being are simply being transformed to meet the challenges of the new millennium.

CHAPTER 7

CONCLUSIONS

This book has been about work and well-being. It is these words and this relationship that capture the very essence of the work experience, that is why understanding the nature of the relationship is important. However, we have also explored a subtheme relevant to this relationship, which we have described as "towards a balanced agenda." Why balance? Because the idea of balance, or "fit," frames the way researchers investigate the work–well-being relationship and the way our understanding of that relationship has developed. Yet, in tune with many of the arguments in this book, the idea of balance or "fit" needs now to be reexamined in light of those economic, social, and technological forces which are fundamentally changing the nature of work and the satisfaction we derive from it. For us, and for many of those we have cited, the idea of balance needs now to be extended and considered beyond its more traditional structural boundaries of "person–environment fit." The idea of balance is now seen as something that permeates every facet of what we as researchers and practitioners do, and represents something more than just a framework for understanding how behavior in organizations occurs. So, in drawing this book to a close we want first to explore the new meaning of balance, and then look at four themes that flow from it: meaning, measurement, membership, and moral responsibilities.

BALANCE: TOWARDS A NEW PERSPECTIVE

Balance as we described it in our introduction brings with it a number of meanings, and although the idea of equilibrium is ever-present, reflecting back on what we have written we want to focus on what we consider to be three important themes – evenness, alignment, and consideration – and argue that it is these themes that represent a more contemporary view of balance which better represents the ideas that have been expressed throughout this book. The idea of achieving a "research evenness" is clearly present in the work of those cited, with those arguing for more evenness in focus and approach doing so with as much passion as those arguing that an evenness of focus and approach has always been present, but accepting that it may have been somewhat understated. This does not mean simply replacing one focus or approach with another. If we are to understand the richness and complexity of the work experience then a more inclusive approach is needed so that a more comprehensive understanding emerges. Evenness means that each focus or approach is able to express itself in its own way, whilst recognizing that each is part of a more complex whole and taken together they give a more complete picture.

The second theme, "alignment," seems to have been embraced by researchers in practice, if not in terminology, and relates to the need to continually reevaluate the relevance of theory in relation to the assumptions made about the nature of work and the context within which work is experienced. There is an element of fit here as well, but this time in terms of how well our theories reflect and express the work experience, how long different theories remain relevant, and whether there is a constant need to consider whether our theory, and the measures we use to operationalize them are actually measuring what we think they are, whether they have any relevance to how workers are experiencing work, and where they are leading us in terms of practice and application. Bringing theories into the twenty-first century, reviewing how they are operationalized and applied, and how they express the contemporary work experience, all illustrates why the concept of alignment, through its emphasis on relevance, should now become as much a part of our evaluative techniques as concepts like reliability.

The third theme, "consideration," is used here to signal that in terms of the challenges we face we should look beyond the boundaries of our own discipline, giving attention to what other disciplines can offer to enhance our understanding, what knowledge emerges from practice and how we use and develop that knowledge, and where current methodologies are taking us and what alternative methodologies can provide. The idea of consideration also operates within the boundaries of our own discipline, and here we have an obligation to ensure, as already noted, that different perspectives and approaches are seen as a legitimate part of a web of knowledge and a complexity of experience that offers richness to our understanding and depth to our knowledge. None of these three themes are mutually exclusive. Taken together they provide a context, a way of thinking, and a way of evaluating the progress we have made and its impact on, and relevance to, those whose working lives we study. These three themes provide a context for exploring meaning and measurement, membership, and moral responsibility – issues which researchers need to reflect and act on when exploring work and well-being.

MEANING AND MEASUREMENT

It is clear that a review of work and well-being is also a history of meaning. Therefore, one of the enduring themes running through this book has been the way individuals search for meaning at work and how that meaning colors their work experiences. It is also clear that researchers have begun to explore processes through which meaning is derived and measurement strategies that capture the explanatory potential that resides in such meanings. Meaning and measurement cannot be separated, and emerging from the work of the researchers cited in this book is the call for more ecologically sensitive measures that express how individuals think and feel. As has been argued before, established measurement practices need to be continually assessed to ensure they are measuring what we think they are measuring (Cooper and Dewe 2004; Dewe *et al.* 2010). Such an assessment needs to distinguish between measures that describe a relationship and those that give it meaning, those that impose a reality versus those that allow a reality to emerge, and those that allow a structural understanding of a process versus those that capture the richness and complexity of the process itself.

Meaning is itself a complex concept. The meaning individuals give to events is different from searching for meaning, or sense-making, or identifying what makes work meaningful. Distinguishing between meaning as reminding and meaning as finding (Tennen and Affleck 2005), meaning as managing versus meaning as sustaining, and meaning as a demand versus meaning as a resource is a further reminder of the complexity of the concept. The arrival and emphasis of the positive psychology movement also urges researchers to seek out and distinguish between positive and negative meaning, identifying the different emotions that emerge from such meaning and the causal pathways that allow such meanings to be explored. Work and well-being researchers have always looked for an organizing concept around which their research can cohere, assumptions can be made, and boundaries set. Perhaps the time has come to consider whether we should now organize our research around the concept of meaning. The power of meaning as an explanatory variable is a theme running through much of the work reviewed. To adopt such an organizing concept requires nothing short of a reassessment of what we measure and how we measure it, those causal pathways that best express that meaning, and those variables that now best express the work experience.

MEMBERSHIP

Membership is another theme that has emerged from the work cited. Membership is best expressed as the different partnerships that need to develop to allow for knowledge transfer, for determining the relevance of what we do, and the obligations we have to those whose working lives we study. None of these themes are mutually exclusive, and so membership also helps in how we confront issues, for example, who decides what needs to be researched, how it needs to be researched, and how the knowledge is transferred and used. The theme of membership also extends out and covers what can be learnt from other disciplines; how their approach would aid our understanding and refine what we do (Coyne and Racioppo 2000). The theme also extends to considering what constitutes a useful contribution; whether the utility of what we research needs extending to ensure that there is a pragmatic engagement with organizations and their problems, and that there is a greater balancing of "methodological rigor and practical relevance" (Corley and Gioia 2011, p. 27), through extending what we mean by relevance to include "generating insight[s] practitioners find useful for understanding their own organizations and situations better than before" (Vermeulen 2007, p. 755). The issue of balance continues to play a role as researchers come to terms with the "competing priorities" of producing excellence in research on the one hand, with ensuring that it reaches those who need to put it into practice (Reay *et al.* 2009, p. 16), recognizing in terms of application the critical importance of "design and presentation" (p. 15), and that what needs to be encouraged is a "collaborative approach to research" where researchers and practitioners come together to identify issues that have a significant practical value (p. 16).

Membership or partnership also applies to evidence-based practice. Reay and her colleagues conclude that if the potential of evidence-based management is to be realized, then more work is needed on determining the nature of the evidence, its strength, the practical recommendations that can be drawn from such evidence, how aware managers and practitioners are that they are the focus of such research findings, and what can be done to enhance the way such evidence is used (Reay *et al.* 2009, pp. 11–15). Here again, it is an issue of balance, where encouraging the adoption of evidence-based practice is set against deriving evidence that is collaboratively developed by researchers and practitioners. It is not just agreeing on "what research" and "what evidence," but when it comes to intervening the evidence itself suggests that partnerships involving a range of disciplines and professionals, addressing in a complementary and consultative way research and organizational issues, and comprehensively drawing on the skills and knowledge of all those involved improve results (Hill *et al.* 2007). What this means is that, for both researchers and practitioners, discipline and organizational boundaries are changing, and while the ultimate goal of designing meaningful work that allows individuals to flourish and develop remains the same, each party must now look beyond its traditional boundaries and engage in collaborations and consultations which reflect the need for a rebalanced approach.

MORAL RESPONSIBILITIES

Underlying these different themes is the question of what responsibilities we have to those whose working lives we study. If we express moral responsibility in terms of ethics then it is clear that we have responsibilities across all the areas we have been discussing. These would include: continually assessing the values and ideologies that surround our research and theory (Ghoshal 2005), accepting that ethically in taking a particular standpoint we should "take responsibility for the impact (or lack of it) of our scholarship on the world" (Adler and Jermier 2005, p. 942), recognize that while the rigor–relevance debate "has persisted for several decades without substantive action" (Gulati 2007, p. 777) it is now ethically correct that "rigor and relevance" be "jointly valued" (Tushman and O'Reilly 2007, p. 772), and that when questioning the "self-serving ideologies" which have surrounded organizational leadership (Ashford and Anand, 2003, p. 1) it is clear that we have an ethical responsibility to return to leadership that infuses "purpose and meaning into the organizational experience" (Podolny *et al.* 2005, p. 5) and begins to reestablish the importance of meaningful actions and the necessity of an authentic leadership style (Avolio and Gardener 2005).

Considering our moral responsibilities from an ethical standpoint also requires that we continue to review and evaluate our competence to do research at a personal level, ensuring that by meeting the needs of one group through the questions we ask and the measures we use we are not failing in our responsibilities to another (Cooper and Dewe 2004), that we shed any sense of "methodological preciousness" (Lazarus 1999) which suggests that there is one best way to do research and simply leads to a narrowness of interest and purpose, and that we balance our responsibilities to contribute to the practice of management with responsibilities we have to contribute to "public policies promoting human welfare" (Brief and Cortina 2000, p. 4) that do not always attract the attention they deserve. As much of the work cited suggests, change is occurring: researchers are using their creative talents to identify ways forward, and are engaging in robust, and at times passionate, debate about how such change is accepted and operationalized. However, this change is something that should be engaged in by all and not simply be left to the few, for to do so would be to maintain a status quo that is constantly being questioned in terms of its moral, ethical, empirical, and practical relevance.

REFERENCES

Adler, P. and Jermier, J. (2005) Developing a field with more soul: Standpoint theory and public policy research for management scholars. *Academy of Management Journal* 48, 941–944.

Aldwin, C. M. (2000) *Stress, coping, and development: An integrative perspective.* New York: The Guilford Press.

Aldwin, C. M. (2009) *Stress, coping, and development: An integrative perspective,* 2nd edn. New York: The Guilford Press.

Alexandrova, A. (2005) Subjective well-being and Kuhneman's "objective happiness." *Journal of Happiness Studies* 6, 301–324.

Ambrose, M. L. and Kulik, C. T. (1999) Old friends, new faces: Motivation research in the 1990s. *Journal of Management* 25, 231–292.

Antoniou, A. and Cooper, C. L. (eds.) (2005) *Research Companion to Organizational Health Psychology.* Cheltenham: Edward Elgar.

Arnold, J., Cooper, C., and Robertson, I. T. (1998) *Work psychology: Understanding human behaviour in the workplace.* Harlow: Financial Times/Prentice Hall.

Aronson, E. (2001) Integrating leadership styles and ethical perspectives. *Canadian Journal of Administrative Sciences* 18, 244–256.

Ashford, B. E. and Anand, V. (2003) The normalization of corruption in organizations. *Research in Organizational Behavior* 25, 1–52.

Ashforth, B. A. and Humphrey, R. H. (1995) Emotion in the workplace: A reappraisal. *Human Relations* 48, 97–125.

Ashforth, B. A. and Kreiner, G. L. (2002) Normalizing emotions in organizations: Making the extraordinary seem ordinary. *Human Resource Management Review* 12, 215–235.

Aspinwall, L. G. (2011) Future-oriented thinking, proactive coping and the management of potential threats to health and well-being. In S. Folkman (ed.) *The Oxford handbook of stress, health, and coping.* (pp. 334–365). Oxford: Oxford University Press.

Aspinwall, L. G. and Taylor, S. (1997) A stitch in time: Self-regulation and proactive coping. *Psychological Bulletin* 121, 417–436.

Avey, J. B., Luthans, F., and Jensen, S. M. (2009) Psychological capital: A positive resource for combating employee stress and turnover. *Human Resource Management* 48, 677–693.

Avolio, B. J. and Gardner W. L. (2005) Authentic leadership development: Getting to the root of positive forms of leadership. *The Leadership Quarterly* 16, 315–338.

Bacon, S. F. (2005) Positive psychology's two cultures. *Review of General Psychology* 9, 181–192.

Bakker, A. B. and Schaufeli, W. B. (2008) Positive organizational behavior: Engaged employees in flourishing organizations. *Journal of Organizational Behavior* 29, 147–154.

Bakker, A. B., Albrecht, S. L., and Leiter, M. P. (2011a) Key questions regarding work engagement. *European Journal of Work and Organizational Psychology* 20, 4–28.

Bakker, A. B., Albrecht, S. L., and Leiter, M. P. (2011b) Work engagement: further reflections on the state of play. *European Journal of Work and Organizational Psychology* 20, 74–88.

Barber, B. (2009) A trade union agenda for good work. In D. Coats (ed.) *Advancing opportunity: The future of good work.* (pp. 66–71). London: The Smith Institute.

Barling, J., Kelloway, E. K., and Frone, M. (2005) Editors' overview: Sources of work stress. In J. Barling, E. K. Kelloway, and M. R. Frone (eds.) *Handbook of work stress.* (pp. 3–5). Thousand Oaks, CA: Sage Publications.

Barsade, S. G. and Gibson, D. E. (2007) Why does affect matter in organizations? *Academy of Management Perspectives* 21, 36–59.

Barsade, S. G., Brief, A. P., and Spataro, S. E. (2003) The affective revolution in organizational behavior: The emergence of a paradigm. In J. Greenberg (ed.) *Organizational behavior: The state of the science.* (pp. 3–52). Mahwah, NJ: Lawrence Erlbaum.

Bar-Tal, Y. and Spitzer, A. (1994) Coping use versus effectiveness as moderating the stress–strain relationship. *Journal of Community and Applied Social Psychology* 4, 91–100.

Beehr, T. A. (1998) Research on occupational stress: An unfinished enterprise. *Personnel Psychology* 51, 835–844.

Beehr, T. A. and Grebner, S. L. (2009) When stress is less (harmful). In A. S. G. Antoniou, C. L. Cooper, G. P. Chrousos, C. D. Spielberger, and M. W. Eysenck (eds.) *Handbook of managerial behavior and occupational stress.* (pp. 20–34). Cheltenham: Edward Elgar.

Beehr, T. A. and McGrath, J. E. (1996) The methodology of research on coping: Conceptual, strategic, and operational-level issues. In M. Zeidner and N. Endler (eds.), *Handbook of coping: Theory, research, applications.* (pp. 65–82). New York: John Wiley.

Beehr, T. A. and Newman, J. E. (1978) Job stress, employee health, and organizational effectiveness: A facet analysis, model, and literature review. *Personnel Psychology* 31, 665–699.

Bellavia, G. M. and Frone, M. R. (2005) Work–family conflict. In J. Barling, E. K. Kelloway, and M. R. Frone (eds.), *Handbook of work stress.* (pp. 113–147). Thousand Oaks, CA: Sage Publications.

Belschak, F. K., Den Hartog, D. N., and Fay, D. (2010) Exploring positive, negative and context-dependent aspects of proactive behaviors at work. *Journal of Occupational and Organizational Psychology* 83, 267–273.

Berg, C. A., Weibe, D. J., Bloor, L., Bradstreet, C., Upchurch, R., Hayes, J., Stephenson, R., Nail, L., and Patton, G. (2008) Collaborative coping and daily mood in couples dealing with prostate cancer. *Psychology and Aging* 23, 505–516.

Bernstein, S. D. (2003) Positive organizational scholarship: Meet the movement. *Journal of Management Inquiry* 12, 266–271.

Bevan, S. (2010) *The business case for employee wellbeing*. A report prepared for Investors in People. London: The Work Foundation.

Bhagat, R. S., Allie, S. M., and Ford, D. L. (1991) An enquiry into the moderating role of styles of coping. In P. L. Perrewé (ed.), *Handbook on job stress* [Special Issue]. *Journal of Social Behaviour and Personality* 6, 163–185.

Billings, A., and Moos, R. (1984) Coping, stress and social resources among depression. *Journal of Personality and Social Psychology* 46, 877–891.

Biron, C., Cooper, C. L., and Gibbs, P. (2011) Stress interventions versus positive interventions: Apples and oranges. In K. S. Cameron (ed.), *The Oxford handbook of positive organizational scholarship*. (pp. 938–950). Oxford: Oxford University Press.

Black, C. (2008) *Working for a healthier tomorrow: Review of the health of Britain's working age population*. Presented to the Secretary of State for Health and the Secretary of State for Work and Pensions. London: TSO.

Boatman, J. E. and Sinar, E. F. (2011) The path to meaningful evidence. *Industrial and Organizational Psychology* 4, 66–71.

Bohart, A. C. and Greening, T. (2001) Humanistic psychology and positive psychology. *American Psychologist* 56, 81–82.

Bolino, M., Valcea, S., and Harvey, J. (2010) Employee manage thyself: The potentially negative implications of expecting employees to behave proactively. *Journal of Occupational and Organizational Psychology* 83, 325–345.

Bonanno, G. A. (2004) Loss, trauma, and human resilience: Have we under-estimated the human capacity to thrive after extremely adverse events? *American Psychologist* 59, 20–28.

Bonanno, G. A. (2008) Loss, trauma, and human resilience: Have we under-estimated the human capacity to thrive after extremely aversive events? *Psychological Trauma: Theory, Research, Practice, and Policy* Vol. S(1), 101–113.

Bowles, D. and Cooper, C. L. (2009) *Employee Morale: Driving performance in challenging times*. Basingstoke: Palgrave Macmillan.

Brewster-Smith, M. (2003) Positive Psychology: Documentation of a burgeoning movement. *American Journal of Psychology* 116, 159–163.

Brief, A. P. and Cortina, J. (2000) Research ethics: A place to begin. *The Academy of Management Research Methods Divisional Newsletter* 15, 1; 4; 11–12.

Brief, A. P. and George, J. M. (1991) Psychological stress and the workplace: A brief comment on Lazarus' outlook. In P. L. Perrewé (ed.), *Handbook on job stress* [Special Issue]. *Journal of Social Behaviour and Personality* 6, 15–20.

Brief, A. P. and Weiss, H. M. (2002) Organizational behavior: Affect in the workplace. *Annual Review of Psychology* 53, 279–307.

Briner, R. B. and Rousseau, D. M. (2011a) Evidence-based I-O Psychology: Not there yet. *Industrial and Organizational Psychology* 4, 3–22.

Briner, R. B. and Rousseau, D. M. (2011b) Evidence-based I-O Psychology: Not there yet but now a little closer. *Industrial and Organizational Psychology* 4, 76–82.

Brinkley, I., Fauth, R., Mahdon, M., and Theodoropoulou, S. (2010) *Is knowledge work better for us? Knowledge workers, good work and wellbeing.* London: The Work Foundation.

Brough, P., O'Driscoll, M. P., Kalliath, T., Cooper, C. L., and Poelmans, S. A. Y. (eds.) (2009) *Workplace psychological health: Current research and practice.* Cheltenham: Edward Elgar.

Brown, A., Charlwood, C., Forde, C., and Spencer, D. (2006) *Changing job quality in Great Britain 1998–2004.* DTI: Employment Relations Research Series No 70, London.

Burke, R. J. (1988) Sources of managerial and professional stress in large organizations. In C. L. Cooper and R. Payne (eds.), *Causes, coping and consequences of stress at work.* (pp. 77–114). Chichester: John Wiley.

Burke, R. J. (2002) Work stress and coping in organizations: Progress and prospects. In E. Frydenberg (ed.), *Beyond coping: Meeting goals, visions, and challenges.* (pp. 83–106). Oxford: Oxford University Press.

Burke, R. and Cooper, C. (eds.) (2008) *The long work hours culture: Causes, consequences, and choices.* Bingley: Emerald.

Cameron, K. S., and Caza, A. (2004) Contributions to the discipline of Positive Organizational scholarship. *American Behavioral Scientist* 47, 731–739.

Cameron, K. S., Dutton, J. E., and Quinn, R. E. (2003) *Positive organizational scholarship: Foundations of a new discipline.* San Francisco: Berrett-Koehler.

Cassell, C. (2011) Evidenced based I-O Psychology: What do we lose on the way? *Industrial and Organizational Psychology* 4, 23–26.

Cassidy, T. (1999) *Stress, cognition and health.* London: Routledge.

Catano, V. M. (2011) Evidence-based I-O Psychology: Lessons from clinical psychology. *Industrial and Organizational Psychology* 4, 45–48.

Chandola, T. (2010) *Stress at work.* A report prepared for the British Academy. London: British Academy.

Chartered Institute of Personnel and Development (2002) *Sustaining success in difficult times:* Research summary. London: CIPD.

Chartered Institute of Personnel and Development (2007) *A barometer of HR trends and prospects 2007*: Overview of CIPD surveys. CIPD Chartered Institute of Personnel and Development, London.

Chartered Institute of Personnel and Development (2011) *Preventing stress: promoting positive manager behaviour.* Research Insight July CIPD.

Cheng, G. H-L., and Chan, D. K-S., (2008) Who suffers more from job insecurity? A meta-analytic review. *Applied Psychology: An international review* 57, 272–303.

Coats, D. (2009) Good work in recessionary times. In D. Coats (ed.), *Advancing opportunity: The future of good work.* (pp. 6–12). London: The Smith Institute.

Coats, D., and Lekhi, R. (2008) *"Good Work": job quality in a changing economy.* London: The Work Foundation.

Collins Dictionary and Thesaurus (1992) Glasgow: HarperCollins.

Confederation of British Industry (2007) *Employment trends survey 2007: Fit for Business.* London.

Constable, S., Coats, D., Bevan, S., and Mahdon, M. (2009) *Good jobs.* London: The Work Foundation.

Cooper, C. L. and Cartwright, S. (1994) Healthy mind, healthy organization – A proactive approach to occupational stress. *Human Relations* 47, 45–471.

Cooper, C. L. and Dewe, P. (2004) *Stress: A brief history*. Oxford: Blackwell.

Cooper, C. L. and Dewe, P. (2008) Well-being: Absenteeism, presenteeism, costs and challenges. *Occupational Medicine* 58, 522–524.

Cooper, C. L. and Marshall, J. (1976) Occupational sources of stress: a review of the literature relating to coronary heart disease and mental ill health. *Journal of Occupational Psychology* 49, 11–28.

Cooper, C. L., Dewe, P., and O'Driscoll, M. (2001) *Organizational Stress: A review and critique of theory, research, and applications*. Thousand Oaks, CA: Sage.

Coovert, M. D., Thompson, L. F., and Craiger, J. P. (2005) Technology. In J. Barling, E. K. Kelloway, and M. R. Frone (eds.) *Handbook of work stress*. (pp. 299–324). Thousand Oaks, CA: Sage.

Corley, K. G. and Gioia, D. A. (2011) Building theory about theory building: What constitutes a theoretical contribution? *Academy of Management Review* 36, 12–32.

Costa, P. T., Somerfield, M. R., and McCrae, R. R. (1996) Personality and coping: A reconceptualization. In M. Zeidner and N. M. Endler (eds.), *Handbook of coping: Theory, research, applications*. (pp. 44–61). New York: John Wiley.

Cousins, R., Mackay, C. J., Clarke, S. D., Kelly, C., Kelly, P. J., and McCaig, R. H. (2004) "Management standards" and work related stress in the UK: Practical development. *Work and Stress* 18, 113–136.

Coutu, D. L. (2002) How resilience works. *Harvard Business Review* 80, 46–55.

Cox, T. (1978) *Stress*. New York: Macmillan.

Coyle, D. and Quah, D. (2002) *Getting the measure of the new economy*. London: The Work Foundation.

Coyne, J. C. (1997) Improving coping research: Raze the slum before any more building! *Journal of Health Psychology* 2, 153–155.

Coyne, J. C. and Gottlieb, B. H. (1996) The mismeasure of coping by checklist. *Journal of Personality* 64, 959–991.

Coyne, J. C. and Racioppo, M. (2000) Never the twain shall meet? Closing the gap between coping research and clinical intervention research. *American Psychologist* 55, 655–664.

Cronin, M. A. and Klimoski, R. (2011) Broadening the view of what constitutes "evidence." *Industrial and Organizational Psychology* 4, 57–61.

Cropanzano, R., Goldman, B. M., and Benson, L. (2005) Organizational justice. In J. Barling, E. K. Kelloway, and M. R. Frone (eds.) *Handbook of work stress*. (pp. 63–87). Thousand Oaks, CA: Sage.

Csikszentmihalyi, M. (2003) Legs or wings? A reply to Richard Lazarus. *Psychological Inquiry* 14, 113–115.

Daniels, K. (2006) Rethinking job characteristics in work stress research. *Human Relations* 59, 267–290.

Davis, C. G., Nolen-Hoeksema, S., and Larson, J. (1998) Making sense of loss and benefit from the experience: Two construals of meaning. *Journal of Personality and Social Psychology* 75, 561–574.

Davis, J. S. (2010) Building the positive workplace: A preliminary report from the field. In P. A. Linley, S. Harrington, and N. Garcea (eds.) *Oxford handbook of positive psychology and work.* (pp. 289–298). Oxford: Oxford University Press.

DeAngelis, T. (2007) America: a toxic lifestyle. *Monitor on psychology* 38, 50.

Deci, E. L. and Ryan, R. M. (2000) The "what" and "why" of goal pursuits: Human needs and the self-determination of behavior. *Psychological Inquiry* 11, 227–268.

Dent, E., Higgins, M., and Wharf, D. (2005) Spirituality and leadership: An empirical review of definitions, distinctions, and embedded assumptions. *The Leadership Quarterly* 16, 625–653.

Dewe, P. (2001) Determinants of coping: Some alternative explanations and measurement issues. *Psychological Reports* 88, 832–834.

Dewe, P. (2003) A closer examination of the patterns when coping with work-related stress: Implications for measurement. *Journal of Occupational and Organizational Psychology* 76, 517–524.

Dewe, P. (2008) Positive coping strategies at work. In A. Kinder, R. Hughes, and C. Cooper (eds.), *Employee well-being support: A workplace resource.* (pp. 91–98). Chichester: John Wiley.

Dewe, P. and Brook, R. (2000) Sequential tree analysis of work stressors: exploring score profiles in the context of the stressor–strain relationship. *International Journal of Stress Management* 7, 1–18.

Dewe, P. and Cooper, C. (2007) Coping research and measurement in the context of work related stress. In G. Hodgkinson and J. Kevin Ford (eds.), *International Review of Industrial and Organizational Psychology* 22, 141–191.

Dewe, P., O'Driscoll, M., and Cooper, C. (2010) *Coping with work stress: A review and critique.* Chichester: Wiley-Blackwell.

Diener, E. (1984) Subjective well-being. *Psychological Bulletin* 95, 542–575.

Diener, E. (2000) Subjective well-being: The science of happiness and a proposal for a national index. *American Psychologist* 55, 34–43.

Diener, E. (2003) What is positive about Positive Psychology: The curmudgeon and pollyanna. *Psychological Inquiry* 14, 115–120.

Diener, E., Lucas, R. E., and Scollon, C. N. (2006) Beyond the hedonic treadmill: Revising the adaptation theory of well-being. *American Psychologist* 61, 305–314.

Diener, E., Oishi, S., and Lucas, R. E. (2003) Personality, culture, and subjective well-being: Emotional and cognitive evaluations of life. *Annual Review of Psychology* 54, 403–425.

Diener, E., Sapyta, J., and Suh, E. (1998) Subjective well-being is essential to well-being. *Psychological Inquiry* 9, 33–37.

Diener, E., Suh, E. M., Lucas, R. E., and Smith, H. L. (1999) Subjective well-being: Three decades of progress. *Psychological Bulletin* 125, 276–302.

Dolan, P., Peasgood, T., and White, M. (2008) "Do we really know what makes us happy" A review of the economic literature on the factors associated with subjective wellbeing. *Journal of Economic Psychology* 29, 94–122.

Donaldson, L. (2005) For positive management theories while retaining science: Reply to Ghoshal. *Academy of Management Learning and Education* 4, 109–113.

Dutton, J. E. (2003) Breathing life into organizational studies. *Journal of Management Inquiry* 12, 5–19.

Dutton, J. and Glynn, M. (2008) Positive Organizational Scholarship. In C. Cooper and J. Barling (eds.), *Handbook of Organizational Behavior.* (pp. 693–712). Thousand Oaks, CA: Sage.

Edwards, J. R. and Cooper, C. L. (1988) The impacts of positive psychological states on physical health: A review and theoretical framework. *Social Science and Medicine* 27, 1447–1459.

Elfenbein, H. A. (2007) Emotions in organizations: A review and theoretical integration. *The Academy of Management Annals* 1, 315–386.

Emery, F. E. and Trist, E. L. (1960) Socio-technical systems. In C. H. Churchman and M. Verhulst (eds.) *Management science, models and techniques* 2. (pp. 83–97). New York: Pergamon.

Eschleman, K. J., Bowling, N. A., and Alarcon, G. M. (2010) A meta-analytic examination of hardiness. *International Journal of Stress Management* 17, 277–307.

Ferris, G., Brouer, R. L., Laird, M. D., and Hochwarter, W. A. (2005) The consequences of organizational politics perceptions as a workplace stressor. In A. M Rossi, P. Perrewe, and S. Sauter (eds.), *Stress and the quality of working life: Current perspectives in occupational health.* (pp. 155–165). Greenwich, CT: Information Age.

Fineman, S. (2004) Getting the measure of emotion – and the cautionary tale of emotional intelligence. *Human Relations* 57, 719–740.

Fineman, S. (2006) On being positive: Concerns and Counterpoints. *Academy of Management Review* 31, 270–291.

Fleury, J. (1998) On promoting positive human health. *Psychological Inquiry* 9, 40–43.

Folkman, S. (1982) An approach to the measurement of coping. *Journal of Occupational Behaviour* 3, 95–107.

Folkman, S. (1992) Improving coping assessment: Reply to Stone and Kennedy-Moore. In H. S. Friedman (ed.), *Hostility, coping and health.* pp. 215–223. Washington: American Psychological Association.

Folkman, S. (2011) Stress, health, and coping: Synthesis, commentary, and future directions. In S. Folkman (ed.) *The Oxford handbook of stress, health, and coping.* (pp. 453–462). Oxford: Oxford University Press.

Folkman, S. and Lazarus, R. S. (1984) *Stress, appraisal and coping.* New York: Springer.

Folkman, S. and Lazarus, R. S. (1991) Coping and emotion. In A. Monat and R. S. Lazarus (eds.), *Stress and coping: An anthology.* (pp. 207–227). New York: Columbia University Press.

Folkman, S. and Moskowitz, J. T. (2000) The context matters. *Personality and Social Psychology Bulletin* 26, 150–151.

Folkman, S. and Moskowitz, J. T. (2003) Positive Psychology from a coping perspective. *Psychological Inquiry* 14, 121–125.

Folkman, S. and Moskowitz, J. T. (2004) Coping: Pitfalls and promise. *Annual Review of Psychology* 55, 745–774.

Folkman, S. and Moskowitz, J. T. (2007) Positive affect and meaning-focused coping, during significant psychological stress. In M. Hewstone, H. A. W. Schut, J. B. F de Wit, K. van den Bos, and M. S. Stroebe (eds.), *The scope of social psychology: Theory and applications.* (pp. 193–208). Hove and New York: Psychology Press.

Foresight Mental capital and Wellbeing Project (2008) *Final project Report.* London: The Government Office for Science.

Fox, S. and Spector, P. E. (2002) Emotions in the workplace: The neglected side of organizational life introduction. *Human Resource Management Review* 12, 167–171.

Fredrickson, B. L. (1998) What good are positive emotions? *Review of General Psychology* 2, 300–319.

Fredrickson, B. L. (2000) Cultivating positive emotions to optimize health and well-being. *Prevention and Treatment* 3, Article 1a, 1–25.

Fredrickson, B. L. (2000a) Cultivating research on positive emotions. *Prevention and Treatment* 3, Article 7, 1–5.

Fredrickson, B. L. (2001) The role of positive emotions in positive psychology: The broaden-and-build theory of positive emotions. *American Psychologist* 56, 218–226.

Fredrickson, B. L. (2003a) Positive emotions and upward spirals in organizations. In K. S. Cameron, J. E. Dutton, and R. E. Quinn (eds.), *Positive Organizational Scholarship: Foundations of a new discipline.* (pp. 163–175). San Francisco: Berrett-Koehler.

Fredrickson, B. L. (2003b) The value of positive emotions. *American Scientist* 91, 330–335.

Fredrickson, B. L. (2005) Positive emotions. In C. R. Snyder and S. J. Lopez (eds.), *Handbook of Positive Psychology.* (pp. 120–134). Oxford: Oxford University Press.

Fredrickson, B. L. (2006) Unpacking positive emotions: Investigating the seeds of human flourishing. *The Journal of Positive Psychology* 1, 57–59.

Fredrickson, B. L. (2009) *Positivity.* Oxford: Oneworld Publications.

Fredrickson, B. L. and Branigan, C. (2005) Positive emotions broaden the scope of attention and thought–action repertoires. *Cognition and Emotion* 19, 313–332.

Fredrickson, B. L. and Losada, M. F. (2005) Positive affect and the complex dynamics of human flourishing. *American Psychologist* 60, 678–686.

Frese, M. and Fay, D. (2001) Personal initiative: An active performance concept for work in the 21st Century. *Research in Organizational Behavior* 23, 133–187.

Frese, M. and Zapf, D. (1999) On the importance of the objective environment in stress and attribution theory. Counterpoint to Perrewe and Zellars. *Journal of Organizational Behavior* 20, 761–765.

Freund, A. M. and Riediger, M. (2001) What I have and what I do – The role of resource loss and gain throughout life. *Applied Psychology: An international review* 50, 370–380.

Fried, Y., Levi, A. S., and Laurence, G. (2008) Motivation and job design in the new world of work. In C. Cooper and S. Cartwright (eds.), *The Oxford handbook of personnel psychology.* (pp. 586–613). Oxford: Oxford University Press.

Fry, L. W. (2005) Toward a theory of ethical and spiritual well-being, and corporate social responsibility through spiritual leadership. In R. A. Giacalone and C. L. Jurkiewicz (eds.), *Positive psychology in business ethics and corporate responsibility.* Greenwich, CT: Information Age.

Frydenberg, E. (2002) Success and achievement: Factors that contribute to positive outcomes. In E. Frydenberg (ed.) *Beyond coping: Meeting goals, visions, and challenges.* (pp. 219–240). New York: Oxford University Press.

Fulmer, R. M. (2004) The challenge of ethical leadership. *Organizational Dynamics* 33, 307–317.

Gable, S. L. and Haidt, J. (2005) What (and why) is Positive Psychology? *Review of General Psychology* 9, 102–110.

Gallup Management Journal (2007) Hope, optimism, and other business assets: Why "psychological capital" is so valuable to your company. A GMJ/Q&A with Fred Luthans. January 11, 2007.

Gapper, J. (2005) Comment on Sumantra Ghoshal's "Bad management theories are destroying good management practices." *Academy of Management Learning and Education* 4, 101–103.

Garcea, N., Harrington, S., and Linley, P. A. (2010) Building positive organizations. In P. A. Linley, S. Harrington, and N. Garcea. (eds.) *Oxford handbook of positive psychology and work.* (pp. 323–333). Oxford: Oxford University Press.

Gardner, W. L. and Schermerhorn, J. R. (2004) Performance gains through positive organizational behavior and authentic leadership. *Organizational Dynamics* 33, 270–281.

Gardner, W. L., Avolio, B. J., Luthans, F., May, D. R., and Walumbwa, F. (2005) "Can you see the real me?" A self-based model of authentic leader and follower development. *The Leadership Quarterly* 16, 343–372.

George, J. (2004) Book Review: Positive Organizational Scholarship: Foundations of a new discipline. *Administrative Science Quarterly* 49, 325–330.

George, J. M. (2011) The wider context, costs, and benefits of work engagement. *European Journal of Work and Organizational Psychology* 20, 53–59.

Ghoshal, S. (2005) Bad management theories are destroying good management practices. *Academy of Management Learning and Education* 4, 75–91.

Giacalone, R. A., Jurkiewicz, C. L., and Dunn, C. (2005) *Positive psychology in business ethics and corporate responsibility.* Charlotte, NC: Information Age.

Glowinkowski, S. P. and Cooper, C. L. (1985) Current issues in organizational stress research. *Bulletin of the British Psychological Society* 38, 212–216.

Grant, A. M. (2007) Relational job design and the motivation to make a prosocial difference. *Academy of Management Review* 32, 393–417.

Grant, A. M. (2008a) Designing jobs to do good: Dimensions and psychological consequences of prosocial job characteristics. *The Journal of Positive Psychology* 3, 19–39.

Grant, A. M. (2008b) Does intrinsic, motivation fuel the prosocial fire? Motivational synergy in predicting persistence, performance, and productivity. *Journal of Applied Psychology* 93, 48–58.

Grant, A. M. and Ashford, S. J. (2008) The dynamics of proactivity at work. *Research in Organizational Behavior* 28, 3–34.

Grant, A. M. and Parker, S. K. (2009) Redesigning work design theories: The rise of relational and proactive perspectives. *The Academy of Management Annals* 3, 317–375.

Grant, A. M. and Spence, G. B. (2010) Using coaching and positive psychology to promote a flourishing workforce: A model of goal-striving and mental health. In P. A. Linley, S. Harrington, and N. Garcea (eds.), *Oxford handbook of positive psychology and work.* (pp. 175–188). Oxford: Oxford University Press.

Grant, A. M., Christianson, M. K., and Price, R. H. (2007) Happiness, health, or relationships? Managerial practices and employee well-being tradeoffs. *Academy of Management Perspectives* 21, 51–63.

Grant, A. M., Fried, Y., and Juillerat, T. (2008) Work matters: Job design in classic and contemporary perspectives. In S. Zedeck (ed.), *APA Handbook of Industrial and Organizational Psychology* 1. (pp. 417–453). Washington, DC: American Psychological Association.

Grant, A. M., Fried, Y., Parker, S. K., and Frese, M. (2010) Putting job design in context: Introduction to the special issue. *Journal of Organizational Behavior* 31, 145–157.

Grant, J. M. (2000) Proactive behavior in organizations. *Journal of Management* 26, 435–462.

Greenglass, E. R. (2002) Proactive coping and quality of life management. In E. Frydenberg (ed.), *Beyond coping: Meeting goals, visions, and challenges.* (pp. 37–62). New York: Oxford University Press.

Griffin, M. A., Neal, A., and Parker, S. K. (2007) A new model of work role performance: Positive behavior in uncertain and interdependent contexts. *Academy of Management Journal* 50, 327–347.

Gulati, R. (2007) Tent poles, tribalism, and boundary spanning: The rigor-relevance debate in management research. *Academy of Management Journal* 50, 775–782.

Hackman, J. R. (2009a) The perils of positivity. *Journal of Organizational Behavior* 30, 309–319.

Hackman, J. R. (2009b) The point of POB: Rejoiner. *Journal of Organizational Behavior* 30, 321–322.

Hackman, J. R. and Lawler, E. E. (1971) Employee reactions to job characteristics. *Journal of Applied Psychology* 55, 259–286.

Hackman, J. R. and Oldham, G. R. (1976) Motivation through the design of work: Test of a theory. *Organizational Behavior and Human Performance* 16, 250–279.

Hackman, J. R. and Oldham, G. R. (1980) *Work design.* Reading, MA: Addison-Wesley.

Haidt, J. (2000) The positive emotion of elevation. *Prevention and Treatment* 3, Article 3, 1–5.

Halbesleben, J. R. B. (2011) The consequences of engagement: The good, the bad, and ugly. *European Journal of Work and Organizational Psychology* 20, 68–73.

Hambrick, D. C. (2005) Just how bad are our theories? A response to Ghoshal. *Academy of Management Learning and Education* 4, 104–107.

Harris, J. (1991) The utility of the transactional approach for occupational stress research. In P. Perrewé (ed.), *Handbook on job stress* [Special Issue]. *Journal of Social Behavior and Personality* 6, 21–29.

Harris, K. and Kacmar, K. M. (2005) Organizational politics. In J. Barling, E. K. Kelloway, and M. R. Frone (eds.), *Handbook of work stress.* (pp. 353–374). Thousand Oaks: Sage.

Haward, L. (1960) The subjective meaning of stress. *British Journal of Psychology* 33, 185–194.

Hayman, A. (2008) Major job losses forecast for all of England. *Regeneration and Renewal*, November 7, 2008. http://www.egen.net/news/Email/ThisArticle/859991/. [accessed December 5 , 2011].

Held, B. (2004) The negative side of Positive Psychology. *Journal of Humanistic Psychology* 44, 9–46.

Helgeson, V. S. (2011) Gender, stress, and coping In S. Folkman (ed.), *The Oxford handbook of stress, health, and coping.* (pp. 63–85). Oxford: Oxford University Press.

Hellgren, J., Sverke, M., and Naswall, K. (2008) Changing work roles: new demands and challenges. In K. Naswall, J. Hellgren, and M. Sverke (eds.), *The individual in the changing work life.* (pp. 46–66). Cambridge: Cambridge University Press.

Herzberg, F. (1966) *Work and the nature of man.* Oxford: World Publishing.

Hill, D., Tyers, L. D., and James, L. (2007) *What works at work?* Health Work and Well-being Report: Institute for Employment Studies: November.

Hobfoll, S. E. (1989) Conservation of resources: A new attempt at conceptualizing stress. *American Psychologist* 44, 513–524.

Hobfoll, S. E. (2001) The influence of culture, community, and the nested-self in the stress process: Advancing conservation of resources theory. *Applied Psychology: An international review* 50, 337–421.

Hobfoll, S. E. (2011) Conservation of resources theory: Its implications for stress, health, and resilience. In S. Folkman (ed.), *The Oxford handbook of stress, health, and coping.* (pp. 127–147). Oxford: Oxford University Press.

Hodges, T. D. and Asplund, J. (2010) Strengths development in the workplace. In P. A. Linley, S. Harrington, and N. Garcea (eds.), *Oxford handbook of positive psychology and work.* (pp. 213–220). Oxford: Oxford University Press.

Hodges, T. D. and Clifton, D. O. (2004) Strengths-based development in practice. In P. A. Linley and S. Joseph (eds.), *Positive psychology in practice.* (pp. 256–268). Hoboken, NJ: John Wiley.

Hodgkinson, G. P. (2011) Why evidence-based practice in I-O Psychology is not there yet: Going beyond systematic reviews. *Industrial and Organizational Psychology* 4, 49–53.

Holroyd, K. and Lazarus, R. (1982) Stress, coping and somatic adaptation. In L. Goldberger and S. Breznitz (eds.), *Handbook of stress: Theoretical and clinical aspects.* (pp. 21–35). New York: Free Press.

Humphrey, S. E., Nahrgang, J. D., and Morgeson, F. P. (2007) Integrating motivational, social, and contextual work design features: A meta-analytic

175

summary and theoretical extension of the work design literature. *Journal of Applied Psychology* 92, 1332–1356.

Inness, M. and Barling, J. (2005) Terrorism. In J. Barling, E. K. Kelloway, and M. R. Frone (eds.), *Handbook of work stress.* (pp. 375–397). Thousand Oaks: Sage.

James, W. (1902) *The varieties of religious experience: A study in human nature.* New York: Longmans, Green and Co.

Jones, A., Visser, F., Coats, Bevan, S., and McVerry, A. (2007) *Transforming work: reviewing the case for change and new ways of working.* Working Paper Series No. 60. London: The Work Foundation.

Jones, F. and Bright, J. (2001) *Stress: Myth, theory and research.* Harlow: Prentice-Hall.

Kahn, R., Wolfe, D., Quinn, R., Snoek, J., and Rosenthal, R. (1964) *Organizational stress: Studies in role conflict and ambiguity.* New York: John Wiley.

Kanter, R. M. (2005) What theories do audiences want? Exploring the demand side. *Academy of Management Learning and Education* 4, 93–95.

Kanungo, R. N. (2001) Ethical values of transactional and transformational leaders. *Canadian Journal of Administrative Sciences* 18, 257–265.

Kaplan, H. (1996) Themes, lacunae and directions in research on psychological stress. In H. Kaplan (ed.), *Psychosocial stress: Perspectives on structure, theory, life courses and methods.* (pp. 369–401). New York: Academic Press.

Kasl, S. V. (1983) Perusing the link between stressful life experiences and disease: A time for reappraisal. In C. L. Cooper (ed.), *Stress research: Issues for the eighties.* (pp. 79–102). Chichester: John Wiley.

Kauffman, C., and Scoular, A. (2004) Toward a positive psychology of executive coaching. In P. A. Linley and S. Joseph (eds.), *Positive psychology in practice.* (pp. 287–302). Hoboken, NJ: John Wiley.

Kesebir, P. and Diener, E. (2008) In pursuit of happiness: Empirical answers to philosophical questions. *Perspectives on Psychological Science* 3, 117–125.

Keyes, C. L. M. (1998) Social well-being. *Social Psychology Quarterly* 61, 121–140.

Keyes, C. L. M. (2002) The mental health continuum: From languishing to flourishing in life. *Journal of Health and Social Research* 43, 207–222.

Keyes, C. L. M. and Lopez, S. J. (2005) Toward a science of mental health: Positive directions in diagnosis and interventions. In C. R. Snyder and S. Lopez (eds.), *Handbook of positive psychology.* (pp. 45–59). Oxford: Oxford University Press.

Keyes, C. L., Shmotkin, D., and Ryff, C. D. (2002) Optimizing well-being: The empirical encounter of two traditions. *Journal of Personality and Social Psychology* 82, 1007–1022.

King, L. A. (2000) Why happiness is good for you: A commentary on Fredrickson. *Prevention and Treatment* 3, Article 4, 1–4.

King, L. A. (2003) Some truths behind the trombones? *Psychological Inquiry* 14, 128–131.

Kinder, A., Hughes, R., and Cooper, C. L. (eds.) (2008) *Employee well-being support: A workplace support.* Chichester: John Wiley.

Kivimaki, M. *et al.* (2003) Temporary employment and risk of overall and cause specific mortality. *American Journal of Epidemiology* 158 (7), 663–668.

Kobasa, S. C. (1979) Stressful life events, personality and health: An inquiry into hardiness. *Journal of Personality and Social Psychology* 37, 1–11.

Kobasa, S. C. (2003) Stress hardiness. *Consciousone*. http://www.consciousone. com/authorarticles.cfm?aid=53andpartid=138 [accessed December 6, 2011].

Kobasa, S. C., and Maddi, S. R. (1977) Existential personality theory. In R. J. Corsini (ed.), *Current personality theories*. (pp. 243–276). Itasca, IL: F. E. Peacock.

Kobasa, S. C., Maddi, S. R., and Kahn, S. (1982) Hardiness and health: A prospective study. *Journal of Personality and Social Psychology* 42, 168–177.

Koltko-Rivera, M. K. (2006) Rediscovering the later version of Maslow's hierarchy of needs: Self-transcendence and opportunities for theory, research, and unification. *Review of General Psychology* 10, 302–317.

Kompier, M., and Cooper, C. (eds.) (1999) *Preventing stress, improving productivity*. London: Routledge.

Latack, J. and Havlovic, S. (1992) Coping with job stress: A conceptual evaluation framework for coping measures. *Journal of Organizational Behavior* 13, 479–508.

Layard, R. (2006) Happiness and public policy. *Economic Journal* 116, 24–33.

Lazarus, R. S. (1966) *Psychological stress and the coping process*. New York: McGraw-Hill.

Lazarus, R. S. (1990) Theory-based stress measurement. *Psychological Inquiry* 1, 3–12.

Lazarus, R. S. (1991) Psychological stress in the workplace. *Journal of Social Behavior and Personality* 6, 1–13.

Lazarus, R. S. (1993a) Coping theory and research: Past, present and future. *Psychosomatic Medicine* 55, 234–247.

Lazarus, R. S. (1993b) From psychological stress to the emotions: A history of changing outlooks. *Annual Review of Psychology* 44, 1–21.

Lazarus, R. S. (1995) Vexing research problems inherent in cognitive-mediational theories of emotion – and some solutions. *Psychological Inquiry* 6, 183–196.

Lazarus, R. S. (1997) Hurrah for a systems approach. *Journal of Health Psychology* 2, 158–160.

Lazarus, R. S. (1998) *Fifty years of the research and theory of R. S. Lazarus: An analysis of historical and perennial issues*. Mahwah, NJ: Lawrence Erlbaum.

Lazarus, R. S. (1999) *Stress and emotion: a new synthesis*. London: Free Association.

Lazarus, R. S. (2000) Toward better research on stress and coping. *American Psychologist* 55, 665–673.

Lazarus, R. S. (2001a) Conservation of resources theory (COR): Little more than words masquerading as a new theory. *Applied Psychology: An International Review* 50, 381–391.

Lazarus, R. S. (2001b) Relational meaning and discrete emotions. In K. Scherer, A. Schorr, and T. Johnstone (eds.), *Appraisal processes in emotion: Theory, methods, research*. (pp. 37–67). New York: Oxford University Press.

Lazarus, R. S. (2003a) Does the Positive Psychology movement have legs? *Psychological Inquiry* 14, 93–109.

Lazarus, R. S. (2003b) The Lazarus manifesto for Positive Psychology and Psychology in general. *Psychological Inquiry* 14, 173–189.

Lazarus, R. S. and Cohen-Charash, Y. (2001) Discrete emotions in organizational life. In R. Payne and C. Cooper (eds.), *Emotions at work: theory, research and applications for management.* (pp. 45–81). Chichester: John Wiley.

Lazarus, R. S. and Folkman, S. (1984) *Stress, appraisal and coping.* New York: Springer.

Lazarus, R. S. and Folkman, S. (1991) The concept of coping. In A. Monet and R. S. Lazarus (eds.), *Stress and coping: An anthology.* (pp. 189–206). New York: Columbia University Press.

Lee, F., Caza, A., Edmondson, A., and Thomke, S. (2003) New knowledge creation in organizations. In K. Cameron, J. Dutton, and R. E. Quinn (eds.), *Positive organizational scholarship.* (pp. 194–206). San Francisco: Berrett-Koehler.

Linley, P. A. and Joseph, S. (2004a) Applied positive psychology: A new perspective for professional practice. In P. A. Linley and S. Joseph (eds.), *Positive psychology in practice.* (pp. 3–12). Hoboken, NJ: John Wiley.

Linley, P. A. and Joseph, S. (eds.) (2004b) *Positive psychology in practice.* Hoboken, NJ: John Wiley.

Linley, P. A. and Joseph, S. (2005) The human capacity for growth through adversity. *American Psychologist* 60, 262–264.

Linley, P. A., Joseph, S., Harrington, S., and Wood, A. M. (2006) Positive Psychology: Past, present, and (possible) future. *Journal of Positive Psychology* 1, 3–16.

Locke, E. A. (1976) The nature and causes of job satisfaction. In M. Dunnette (ed.), *Handbook of Industrial and Organizational Psychology.* (pp. 1297–1349). Chicago: Rand-McNally.

Logsdon, J. M. and Young, J. E. (2005) Executive influence on ethical culture. In R. A. Giacalone, C. L. Jurkiewicz, and C. Dunn (eds.), *Positive psychology in business ethics and corporate responsibility.* (pp. 103–122). Charlotte, NC: Information Age.

Long, B. (1993) Coping strategies of male managers: A prospective analysis of predictors of psychosomatic symptoms and job satisfactions. *Journal of Vocational Behavior* 42, 184–199.

Lorenzi, P. (2004) Managing for the common good: Prosocial Leadership. *Organizational Dynamics* 33, 282–291.

Lucas, R. E., Diener, E., and Suh, E. (1996) Discriminant validity of well-being measures. *Journal of Personality and Social Psychology* 71, 616–628.

Lundberg, U. and Cooper, C. L. (2010) *The Science of Occupational Health: Stress, Psychobiology and the New World of Work.* Oxford: Wiley-Blackwell.

Luthans, F. (2002a) The need for and meaning of positive organizational behavior. *Journal of Organizational Behavior* 23, 695–706.

Luthans, F. (2002b) Positive Organizational Behavior: Developing and managing psychological strengths. *Academy of Management Executive* 16, 57–72.

Luthans, F. and Avolio, B. J. (2003a) Authentic leadership development. In K. Cameron, J. Dutton, and R. E. Quinn (eds.), *Positive organizational scholarship.* (pp. 241–258). San Francisco: Berrett-Koehler.

Luthans, F. and Avolio, B. J. (2003b) Inquiry unplugged: Building on Hackman's potential perils of POB. *Journal of Organizational Behavior* 30, 323–328.

Luthans, F. and Avolio, B. J. (2009a) Inquiry unplugged: Building on Hackman's potential perils of POB. *Journal of Organizational Behavior* 30, 323–328.

Luthans, F. and Avolio, B. J. (2009b) The "point" of Positive Organizational Behavior. *Journal of Organizational Behavior* 30, 291–307.

Luthans, F. and Youssef, C. M. (2004) Investing in people for competitive advantage. *Organizational Dynamics* 33, 143–160.

Luthans, F., Luthans, K. W., and Luthans, B. C. (2004) Positive psychological capital: Beyond human and social capital. *Business Horizons* 47, 45–50.

Luthans, F., Vogelgesang, G. R., and Lester, P. B. (2006) Developing the psychological capital of resiliency. *Human Resources Development Review* 5, 25–44.

Luthans, F., Youssef, C. M., and Avolio, B. J. (2007a) *Psychological capital: Developing the human edge.* Oxford: Oxford University Press.

Luthans, F., Avolio, B. J., Avey, J. B., and Norman, S. M. (2007b) Psychological capital: Measurement and relationship with performance and job satisfaction. *Personnel Psychology* 60, 541–572.

Lyubomirsky, S. L. (2000) On studying positive emotions. *Prevention and Treatment* 3, Article 5, 1–5.

Lyubomirsky, S. L. (2001) Why are some people happier than others? The role of cognition and motivational processes in well-being. *American Psychologist* 56, 239–249.

Lyubomirsky, S. and Abbe, A. (2003) Positive Psychology's legs. *Psychological Inquiry* 14, 132–136.

Lyubomirsky, S., Sheldon, K. M., and Schkade, D. (2005) Pursuing happiness: The architecture of sustainable change. *Review of General Psychology* 9, 111–131.

Mackay, C. J., Cousins, R., Kelly, P. J., Lee, S., and McCaig, R. H. (2004) Management standards and work-related stress in the UK: Policy background and science. *Work and Stress* 18, 91–112.

Maddi, S. R. (1999a) Comments on trends in hardiness research and theorizing. *Consulting Psychology Journal* 51, 67–71.

Maddi, S. R. (1999b) The personality construct of hardiness: 1. Effects on experiencing, coping, and strain. *Consulting Psychology Journal* 51, 83–94.

Maddi, S. R. (2002) The story of hardiness: Twenty years of theorizing, research and practice. *Consulting Psychology Journal* 54, 173–185.

Maddi, S. R. (2005) On hardiness and other pathways to resilience. *American Psychologist* 60, 261–262.

Maddi, S. R. (2006) Hardiness: The courage to grow from stresses. *The Journal of Positive Psychology* 1, 160–168.

Maddi, S. R. and Hightower, M. (1999) Hardiness and optimism as expressed in coping patterns. *Consulting Psychology Journal* 52, 95–105.

Maddi, S. R. and Khoshaba, D. M. (1994) Hardiness and mental health. *Journal of Personality Assessment* 63, 265–274.

Maddi, S. R., Khoshaba, D. M., and Pammenter, A. (1999) The hardy organization: Success by turning change to advantage. *Consulting Psychology Journal* 51, 117–124.

179

Marianetti, O. and Passmore, J. (2010) Mindfulness at work: Paying attention to enhance well-being and performance. In P. A. Linley, S. Harrington, and N. Garcea (eds.), *Oxford handbook of positive psychology and work*. (pp. 189–200). Oxford: Oxford University Press.

Maslow, A. H. (1954) *Motivation and personality*. New York: Harper.

Maslow, A. H. (1968) *Toward a psychology of being*. New York: Van Nostrand Reinhold.

Mason, J. (1971) A re-evaluation of the concept of "non-specificity" in stress theory. *Journal of Psychiatric Research* 8, 323–353.

Masten, A. S. (2001) Ordinary magic: Resilience process in development. *American Psychologist* 56, 227–239.

Masten, A. S. and Reed, M. J. (2005) Resilience in development. In C. R. Snyder and S. Lopez (eds.), *Handbook of positive psychology*. (pp. 74–88). Oxford: Oxford University Press.

May, D. R., Chan, A. Y. L., Hodges, T. D., and Avolio B. J. (2003) Developing the moral component of authentic leadership. *Organizational Dynamics* 32, 247–260.

McCullough, M. and Snyder, C. (2000) Classical sources of human strength: Revisiting an old home and building a new one. *Journal of Social and Clinical Psychology* 19, 1–10.

McGrath, J. E. (1976) Stress and behavior in organizations. In M. Dunnette (ed.), *Handbook of industrial and organizational psychology*. (pp. 1351–1395). Chicago: Rand McNally.

McVeigh, T. (2011) Cameron measuring "wrong type of happiness." *The Observer* Sunday April 10, 2011. p. 19.

Mintzberg, H. (2005) How inspiring. How sad. Comment on Sumantra Ghoshal's paper. *Academy of Management Learning and Education* 4, 108.

Morgeson, F. P. and Humphrey, S. E. (2006) The Work Design Questionnaire (WDQ): Developing and validating a comprehensive measure for assessing job design and the nature of work. *Journal of Applied Psychology* 91, 1321–1339.

Moskowitz, J. T. and Epel, E. S. (2006) Benefit finding and diurnal cortisol slope in maternal caregivers: A moderating role for positive emotions. *The Journal of Positive Psychology* 1, 83–91.

Mullins, L. (2002) *Management and Organizational Behaviour*. Harlow: Financial Times/Prentice-Hall.

Murphy, L., Hurrell, J., Sauter, S., and Keita, C. (eds.) (1995) *Job Stress Interventions*. Washington, DC: American Psychological Association.

Myers, D. G. (2000) Feeling good about Fredrickson's positive emotions. *Prevention and Treatment* 3, Article 2, 1–4.

Neenan, M. (2009) *Developing resilience: A cognitive-behavioural approach*. London: Routledge.

Nelson, D. and Cooper, C. L. (2007) Positive Organizational Behaviour: An Exclusive view. In D. Nelson and C. Cooper (eds.), *Positive Organizational Behaviour*. (pp. 3–8). London: Sage.

Nelson, D. L. and Simmons, B. L. (2003) Health psychology and work stress: A more positive approach. In J. C. Quick and L. E. Tetrick (eds.), *Handbook of occupational psychology.* (pp. 97–119). Washington, DC: American Psychological Society.

Nelson, D. L. and Simmons, B. L. (2004) Eustress: An elusive construct, an engaging pursuit. In P. L. Perrewe and D. C. Ganster (eds.), *Research in occupational stress and well being.* Vol 3. (pp. 265–322). Amsterdam: Elsevier JAL.

Nelson, D. L., Little, L. M., and Frazier, M. (2008) Employee well-being: The heart of positive organizational behavior. In A. Kinder, R. Hughes, and C. L. Cooper (eds.), *Employee well-being support: A workplace resource.* (pp. 51–60). Chichester: John Wiley.

Newton, T. (1995) *"Managing" stress: Emotion and power at work.* London: Sage.

Nielsen, K., Taris, T., and Cox, T. (2010) The future of organizational interventions: Addressing the challenges of today's organizations. *Work and Stress* 24, 219–233.

Nigam, J. A. S., Murphy, L. R., and Swanson, N. G. (2003) Are stress management programs indicators of good places to work? Results of a national survey. *International Journal of Stress Management* 10, 345–360.

Nord, W. (2005) Treat and some treatments: Responses by Kanter, Pfeffer, Gapper, Hambrick, Mintzberg, and Donaldson to Ghoshal's "Bad management theories are destroying good management practices." *Academy of Management Learning and Education* 4, 92.

Oakland, S. and Ostell, A. (1996) Measuring coping: A review and critique. *Human Relations* 49, 133–155.

O'Brien, T. and DeLongis, A. (1996) The interactional context of problem-, emotion-, and relationship-focused coping: The role of the big-five personality factors. *Journal of Personality* 64, 775–813.

Oldham, G. R. (1996) Job Design. In C. L. Cooper and I. V. Robertson (eds.), *International Review of Industrial and organizational Psychology* 11. (pp. 33–60). Chichester: John Wiley.

Oldham, G. R. and Hackman, J. R. (2010) Not what it was and not what it will be: The future of job design research *Journal of Organizational Behavior* 31, 463–479.

Ong, A. D., Bergeman, C. S., Bisconti, T. L., and Wallace, K. A. (2006) Psychological resilience, positive emotions, and successful adaptation to stress in later life. *Journal of Personality and Social Psychology* 91, 730–749.

Oswald, A. and Wu, S. (2010) Objective confirmation of subjective measures of human well-being. *Science* 327, 576–579.

Overell, S. (2008) *Inwardness: The rise of meaningful work.* London: The Work Foundation.

Packman, C. and Webster, S. (2009) *Psychosocial working conditions in Britain in 2009.* Statistics Branch: Health and Safety Executive: September 2009.

Page, L. F. and Donohue, R. (2004) Positive psychological capital: A preliminary exploration of the construct. *Department of Management Working Paper Series,* Working Paper 51/04, October. University of Melbourne.

Park, C. and Folkman, S. (1997) Meaning in the context of stress and coping. *Review of General Psychology* 1, 115–144.

Parker, S. K. and Griffin, M. A. (2011) Understanding active psychological states: Embedding engagement in a wider nomological net and closer attention to performance. *European Journal of Work and Organizational Psychology* 20, 60–67.

Parker, S. K. and Ohly, S. (2008) Designing motivating jobs: An expanded framework for linking work characteristics and motivation. In R. Kanfer, G. Chen, and R. D. Pritchard (eds.), *Work motivation: Past, present, and future.* (pp. 233–284). Abingdon: Routledge/Taylor and Francis.

Parker, S. and Wall, T. (1998) *Job design: Organizing work to promote well-being and effectiveness.* London: Sage.

Parker, S. K., Bindl, U. K., and Strauss, K. (2010) Making things happen: A model of proactive behaviour. *Journal of Management* 36, 827–856.

Parker, S. K., Wall, T. D., and Cordery, J. L. (2001) Future work design research and practice: Towards an elaborated model of work design. *Journal of Occupational and Organizational Psychology* 74, 413–440.

Parker, S. K., Williams, H. M., and Turner, N. (2006) Modeling the antecedents of proactive behavior at work. *Journal of Applied Psychology* 91, 636–652.

Parsonage, M. (2010) *The organizational costs of mental ill health.* (Centre for Mental Health) Presentation: Academy of Social Science: October 20, 2010.

Pawelski, J. O. and Prilleltensky, I. (2005) That at which all things aim. In R. A. Giacalone, C. L. Jurkiewicz, and C. Dunn (eds.), *Positive psychology in business ethics and corporate responsibility.* (pp. 191–208). Charlotte, NC: Information Age.

Pekrun, R. and Frese, M. (1992) Emotions in work and achievement. In C. Cooper and I Robertson (eds.), *International Review of Industrial and Organizational Psychology* 7. (pp. 153–200). Chichester: John Wiley.

Peterson, C. and Park, N. (2003) Positive Psychology as the evenhanded positive psychologist views it. *Psychological Inquiry* 14, 143–147.

Peterson, C. M. and Seligman, M. E. P. (2003) Positive organizational studies: Lessons from positive psychology. In K. Cameron, J. Dutton, and R. E. Quinn (eds.), *Positive organizational scholarship.* (pp. 14–27). San Francisco: Berrett-Koehler.

Peterson, C., Park, N., and Seligman, E. P. (2005) Orientations to happiness and life satisfaction: The full life versus the empty life. *Journal of Happiness Studies* 6, 25–41.

Peterson, C., Park, N., Hall, N., and Seligman, M. (2009) Zest and work. *Journal of Organizational Behavior* 30, 161–172.

Pfeffer, J. (2005) Why do bad management theories persist? A comment on Ghoshal. *Academy of Management Learning and Education* 4, 96–100.

Podolny, J. M., Khurana, R., and Hill-Pooper, M. (2005) Revisiting the meaning of leadership. *Research in Organizational Behavior* 26, 1–36.

Powdthavee, N. (2010) *The happiness equation.* London: Icon Books.

Pratt, M. G. and Ashforth (2003) Fostering meaningfulness in working and at work. In K. S. Cameron, J. E. Dutton, and R. E. Quinn (eds.), *Positive organizational scholarship.* (pp. 309–327). San Francisco: Berrett-Koehler.

Price, T. L. (2003) The ethics of authentic transformational leadership. *The Leadership Quarterly* 14, 67–81.

Quick, J. C. and Gavin, J. H. (2001) Four perspectives on conservation of resources theory: A commentary. *Applied Psychology: An International Review* 50, 392–400.

Quick, J. C. and Macik-Frey, M. (2007) Healthy productive work: Strength through communication, competence and interpersonal interdependence. In D. Nelson and C. Cooper (eds.), *Positive organizational behaviour.* (pp. 25–39). London: Sage.

Quick, J. C. and Tetrick, L. E. (eds.) (2003) *Handbook of occupational health psychology.* Washington, DC: American Psychological Association.

Quick, J. C., Quick, J. D., Nelson, D. L., and Hurrell, J. J. (eds.) (1997) *Preventive stress management in organizations.* Washington, DC: American Psychological Association.

Quick, J., Cooper, C., Gibbs, P., Little, L., and Nelson, D. (2010) Positive Organizational Behavior at work. In G. Hodgkinson and J. Ford (eds.), *International review of industrial and organizational psychology* 25. (pp. 253–291). Chichester: John Wiley.

Rand, K. and Snyder, C. (2003) A reply to Dr Lazarus, the evocator emeritus. *Psychological Inquiry* 14, 148–153.

Rank, J., Pace, V. L., and Frese, M. (2004) Three avenues for future research on creativity, innovation and initiative. *Applied Psychology: An International Journal* 53, 518–528.

Rathunde, K. (2000) Broadening and narrowing in the creative process: A commentary on Fredrickson's "Broaden-and-Build" model. *Prevention and Treatment* 3, Article 6, 1–6.

Rathunde, K. (2001) Toward a psychology of optimal human functioning: What Positive Psychology can learn from the "experiential turns" of James, Dewey, and Maslow. *Journal of Humanistic Psychology* 41, 135–153.

Reay, T., Berta, W., and Kohn, M. K. (2009) What's the evidence on evidence-based management? *Academy of Management Perspectives* 23, 5–18.

Resnick, S., Warmoth, A., and Serlin, I. (2001) The Humanistic Psychology and Positive Psychology connection: Implications for Psychotherapy. *Journal of Humanistic Psychology* 41, 73–101.

Richardson, G. E. (2002) The metatheory of resilience and resiliency. *Journal of Clinical Psychology* 58, 307–312.

Roberts, L. M. (2006) Shifting the lens on organizational life: The added value of positive scholarship. *Academy of Management Review* 31, 292–305.

Robertson, I. and Cooper, C. (2011) *Wellbeing: Productivity and happiness at work.* Basingstoke: Palgrave Macmillan.

Rogers, C. (1961) *On becoming a person: A therapist's view of psychotherapy.* Boston: Houghton Mifflin.

Rolfe, H., Foreman, J., and Tylee, A. (2006) *Welfare or farewell? Mental health and stress in the workplace.* Discussion Paper 268: National Institute of Economic and Social Research.

Rose, M. (1988) *Industrial Behaviour.* London: Penguin Business.

Rospenda, K. M. and Richman, J. A. (2005) Harassment and discrimination. In J. Barling, E. K. Kelloway, and M. R. Frone (eds.), *Handbook of work stress*. (pp. 149–188). Thousand Oaks: Sage.

Rousseau, D. M. and Fried, Y. (2001) Location, location, location: Contextualizing organizational research. *Journal of Organizational Behavior* 22, 1–13.

Ryan, R. M. and Deci, E. L. (2000) Self-determination theory and the facilitation of intrinsic motivation, social development and well-being. *American Psychologist* 55, 68–78.

Ryan, R. M. and Deci, E. L. (2001) On happiness and human potentials: A review of research on hedonic and eudaimonic well-being. *Annual Review of Psychology* 52, 141–166.

Ryff, C. D. (1989) Happiness is everything, or is it? Explorations on the meaning of psychological well-being. *Journal of Personality and Social Psychology* 57, 1069–1081.

Ryff, C. D. (2003) Corners of myopia in the Positive Psychology parade. *Psychological Inquiry* 14, 153–159.

Ryff, C. D. and Keyes, L. M. (1995) The structure of psychological well-being revisited. *Journal of Personality and Social Psychology* 69, 719–727.

Ryff, C. D. and Singer, B. (1998a) Human health: new directions for the next millennium. *Psychological Inquiry* 9, 69–85.

Ryff, C. D. and Singer, B. (1998b) The contours of positive human health. *Psychological Inquiry* 9, 1–28.

Sainsbury Centre for Mental Health (2007) *Mental health at work: Developing the business case*. Policy Paper 8. London: Sainsbury Centre for Mental Health.

Schaubroeck, J. (1999) Should the subjective be the objective? On studying mental processes, coping behavior, and actual exposures in organizational stress research. *Journal of Organizational Behavior* 20, 753–760.

Schat, A. C. H. and Kelloway, E. K. (2005) Workplace aggression. In J. Barling, E. K. Kelloway, and M. R. Frone (eds.), *Handbook of work stress*. (pp. 189–218). Thousand Oaks: Sage.

Schaufeli, W. B. and Salanova, M. (2011) Work engagement: On how to better catch a slippery concept. *European Journal of Work and Organizational Psychology* 20, 39–46.

Schaufeli, W. B., Taris, T. W., and Rhenen, W. (2008) Workaholism, burnout and work engagement: Three of a kind or three different kinds of employee well-being? *Applied psychology: An international review* 57, 173–203.

Schaufeli, W. B., Salanova, M., Gonzalez-Roma, V., and Bakker, A. B. (2002) The measurement of engagement and burnout: A two sample confirmatory factor analytic approach. *Journal of Happiness Studies* 3, 71–92.

Schwarzer, R. (2001) Stress, resources and proactive coping. *Applied Psychology: An international review* 50, 400–407.

Schwarzer, R. (2004) Manage stress at work through preventive and proactive coping. In E. A. Locke (ed.), *The Blackwell handbook of principles of organizational behaviour*. (pp. 342–355). Oxford: Blackwell.

Schwarzer, R. and Taubert, S. (2002) Tenacious goal pursuits and strivings: Toward personal growth. In E. Frydenberg (ed.), *Beyond coping: meeting goals, visions, and challenges*. (pp. 19–35). Oxford: Oxford University Press.

Sears, L. (2010) *Next generation HR: Time for change – Toward a next generation for HR.* London: CIPD.

Seligman, M. E. P. (2005) Positive Psychology, positive prevention and positive therapy. In C. Snyder and S. Lopez (eds.), *Handbook of positive psychology.* (pp. 3–9). Oxford: Oxford University Press.

Seligman, M. E. P. (2008) Positive health. *Applied Psychology: An International Review* 57, 3–18.

Seligman, M. E. P. (2011) *Flourish: A new understanding of happiness and well-being and how to achieve them.* London: Nicholas Brealey.

Seligman, M. E. P. and Csikszentmihalyi, M. (2000) Positive psychology: An introduction. *American Psychologist* 55, 5–14.

Seligman, M. E. P. and Csikszentmihalyi, M. (2001) Reply to comments. *American Psychologist* 56, 89–90.

Seligman, M. E. P. and Pawelski, J. (2003) Positive Psychology: FAQs. *Psychological Inquiry* 14, 159–163.

Seligman, M. E. P., Steen, T., Park, N., and Peterson, C. (2005) Positive psychology progress: Empirical validation of interventions. *American Psychologist* 60, 410–421.

Selye, H. (1984) *The stress of life.* Revised edition. New York: McGraw-Hill.

Seymour, L. and Grove, B. (2005) *Workplace interventions for people with common mental health problems: Evidence review and recommendations.* London: British Occupational Health Research Foundation.

Shaw Trust (2006) *Mental Health: The last workplace taboo: Independent research into what British business thinks.* Commissioned by the Shaw Trust. Conducted and Written by Future Foundation.

Sheldon, K. M. and King, L. (2001) Why Positive Psychology is necessary. *American Psychologist* 56, 216–217.

Shiota, M. N., Keltner, D., and John, O. P. (2006) Positive emotion dispositions differentially associated with Big Five personality and attachment style. *The Journal of Positive Psychology* 1, 61–71.

Shorey, H. S., Rand, K. L., and Snyder, C R. (2005) The ethics of hope. In R. A. Giacalone, C. L. Jurkiewicz, and C. Dunn (eds.), *Positive psychology in business ethics and corporate responsibility.* (pp. 249–264). Charlotte, NC: Information Age.

Simmons, B. L. and Nelson, D. L. (2007) Eustress at work: Extending the holistic stress model. In D. L. Nelson and C. L. Cooper (eds.), *Positive organizational behaviour.* (pp. 40–53). London: Sage.

Simonton, D. and Baumeister, R. (2005) Positive Psychology at the summit. *Review of General Psychology* 9, 99–102.

Snyder, C. (1999) *Coping: The psychology of what works.* New York: Oxford University Press.

Snyder, C. (ed.) (2001) *Coping with stress: effective people and processes.* Oxford: Oxford University Press.

Snyder, C. R. and Lopez, S. (2005a) *Handbook of positive psychology.* Oxford: Oxford University Press.

Snyder, C. R. and Lopez, S. (2005b) The future of Positive Psychology: A declaration of independence. In C. R. Snyder and S. J. Lopez (eds.),

Handbook of positive psychology. (pp. 751–767). Oxford: Oxford University Press.

Snyder, C. R. and Lopez, S. (2007) *Positive Psychology: The scientific and practical explorations of human strengths.* Thousand Oaks: Sage.

Somerfield, M. (1997a) The future of coping research as we know it: A response to commentaries. *Journal of Health Psychology* 2, 173–183.

Somerfield, M. (1997b) The utility of systems models of stress and coping for applied research. *Journal of Health Psychology* 2, 133–151.

Somerfield, M. and McCrae, R. (2000) Stress and coping research: Methodological challenges, theoretical advances. *American Psychologist* 55, 620–625.

Sora, B. *et al.* (2009) Job insecurity climate's influence on employees' job attitudes. *European Journal of Work and Organizational Psychology* 18 (2), 125–147.

Spector, P. E. and Jex, S. M. (1998) Development of four self-report measures of job stressors and strain: Interpersonal conflict at work scale, organizational constraints scale, quantitative workload inventory and physical symptoms inventory. *Journal of Occupational Health Psychology* 3, 356–367.

Spreitzer, G. M. and Sonenshein, S. (2003) Positive deviance and extraordinary organizing. In K. S. Cameron, J. E. Dutton, and R. E. Quinn (eds.), *Positive organizational psychology.* (pp. 207–224). San Francisco: Berrett-Koehler.

Spreitzer, G. M. and Sonenshein, S. (2004) Toward the construct definition of positive deviance. *American Behavior Scientist* 47, 828–847.

Spreitzer, G., Sutcliffe, K., Dutton, J., Sonenshein, and Grant, A. M. (2005) A socially embedded model of thriving at work. *Organizational Science* 16, 637–549.

Stanton, A. L., Parsa, A., and Austenfeld, J. L. (2005) The adaptive potential of coping through emotional approach. In C. R. Snyder and S. J. Lopez (eds.), *Handbook of positive psychology.* (pp. 148–158). Oxford: Oxford University Press.

Stanton, A. L., Kirk, S. B., Cameron, C. L., and Danoff-Burg, S. (2000) Coping through emotional approach: Scale construction and validation. *Journal of Personality and Social Psychology* 78, 1150–1169.

Stone, A. and Kennedy-Moore, E. (1992) Assessing situational coping: Conceptual and methodological considerations. In H. Friedman (ed.), *Hostility coping and health.* (pp. 203–214). Washington, DC: American Psychological Association.

Suls, J. and David, P. (1996) Coping and personality: Third time's the charm? *Journal of Personality* 64, 993–1005.

Suls, J., David, J., and Harvey, J. (1996) Personality and coping: Three generations of research. *Journal of Personality* 64, 711–735.

Sulsky, L. and Smith, C. (2005) *Work stress.* Belmont, CA: Thomson-Wadsworth.

Sutcliffe, K. M. and Vogus, T. J. (2003) Organizing for resilience. In K. S. Cameron, J. E. Dutton, and R. E. Quinn (eds.), *Positive organizational scholarship.* (pp. 94–110). San Francisco: Berrett-Koehler.

Sweeney, K. (2010)*The health and safety executive: Statistics 2009/2010. A national statistics publication.* London: Health and Safety Executive.

Taylor, E. (2001) Positive psychology and humanistic psychology: A reply to Seligman. *Journal of Humanistic Psychology* 41, 13–29.

Taylor, R. (2005) *Britain's world of work-myths and realities*. An ESRC Future of Work Programme Seminar Series. Swindon: ESRC.

Taylor, S. E. and Sherman, D. K. (2004) Positive psychology and health psychology: A fruitful liaison. In P. A. Linley and S. Joseph (eds.), *Positive psychology in practice*. (pp. 305–319). Hoboken, NJ: John Wiley.

Tedeschi, R. G. and Kilmer, R. P. (2005) Assessing strengths, resilience and growth to guide clinical interventions. *Professional Psychology Research and Practice* 36, 230–237.

Tennen, H. and Affleck, G. (2003) While accentuating the positive, don't forget the negative or Mr. In-between. *Psychological Inquiry* 14, 163–169.

Tennen, H. and Affleck, G. (2005) Benefit-finding and benefit-reminding. In C. R. Snyder and S. J. Lopez (eds.), *Handbook of positive psychology*. (pp. 584–597). Oxford: Oxford University Press.

Tennen, H., Affleck, G., Armeli, S., and Carney, M. (2000) A daily process approach to coping. *American Psychologist* 55, 626–636.

Thayer, A. L., Wildman, J. L., and Salas, E. (2011) I-O Psychology: We have the evidence; we just don't use it (or care to) *Industrial and Organizational Psychology* 4, 32–35.

Thomas, J. P., Whitman, D. S., and Viswesvaran, C. (2010) Employee proactivity in organizations: A comparative meta-analysis of emergent proactive constructs. *Journal of Occupational and Organizational Psychology* 83, 275–300.

Thompson, M. and Cooper, C. L. (2001) A rose by any other name...: A commentary on Hobfoll's conservation of resources theory. *Applied Psychology: An International Review* 50, 408–418.

Totterdell, P. (2005) Work schedules. In J. Barling, E. K. Kelloway, and M. R. Frone (eds.), *Handbook of work stress*. (pp. 35–62). Thousand Oaks: Sage.

Trenberth, L. and Dewe, P. (2006) Understanding the experience of stressors: The use of sequential tree analysis for exploring the patterns between various work stressors and strain. *Work and Stress* 20, 191–209.

Trevino, L. K. and Brown, M. E. (2007) Ethical leadership: A developing construct. In D. L. Nelson and C. L. Cooper (eds.), *Positive organizational behaviour*. (pp. 101–116). London: Sage.

Tugade, M. M. and Fredrickson, B. L. (2004) Resilient individuals use positive emotions to bounce back from negative experiences. *Journal of Personality and Social Psychology* 86, 320–333.

Tugade, M. M. and Fredrickson, B. L. (2006) Regulation of positive emotions: Emotion regulation strategies that promote resilience. *Journal of Happiness Studies* 8, 311–333.

Turner, A. N. and Lawrence, P. R. (1965) *Industrial jobs and the worker*. Cambridge, MA: Harvard University Press.

Turner, N., Barling, J., and Zacharatos, A. (2002) Positive psychology at work. In C. Snyder and S. Lopez (eds.), *Handbook of positive psychology*. (pp. 715–728). Oxford: Oxford University Press.

Tushman, M. and O'Reilly, C. (2007) Research and relevance: Implications of Pasteur's quadrant for doctoral programs and faculty development. *Academy of Management Journal* 50, 769–774.

Vermeulen, F. (2007) "I shall not remain insignificant": Adding a second loop to matter more. *Academy of Management Journal* 50, 754–761.

Waddell, G. and Burton, A. K. (2006) *Is work good for your health and well-being?* London: The Stationery Office.

Waddock, S. (2005) Positive psychology of leading corporate citizenship. In R. A. Giacalone, C. L. Jurkiewicz, and C. Dunn (eds.), *Positive psychology in business ethics and corporate responsibility.* (pp. 24–45). Charlotte, NC: Information Age.

Wainwright, D. and Calman, M. (2002) *Work Stress: The making of a modern epidemic.* Buckingham: Open University Press.

Walsh, J. P., Weber, K., and Margolis, J. D. (2003) Social issues and management: Our lost cause found. *Journal of Management* 29, 859–881.

Warr, P. B. (1987) *Work, unemployment and mental health.* Oxford: Oxford University Press.

Warr, P. B. (1990) The measurement of well-being and other aspects of mental health. *Journal of Occupational Psychology* 63, 193–210.

Warr, P. B. (1994) A conceptual framework for the study of work and mental health. *Work and Stress* 8, 84–97.

Warr, P. B. (2007) *Work, happiness and unhappiness.* Mahwah, NJ: Lawrence Erlbaum.

Warr, P. B. and Clapperton, G. (2010) *The joy of work*: *Jobs, happiness, and you.* London: Routledge.

Waterman, A. S. (1993) Two conceptions of happiness: Contrasts of personal expressiveness (eudaimonic) and hedonic enjoyment. *Journal of Personality and Social Psychology* 64, 678–691.

Waugh, C. E. and Fredrickson, B. L. (2006) Nice to know you: Positive emotions; self–other overlap, and complex understanding in the formation of a new relationship. *The Journal of Positive Psychology* 1, 93–106.

Weiss, H. M. (2002) Deconstructing job satisfaction: Separating evaluations, beliefs and affective experiences. *Human Resource Management Review* 12, 173–194.

Whetstone, J. T. (2002) Personalism and moral leadership: The servant leader with a transforming vision. *Business Ethics: A European Review* 11, 385–392.

Whittington, J. L. (2004) Corporate executives as beleaguered rulers: The leader's motive matters. *Problems and Perspectives in Management* 3, 163–169.

Wilkes, G. (2002) Introduction: A second generation of resilience research. *Journal of Clinical Psychology* 58, 229–237.

Wong, W., Albert, A., Huggett, M., and Sullivan, J. (2009) *Quality people management for quality outcomes: The future of HR review of evidence on people management.* London: The Work Foundation.

Wright, T. A. (2003) Positive Organizational Behavior: An idea whose time has come. *Journal of Organizational Behavior* 24, 437–442.

Wright, T. A. (2006) To be or not to be [happy]: The role of employee well-being. *Academy of Management Perspectives* 20, 118–120.

Wright, T. A. and Quick, J. C. (2009) The emerging positive agenda in organizations: Greater than a trickle, but not yet a deluge. *Journal of Organizational Behavior* 30, 147–159.

Youssef, C. M. and Luthans, F. (2005) A positive organizational behavior approach to ethical performance. In R. A. Giacalone, C. L. Jurkiewicz, and C. Dunn (eds.), *Positive psychology in business ethics and corporate responsibility.* (pp. 1–21). Charlotte, NC: Information Age.

Youssef, C. M. and Luthans, F. (2007) Positive organizational behavior in the workplace: The impact of hope, optimism, and resilience. *Journal of Management* 33, 774–800.

Zapf, D. (2002) Emotion work and psychological well-being: A review of the literature and some conceptual considerations. *Human Resource Management Review* 12, 237–268.

Zapf, D. and Holz, M. (2006) On the positive and negative effects of emotion work in organizations. *European Journal of Work and Organizational Psychology* 15, 1–28.

Zeidner, M. and Saklofske, D. (1996) Adaptive and maladaptive coping. In M. Zeidner and N. Endler. (eds.), *Handbook of coping: Theory, research, applications.* (pp. 505–531). New York: John Wiley.

Zelenski, J. M., Murphy, S. A., and Jenkins, D. A. (2008) The happy–productive worker thesis revisited. *Journal of Happiness Studies* 9, 521–537.

INDEX

Note: page numbers in italics refer to summary tables